11081
11.95

Murde

Capital Murder

by

DAVID CRUMP
and
GEORGE JACOBS

Copyright 1977
by
Texian Press

Library of Congress Catalog Card No.
77-81607

ISBN
0-87244-046-X

Published
by

Waco, Texas

Bound
by
Library Binding Company
Waco, Texas

This book is dedicated
with gratitude and affection
to the Houston police officers we have known,
who, by and large,
do a professional job
under impossible conditions.
And, especially, it is dedicated
to Houston Police Officer George G. Rojas,
who risked his life in the line of duty
to arrest accused capital murderer Bernardino Sierra
on June 22, 1974,
and who later gave his life in the line of duty
on January 28, 1976
while attempting to arrest accused capital murderer
Alejandro Cevallos.
We would have liked to have known him better.

—D.C.
G.J.

FOREWORD: BEFORE THE EXECUTION

The convict's head has been shaved to provide a better electrical connection. Cotton has been stuffed into his nose to stem the hemorrhaging that will inevitably occur. From another room, behind a one-way mirror, the executioner turns a switch, and the first flash of electricity—1800 volts—passes through the condemned man's body. The shock is so powerful that it raises him from the chair like a puppet, in spite of the restraints that hold him down.

An instant later, the convict's heart stops. His blood heats to a temperature of more than two hundred degrees Fahrenheit. Within the confines of his brain, the blood literally, actually boils.

The killing force is decreased to 200 volts, then increased to 1200, then shut off; and the attending physician steps forward to examine the corpse. When he pronounces the convict legally dead, the body is taken out by another door. There is very little ceremony. The whole process lasts about five or six minutes.

That is what an execution is like.

And even if it is done by a painless drug injection, as some have suggested, the death penalty is an ugly prospect.

Why do we do it? Why, today, do we use a form of sentencing that so many people disagree with, that so many people have condemned, that so many people believe is brutal, totalitarian, discriminatory, unconstitutional and unfair?

That is what this book is about.

Today, capital punishment is a bigger issue than ever before, because the Supreme Court has decided that the death penalty is constitutional. In some states, executions are beginning again. The first person to be executed in nearly a decade, Gary Gilmore, faced a Utah firing squad in early

1977. In short, the scene of the convict restrained in the electric chair has ceased to be a mental image today. It has become a reality.

And so the question today has taken on a new urgency: Why *do* we use capital punishment?

The answer, I think, is that the process of execution is only part of the capital punishment issue.

Behind every execution, there is another story. There is the story of the crime and the trial that happened *before* the execution. And that story is the "why" that lies behind capital punishment.

But let me take a minute to introduce myself before I go any farther.

My name is David Crump. I've been an assistant district attorney in Houston, Texas, for most of the past four years. In other words, I'm a prosecutor.

And on two occasions, it's been my job to ask a jury to return a death penalty verdict.

When I got out of law school, I wasn't exactly in favor of capital punishment. And I haven't really changed my mind; I'm still not "in favor" of it. But to be perfectly honest, I had no difficulty in deciding to ask the jury for the death penalty in these two cases. The circumstances of the crimes left me no other choice.

These cases bore absolutely no resemblance to what you might see on an "Owen Marshall" TV show. They were horrible murders. Death was the only sensible verdict to ask the jury to return, however much I may dislike the execution process.

In most states, including Texas, the death penalty only covers a few kinds of murder. Specifically, "capital murder" —the kind of murder that is subject to the death penalty—includes only the most brutal and inexcusable homicides. It includes murder by a prison escapee, murder by a hired killer, murder during rape or robbery—that sort of case. It is stranger-on-stranger murder, committed in cold blood, for the killer's own gratification or gain.

For instance, one fellow I prosecuted had committed a whole series of execution-style robbery murders. He made one of his victims lie on the floor and then shot him in the back of the head. After he was arrested, he committed another murder by suffocating an inmate *inside* the county jail. And later, he told a roomful of television newsmen why he had done it: "for kicks." He added that he enjoyed it, and he "guessed" that he would kill again if given the chance. His story is in this book.

It was a death penalty case—and that was the sentence I asked the jury to return. To me, it didn't make sense to ask for anything less.

You may disagree. And if so, that's fine—because on an issue like the death penalty, everyone has an opinion that differs from everyone else's. Besides, this isn't just a book for death penalty supporters; it's for opponents too. It always surprises me, but I've had people tell me that their opposition to capital punishment was strengthened, rather than weakened, by reading about the cases in this book.

It depends on how you interpret the facts you read about. But in any event, capital punishment—and the crimes that lead to it—are a fact we all need to know about, so we can make an intelligent decision about them.

The fact is, there are, on the average, three to four convicted capital murderers sentenced to death every year in my home town of Houston. At the same time, there are other convicted capital murderers who are spared and sentenced to life imprisonment instead.

This book is the story of some of those capital cases.

When I decided to write this book, I was joined in the effort by my friend George Jacobs, who is also an assistant district attorney in Houston. We are both familiar with the capital murder cases that have been tried in Houston—all too familiar, in fact. We have lived with these cases day and night for years, because we prosecuted some of them on behalf of the people of Texas. We decided that the best way to tell what we know about capital punishment is simply to tell the stories of the Houston cases. These cases could have happened anywhere—in New York, or Los Angeles, or Miami, or any of a thousand other American cities. They just happened to happen here.

We're not going to equivocate. We personally have made the decision, on balance, that we support the death penalty. But we aren't so confident as to think we have all the answers, and the final decision is up to you, not us.

And so our purpose in telling you about these cases isn't just to entertain you. We want you, the reader, to be able to confront these capital cases in the same way we had to—and decide what ought to have been done about them. Is the death of each of these men justified by his alleged crime? Or, to look at it another way, can justice be done without capital punishment?

—David Crump

TABLE OF CONTENTS

Chapter		Page
	Foreword: Before the Execution	v
	List of Illustrations	xi
	PART ONE—From Offense to Trial: The Case of Kenneth Brock	1
1	The Offense and the Arrest	3
2	The Defendant, the Victim and the Investigation	20
3	Preliminary Maneuvering: The Lawyers, The Judge and the Jury	31
4	The Trial	47
5	The Arguments and the Verdict	61
6	The Penalty Hearing	68
7	Epilogue	80
	PART TWO—The Jury and the Life-or-Death Decision	83
8	The Richmond Avenue Murders	87
9	The Trial of John Stiles Griffin	109
10	The Halloween Candy Murder Case	126
11	The Trial of Ronald O'Bryan	145
	PART THREE—The Evidence and the Life or Death Decision	159
12	The Murder of an Old Woman	161
13	The Trial of Gerald Lee Bodde	174
14	The Brady Bunch, Part I: Suppression of the Evidence	194
15	The Brady Bunch, Part II: The Trial of Richard Vargas	216
16	The Brady Bunch, Part III: The Navigation Street Murder	233
17	The Brady Bunch, Part IV: Bernardino Sierra's Plea Bargain	244
	PART FOUR—Of Barbarism—And Justice	259
18	The Dilemma of Capital Punishment	261
19	The Best of the Abolitionist Argument	265
20	The Case for Capital Punishment	272

LIST OF ILLUSTRATIONS

The Kenneth Brock Murder Case—
  "Mug Shot" or booking photograph................15
  Crime scene diagram 16
  Aerial photograph 17
  Surry Road, looking south................17
  Alley, looking west toward woods................17
  Store interior................18
  Police photograph of victim................18
  Physical evidence................19
Counsel for the Prosecution—
  David Crump and George Jacobs 85
  Stu Stewart................85
  Ted Busch................85
  Doug Shaver 85
  Vic Driscoll................85
Counsel for the Defense—
  Victor Blaine................86
  Stuart Kinard................86
  Marvin Teague................86
  Al Thomas and Fred Heacock................86
The John Stiles Griffin Murder Case—
  The homicide scene 104
  Detail of crime scene................104
  Wound chart 105
  Booking picture................105
  Physical evidence—handwriting 106
  Physical evidence—fingerprints 106
  Carolyn Stephenson 107
  The lineup sheet 107
  Detective James Pierce 108
  Officer M. A. Hebert................108
The Halloween Candy Murder Case—
  Funeral of Timothy O'Bryan 142
  The murder weapon 142
  Daynene O'Bryan................143
  Booking photograph 143
  Assistant District Attorney Michael Hinton................144
The Gerald Bodde Murder Case—
  Kidnapped child on witness stand 172
  Booking photograph................172
  The victim, Mrs. Bernice Hartsfield................173

The victim's body, as found in closet	173
The victim's house	173

The Brady Bunch Murder Case—

Homicide scene of Brady Street Murder	211
The Brady Bunch Members	211
Bernardino Sierra	212
Richard Vargas	212
Homicide scene of Middle Street Murder	213
Homicide scene of Almeda Road Murder	213
Homicide scene of Navigation Street Murder	214
Robbery victim of Navigation Street Murder	214
Part of a transcription of Sierra's confession	215
Wounds of one of the victims of the Brady Bunch	215

PART ONE

From Offense to Trial:
The Case of Kenneth Brock

KENNETH BROCK was one of the first persons to be tried in Houston under the Texas capital murder statute.

The Kenneth Brock case was, in most respects, unremarkable. It certainly was not the type of crime to catch the attention of the national press, for example. It was a killing during a robbery, and that is the most common kind of capital murder. It has become so common, indeed, as to exhaust the public imagination.

And yet the very senselessness and stupidity of the offense, alone, was enough to make this killing unique. Because what Kenneth Brock did was to execute a hostage by shooting him, at point blank range, in front of six police officers, who then became the State's principal witnesses in court.

The details of the case are vintage Texas. The defendant was captured after a chase with bloodhounds. A big, colorful defense attorney urged the jurors to begin their deliberations with a prayer for divine guidance. And the prosecutor quoted scripture in his final argument.

This is the story of the murder and of the trial that followed it.

CHAPTER ONE
THE OFFENSE AND THE ARREST

Sergeant P. M. Hogg was the first police officer on the scene. In fact, he "on-viewed" the robbery. In police jargon, that means he happened to see it as it came on view during routine patrol, not in response to a call.

The sergeant would later testify in court, "It didn't strike me as what it was, at the beginning." All he knew was that there was something suspicious going on. As he stopped his blue-and-white police car for a red light, he looked over toward the bright green-and-red neon sign that said "Seven-Eleven" hanging over the convenience store like a beacon in the darkness and rain. What he saw was the store manager walking stiffly out the door while another man, a smaller man, followed him like a shadow.

Sergeant Hogg turned his car sharply and drove into the parking lot in front of the store. Now the two men saw him. The smaller man moved quickly. He got behind the bigger man, the manager, and pulled him beyond the corner of the store. It was clear now to Sergeant Hogg what was happening, because now he saw the gun. The smaller man's hand reached around the heavy body of the store manager as he aimed at the police officer who was only a few feet from him. The hand rose and there was a flash, and Sergeant Hogg heard the reverberating "punch-*bang!*" sound of a .22 pistol being fired at him.

In the alley behind the Seven-Eleven store, the engine of the getaway car was running.

Sergeant Hogg pushed the button to his radio microphone. He gave the location of the store and requested backup to handle a robbery in progress.

The robber scuttled down the side of the store building toward the getaway car with his hostage in tow.

* * *

Inside the store, customer Ella Garver and her husband, Jim Wesley Garver, watched what was happening through the plate glass front of the store. When the two men rounded the corner out of view, they heard the report of the pistol. Still unable to believe that they had walked into a robbery, they stood frozen while the robber took the store manager away.

Jim Wesley Garver had brought his wife from work. She got off a little after one a.m. The Seven-Eleven was open at this hour. As they had walked in from the rainy, pitch-black darkness, they had seen the sandy-haired man standing strangely in front of the counter.

When the man had turned and pointed the gun at them and told them to lie on the floor, their first reaction, Jim Garver later said, was to think that the gun was a toy and that the man was joking. When he convinced them, Jim Garver told him, "Everything's cool, brother." The robber relented. He did not make them lie down. He even showed an odd kind of courtesy, the arbitrary courtesy that comes from violent power. "I don't want *your* money, brother," he reassured the Garvers as he emptied the cash register.

The store manager also reassured the Garvers. He was outwardly calm. Convenience stores like this Seven-Eleven chain were so often the targets of night-time robberies that the manager, Michael Sedita, knew to expect them. He had prepared himself for this. He kept firearms in the store, but being unable to reach them, he cooperated with the robber and was careful to do nothing to excite him.

"Come on," said the robber, as he pushed Michael Sedita in front of him, touching him lightly with the gun.

* * *

Outside the store, four young men sat in their car and watched with the same frozen disbelief as the Garvers.

They had been watching for some time. As they had driven up to the store, they had been surprised to see a sandy-haired man lean from behind the wheel of a white Dodge, bending across the woman who was in the passenger's seat, and fix them with a strange, wooden stare. The white car had gone around the store twice, with the sandy-haired man staring. For a moment, Phil Ochsler and Andy Hart, from where they sat in the front seat of Phil's father's car, thought they recognized him as a boy they went to high school with—but no, it wasn't him. Why, then, was he staring?

A moment later, the sandy-haired man walked around the corner of the store and went in. With his thick, matted hair and heavy beard, he was unmistakably the same man who had driven by. The woman was not with him. Nor was the car in sight.

The young men waited. They could not see inside the store.

It was not until the sandy-haired man walked out with the store manager, and the police car careened into the parking lot, and the robber shot at the officer that Phil Ochsler and Andy Hart were certain what was happening.

* * *

A few blocks north of the robbery, Officer G. W. Cormier sat in his blue-and-white in an Exxon station parking lot. M. J. Orlando, twenty-one years old and a rookie on the force, sat with him. Orlando was still in his probationary period. He had been in his new job less than six months. Cormier, himself only twenty-four, was breaking him in.

Cormier and Orlando sat talking to Officer W. E. Carmichael, who was riding solo in a separate police car.

While they sat there, Sergeant Hogg's call came over the radio, reporting the robbery and requesting backup.

From where they sat at the intersection of East Houston-Dyersdale Road and Tidwell Street, it was just a short drive to the Seven-Eleven at East Houston-Dyersdale and Laura Koppe Boulevard. Cormier and Carmichael each knew Michael Sedita from stopping to check the store nightly. A second after they got the call, they were rolling.

As the three officers raced into the parking lot and slammed on their brakes, they saw Sergeant Hogg at the corner of the store. The sergeant cradled his shotgun, unable to get a shot at the robber—who was holding Michael Sedita between him and the officer.

Hogg knew Michael Sedita too. It was imperative to handle the situation quickly, and yet without frightening the robber. It was also imperative not to allow him to take Michael Sedita away from the scene.

The sergeant therefore waved the other three officers away. "Go around to the rear," he directed. Quickly, the officers got back in their cars, drove around the block and parked the two vehicles where they blocked the robber's exit to the north down Surry Road, which ran behind the store. They dismounted and began to walk south toward the store with their pistols and shotguns in front of them.

Two more officers, J. D. Phillips and P. C. Jalomo, arrived from a side street. Together with Cormier, they hurried toward the rear of the store.

As they reached the alley, they saw a white Dodge Dart with its parking lights on and the motor running. Cormier was the first to realize that it was the getaway car. He spoke to the woman behind the wheel, ordering her out. Instead, as Cormier would later say in a sentence that displayed the terse understatement characteristic of police reports, "the car started pulling away at a high rate of speed." Cormier quickly fired two shots after it. Later, when the case reached court, the robber's lawyer would criticize the policeman for his markmanship, suggesting that he could have done better had he thrown his gun at the vanishing automobile—for in the darkness and rain, shooting with a handgun, Cormier believed that he had missed the car completely.

The getaway driver had escaped.

But the robber himself was boxed in.

In the alley beside the store, the robber heard the squealing tires of the car leaving him. He heard the shots. He had been inching along the alley, burdened with a hostage who outweighed him by nearly a hundred pounds, having to position himself so that he did not expose himself to a clear shot from Sergeant Hogg, who remained at the head of the alley with his shotgun.

Cormier, Phillips and Jalomo reached the end of the alley. A hundred yards away, the distance of a football field, they could see Sergeant Hogg at the other end.

Between them and the sergeant, they saw the robber with his hostage. They were still in the alley.

"Back up," said Michael Sedita. "He has the money. He told me he'd let me go."

"Back up," said the robber, threateningly. "Back up or I'll kill him." He had been left on foot and he was desperate.

"He is crazy," said Michael Sedita to the officers. "He'll kill me."

The officers stopped. Sergeant Hogg, who was proceeding cautiously down the alley toward the robber and his hostage, stopped too.

The robber ordered the policemen to put their guns down. "Or I'll kill him."

The three officers at the Surry Road side of the alley put their guns down on the street and backed away. They let the robber and his hostage past them.

The passageway was narrow. Cormier, Phillips and Jalomo were within ten feet of the robber at one point. They could hear his breathing, and they could hear the heavier breathing of the hostage, Michael Sedita. They could see the robber's eyes, white in the harsh light of a parking lot lamp, and they could see the moisture on his face. With a step or two, they could have reached out and touched him.

But they could do absolutely nothing to free Michael Sedita.

The robber was holding the storekeeper around the neck with his left arm. And his right hand held a pistol at the center of Michael Sedita's chest.

As he passed by the three helpless officers, the robber shifted his position laboriously, pushing Michael Sedita around in front of him in a slow and intricate ballet. As he inched ahead, the robber moved carefully, keeping the hostage always in the line of fire.

As he reached the end of the alley, the robber was obviously thinking about his next move.

There was an open stretch of pavement in front of him. Then there was Surry Road, and beyond that there was a thick wooded area. If he could get into that, the ground would swallow him up. But how would he do it? If he let go of the hostage, would he make it into the woods? And if he did, would he make it out the other side, or would the entire Houston police department be on the scene to surround him?

How would he escape?

The robber reached Surry Road and began pulling his

hostage along it. He wanted to get away from the alley he had come from, away from the shopping center that it was part of, away from the light, away from the police officer's positions—as far away as he could.

When he had gone perhaps fifty feet down Surry Road, away from the alley, the robber paused. He looked at the officers. They were still standing where he had told them to stay. The robber looked quickly toward the woods.

And then he made his decision.

He raised his hand.

He pointed the gun, which he had been holding loosely, against Michael Sedita's chest.

Then, while the officers watched in disbelief, he pulled the trigger.

As Michael Sedita's body slumped against him, the robber slipped off balance for an instant. He looked at the officers again. Then he was running. He jumped over a weed-encrusted ditch on the west side of Surry Road. By this time he was in high grass. A six-foot chain-link fence, with barbed wire on top, stood in his path, but he jumped it without hesitation. He was in a thick, wooded area, with undergrowth and weeds to cover him, seconds after his bullet exploded into Michael Sedita's chest.

The dying man fell, saying, "Oh, my God, I'm hit."

The rookie, Officer Orlando, had never seen anything like this. His stomach was in his mouth. As he would later say in court, "My heart was pounding as fast as it could and I was running as fast as I could." He got to the body of Michael Sedita and started giving him mouth-to-mouth resuscitation.

It took the officers some time to recover. In the confusion, Phillips fired six shots. Carmichael fired twice, then ran to call an ambulance. Jalomo picked up his shotgun and fired twice. But the killer, assisted by the diversion he had created and by the element of surprise, had disappeared.

The officers stood for a moment, helpless, in the middle of Surry Road. When they would testify in court eight months later about the events of that moment, their voices would break and they would be close to tears. It is one thing to investigate a murder. It is quite another to watch one happen a few feet away when you are powerless to prevent it, especially if it is a murder of a man you have known and liked. And as the officers stood on Surry Road by the woods in a mood that was tinged with rage and even fear at the senselessness of it all, the most powerful thought in their minds was a meaningless question: *why?*

Why had it happened?

Why had the robber killed the hostage? Did he just have an itchy trigger finger? Was he crazy? Did he hate cops so much that he could not resist the temptation to do this perverse act in front of them? Was it a question of "manhood" for a punk who wanted to show how dangerous he was? Or was it a colder calculation, based on the knowledge that the officers could neither let him drag the hostage into the woods nor refrain from pursuing him if he left the hostage alive? Was it just a step the small sandy-haired man had taken to enhance his chances for escape?

But at the same time these questions revolved through their minds, the officers knew they would never know the answer. The only answer was that it was one more senseless killing that should not have happened. Michael Sedita was dying. The man who was hiding now in the woods had done it. And that was all anyone could say about it now. The officers fought the weakness in their limbs, fought the rising tide in their stomachs, and tried to do their best at their job.

As backup units began to arrive in large numbers, Sergeant Hogg took steps to cordon off the wooded area into which the killer had fled. There were now perhaps twenty officers surrounding the woods.

Sergeant Hogg returned to the body of the hostage. Michael Sedita was dead. The officers called the Houston homicide division. Then they called the office of the Harris County Medical Examiner.

Had it entered their minds to think ahead to the time the case would be tried in a Texas criminal district court, the officers could not, in their wildest dreams, have imagined the argument the killer's lawyer would make. For he would seek to exonerate the small sandy-haired man from the consequences of his crime by claiming that Michael Sedita's death had been caused by the conduct of the officers themselves.

* * *

M. C. Escobar was the investigator on duty at the Harris County morgue when the call came in. He arrived at Surry

Road at 2:45 a.m., an hour after the murder.

A force of twenty police officers continued to surround the woods into which the killer had fled. Escobar went to work on the body a few feet from the woods.

First, he took photographs of the body from several angles. The police had already taken pictures of it, but Escobar conducted his own investigation. He knew that much of what he did would be duplicative of police efforts. It was simply his job to take nothing for granted. Escobar was part of a tradition of thoroughness and competence that made the Harris County Medical Examiner's Office, then and now, one of the most respected such offices in the nation.

Putting away his camera, Escobar began to catalogue clothing and objects in the vicinity of the body. His efforts memorialized details that would be important to both prosecution and defense. His report indicated the killer's pathway, for example, by noting, "a handful of change in a bag was thrown in a ditch near where the body was found." The report also noted that Escobar found six .38 calibre bullets in the right front trouser pocket of the dead man—a fact of which the defense would make much at trial, because a strange quirk of jury psychology seems to make less culpable the murder of a man who knows the risk of death.

The next step for Escobar was to identify the body. Sometimes, this task can be stubbornly difficult or even impossible. Escobar well remembered the frustration of trying to give names to the mass murder victims of Elmer Wayne Henley (not to mention the strange case of the still unidentified human torso that had been found in the county fully a decade ago and now was affectionately called "Stumpy" by morgue workers). But the case at hand, with a dead man who had worked at a known location, would present no such difficulties. When it developed that the officers themselves could tell Escobar positively the identity of Michael Sedita, the experienced investigator was not surprised.

When he completed his investigation, Escobar placed the corpse on a stretcher. He covered it and gently loaded it into the ambulance. Knowing that the police officers, tough as they were, had been acquainted with the dead man and had seen him killed, Escobar was careful to treat the body with respect.

This attitude of respect was also completely in keeping with tradition. One of the remarkable things about the Harris County Medical Examiner's Office is its workers' sensitivity, in the face of their continuous acquaintance with death, to the feelings of the living for the bodies of the dead.

The officers watched, wordlessly, as Escobar drove away with the body of the man they had seen murdered.

* * *

For a time, the officers waited. They could not see into the wooded area. They could barely move through its thick undergrowth and they could search only slowly, with awareness of the danger they exposed themselves to. An occasional crackle of branches told them the killer was still inside their circle.

Shortly after 3 o'clock in the morning, the search reached its conclusion.

With barking and baying that sounded like explosions in the quiet morning air, a set of bloodhounds under the control of a deputy sheriff started into the woods. The dogs strained and pulled eagerly at their leashes.

The killer had been lying in the underbrush, waiting for an opening. A little movement had allowed him to survey the locations of the surrounding police officers. Perhaps he would have a chance. The woods would hide him well, because they were nearly impenetrable. But now he heard the dogs. Frightened, he began to move. When he reached a ditch and had to cross the road beyond it, he got down on his stomach and began to crawl.

A hundred feet down the road, an electrician named Joe Bill Walker sat in his pickup parked by the side of the road.

By happenstance, Joe Bill Walker would play a major role in this unusual case. His presence was itself the result of pure chance: He had been attracted to the scene by reports on a CB radio. He had a friend who was a wrecker driver, and his friend had been listening to the police band and had told him what was happening. Joe Bill Walker had come out here, to the wooded area near Surry Road, for the excitement it promised to bring. Now, as he sat waiting for something to happen, his eye caught something moving on the road.

The killer was as flat on his stomach as he could get. The

dogs were behind him. But he could not see any police officers in his path ahead. He had almost made it. Almost—

The officers were still surrounding the wooded area, and now the hunted man was outside their cordon. The only thing that stood between him and freedom was this road. Joe Bill Walker, a man searching for adventure at 3 o'clock in the morning, just happened to be in the same place at the same time. It was almost unbelievable, a page right out of a dime-store mystery thriller: Walker, the amateur crime-fighter, was going to be instrumental in apprehending a desperado who had eluded a whole posse of lawmen with helicopters and dogs.

So it was that Joe Bill Walker, at 3 a.m. on a pitch-dark rainy night, had his moment in the sun.

"Here he is!" Walker shouted to the officers. "Here he is!" And he aimed his spotlight on the road.

The killer was startled as the blinding light hit him. The shock made his heart race and he jumped reflexively. He ran across the road. There, there were some small houses, with shapes that looked like bushes, fences, places to hide—

But the dogs were almost on him. As he ran between two of the houses, they were barking explosively behind him, and there were police officers with their guns drawn. The killer had thrown his gun away, but the officers did not know that. The killer had a good chance of getting himself killed if he kept running. Or even if he tried to hide.

He decided to give himself up.

Officer W. R. Lilley was the man who made the arrest, simply because he was the closest officer to the killer when he gave himself up. Lilley was near his patrol car, ready to enter the passageway between the two houses where the killer had disappeared.

What happened next was as unexpected as any of the other events in this strange case. As Lilley prepared himself mentally for entry into a dark space that concealed a killer who, he assumed, was armed and dangerous, he saw the man surrendering to him; and then he was surprised to hear the killer blurt out an unsolicited confession to his crime.

"I observed the actor coming out from the west side of the house and cut across the yard coming toward me with both hands in the air, walking in a southeasterly direction," Lilley later wrote in his report, using the flat jargon characteristic of police documents.

"As he got within 10 feet of me he stated, 'I am the man you are looking for. I shot the store owner,'" Lilley reported.

"*I shot the store owner,*" the man had said.

It was a crucial piece of evidence. It was an unequivocal admission of guilt. When the case got to court, there would be a defensive theory of the case, perhaps mistaken identity, or accidental discharge of the gun, or something else—and this confession would go a long way toward contradicting it. Lilley knew this, although he did not stop now to think about it.

Lilley did not have time to think, either, about the argument the killer's lawyer would make concerning the arrest, when the case reached court. What the lawyer would do, predictably, would be to allege that the police had violated his client's constitutional rights. That argument would be part of an attempt to get evidence about the shooting thrown out of the case and hidden from the jury, so as to give the lawyer a better chance to get the killer acquitted. Lilley could not know, now, that in the process of making that argument, the lawyer would make multiple charges of misconduct against him and others in the handling of the arrest and investigation. Lilley could not know, now, that the lawyer would even argue that Lilley had violated the Supreme Court decision in *Miranda v. Arizona* by hearing the confession before warning the killer of his constitutional rights. It appeared to Lilley that he had acted properly. What could he have done? Should he have interrupted the blurted confession until he had had time to say, "You have the right to remain silent?"

Lilley did not think about that now, as the man walked toward him. He thought about safety, the arrested man's safety and his own, and he thought about getting the man securely into custody to prevent his escaping again. And he thought about identifying the killer, getting his name. And so he spoke to the arrested man, quickly had him frisked, and looked at his personal effects.

Now he had a close look at the man who had committed this senseless crime.

The man's name was Kenneth Brock.

During the coming days, the police would have time to learn a great deal more about Kenneth Brock. Now, Officer

Lilley saw before him a normal-looking, 25-year-old caucasian man, apparently healthy and unremarkable except for a heavy reddish-brown beard and hair that were matted and dirty, as were his clothes. Lilley soon learned that Kenneth Brock already had an established "rap sheet;" his first arrest as an adult had followed just two years after he grew beyond the jurisdiction of the juvenile courts. At the present time, he was AWOL from the marine corps, and he had just recently gotten off probation for burglary.

In the days to come, the police would search Kenneth Brock's apartment and would find a variety of illegal drugs and a syringe of the type used to inject heroin. Using offense reports and line-ups, they would match his name to another robbery of a different store and to an attempted murder, in which he had stabbed a man in front of a number of witnesses, committed just nine days before the murder of Michael Sedita.

Of course, Officer Lilley did not know all these specific details about the man he arrested. He was concerned only with doing his immediate job, for now.

Lilley shouted to the other officers that he had the man in custody. Then, his report reflects, he handcuffed Kenneth Brock and placed him in his patrol car, whereupon Brock was "given legal warning" by Officer Cormier. Cormier read the rights, word by word, from a small blue card, called a "Miranda" card, a copy of which is issued to every Houston police officer to ensure compliance with the decisions of the Supreme Court.

Meanwhile, the body of Michael Sedita was lying in the Houston morgue.*

---

*The following names in this chapter were changed, without alteration of the incidents in which the persons were involved: Ella Garver, Jim Wesley Garver, Phil Ochsler, Andy Hart, Joe Bill Walker, Cynthia Morales.

THE KENNETH BROCK MURDER CASE—State's exhibit 25. This exhibit shows the defendant, Kenneth Brock, under arrest for capital murder. It is a blowup of a "mug shot" or booking photograph that was taken only a few hours after the offense.

THE KENNETH BROCK MURDER CASE—State's exhibit 3 (crime scene diagram). The dotted --- line indicates the path Kenneth Brock followed from the time of his robbery of the "Seven-Eleven" store at bottom until his escape into the woods at top. The stick figure indicates the position of the body immediately after the murder; the X's mark approximate police positions. (The actual State's exhibit 3 was nearly six feet tall. This is a reproduction of its most salient features.)

An aerial photograph of this same crime scene appears on the next page.

THE KENNETH BROCK MURDER CASE—State's exhibit 13. This aerial photograph, taken from a police helicopter, shows the store in the left foreground (on corner), the alley at left center, and Surry Road and the woods in the background.

THE KENNETH BROCK MURDER CASE—State's exhibit 5. This photograph shows Surry Road, looking south from near the murder scene.

THE KENNETH BROCK MURDER CASE—State's exhibit 4. This photograph shows the alley, looking west toward the woods.

THE KENNETH BROCK MURDER CASE—Store interior. The defendant robbed the store manager before shooting him. Notice the open cash drawer.

THE KENNETH BROCK MURDER CASE—police photograph of victim. Michael Sedita was a college graduate who had a promising career before him. The bullet entry wound is circled; the projectile passed through his aorta.

THE KENNETH BROCK MURDER CASE—some of the physical evidence. The murder weapon was a .22 pistol. It was referred to during the trial as a "Saturday Night Special," and it was received into evidence as State's exhibit 21. The victim's smock, which was also introduced into evidence, bears the "7-Eleven" store logo. His white shirt has a hole in the center of the pocket where the fatal bullet entered.

CHAPTER TWO
THE DEFENDANT, THE VICTIM AND THE INVESTIGATION

At the county morgue, the remains of Michael Sedita lay face up, eyes closed, in a room kept at low temperature to retard decomposition. At eleven o'clock in the morning, ten hours after the murder, Doctors G. Sheldon Green and Ethyl Erickson began the autopsy.

Nothing about the Houston morgue is the way one would think it ought to be. It is an oddly tidy place, with an antiseptic white background and small touches of color. Against this clean background, there are rows of battered bodies in different stages of mutilation or decomposition, waiting for the attention of the pathologist. Autopsied bodies, however, seldom have a mutilated appearance when released to a funeral home, at least not attributable to autopsy—because the medical examiner's office takes care to preserve the feelings of relatives to the extent that it is possible.

Perhaps the most surprising thing about the Houston morgue is the persons—and personalities—of the pathology staff. Dr. Ethyl Erickson is a friendly, reassuring, even maternal woman, very feminine, with a ready smile and sense of humor. Of the two, Dr. Green looks more like a scientist should, with his wispy gray goatee and balding head—until, that is, one spots the colorfully informal Western string tie with the turquoise holder that is his trademark. Neither of the doctors, when one comes right down to it, has quite the expected appearance for this unusual line of work.

But be that as it may, their skill as pathologists is clear. When either of them is called to testify, it can take several minutes before he or she finishes listing such credentials as multiple advanced degrees, internships, residencies, medical school professorships, and experience in the field of "forensic pathology"—which is the macabre science of determining cause of death. If asked, "And how many autopsies would you estimate you have performed, doctor?" they would give estimates that ran into the thousands. The doctors' integrity makes them impregnable witnesses and their skill enables them to refute the maxim "dead men tell no tales" when they talk about their work.

And now, under the tutelage of Doctors Green and Erickson, the body of Michael Sedita was about to speak volumes about his killer.

The doctors circled the body and recorded their findings into a gooseneck microphone that hung over the operating table. Before the incision, they made a careful examination of the body—weighing, measuring, examining it all over. They recorded each finding in flat, technical jargon: "The body was that of a well-developed, obese, 31 year-old white man, measuring 71 inches in length and weighing 241 pounds." They catalogued carefully the symptoms of death: "There was fixed rigor mortis and well developed posterior dependent lividity." In other words, the body had stiffened and become discolored.

But the most important external detail was the garishly colored gunshot wound in Michael Sedita's chest. "Over the left pectoral region," Dr. Green dictated, "situated 4 inches below the suprasternal notch and 4½ inches to the left of the midline, there was a gunshot wound of entrance, measuring ¼ inch in diameter and surrounded by charred and abraded skin margins measuring 3/8 inch in diameter. There was no powder stippling. The abdomen was protuberant but soft...."

These findings were of crucial significance. The recording of the location of the wound would allow Dr. Green to turn to the jury ten months hence and point out where the bullet had entered, using his own anatomy as a model. The charring and abrasion were even more important: they indicated that the gun muzzle had been within inches of the skin when fired. The absence of "powder stippling," together with the charring, allowed the examiners to be yet more specific. This evidence indicated a contact wound, in which the gun had been directly against the victim's chest.

Thus the doctors' observations, independently and scientifically made, corroborated the eyewitness accounts of the police officers, whose reports the doctors had not seen.

Now the doctors were ready to make the "Y" shaped incision on the victim's chest that begins the internal examination of a complete autopsy. Through this series of cuts, they would be able to enter the thoracic and abdominal cavities. They began at a point near each shoulder and cut to the middle of the chest. From that point, they cut straight down the center of the abdomen toward the pubic area to form the stem of the "Y".

Upon peeling back the skin, they immediately encountered the damage the bullet had done.

"The rib cage showed, anteriorly, at the level of the 3rd intercostal space, a gunshot wound of entrance," they reported. "The right pleural cavity had about 1 pint of liquid and clotted blood. The left pleural cavity had 1 quart of liquid and clotted blood. . . . A .22 calibre, lead, copper-coated bullet was recovered from the body of the 5th thoracic vertebra, slightly to the right of the midline."

The bullet was "moderately" deformed through its collision with Michael Sedita's backbone. Dr. Green marked it with his initial and the autopsy number so that he would be able to identify it in court. Meanwhile, it would be sent to the ballistics laboratory.

The doctors removed the heart. Routinely, they recorded that it "weighed 440 grams" and that its myocardium was "dark red and beefy." It had been healthy before the murder. But the damage from the bullet was most apparent here: The doctors dictated that at the "origin" of the aorta (*i.e.*, at its junction with the heart), "there was a gunshot wound of entrance with its largest diameter. . .measuring 2 centimeters in length, and with irregular, shaggy edges."

In lay terms, these entries meant that the bullet had torn a half-inch hole through the major connecting artery, right at the side of Michael Sedita's heart.

Now the autopsy was nearly complete. It had been done with care and skill.

If, at trial, there were a defense of accident, a hundred separate details would be available to test this theory. Was it consistent with a bullet trajectory that was "horizontal, from left to right," as the autopsy had shown? With the path of the bullet inside the chest? If there was a claim of self defense, was it consistent with the placing of the gun, with its nearness to the body? The details went on and on.

The doctors removed and examined Michael Sedita's other internal organs, and then got ready to put him back together again.

* * *

Who was Michael Sedita?

The autopsy showed a great deal about the way he died. But what had his life been like?

As the investigation progressed, it became clear that the most noteworthy thing about Michael Sedita's life was its normal, everyday *averageness*. He was born November 1, 1942, the son of Mr. and Mrs. Joseph Sedita. He grew up in a middle-class area of north Houston known as The Heights, an area filled with small but comfortable old homes built during a time when every house was individually designed. Michael Sedita lived nearly all his life on a short, tree-lined street in The Heights called Bay Oaks. At the time of his death, still unmarried, he lived with his mother in that same house in The Heights where he had lived as boy.

He had lived there during high school. He had worked part-time, then, as a machinist's helper. And he worked part-time, as a youth, in a chain of convenience stores operated by the Southland Corporation under the Seven-Eleven trademark.

After graduation from high school, he went to college at the University of Houston. He worked his way through. His studies included basic accounting, management, advertising and merchandising. Finally, he graduated from the University of Houston with an A.B. degree in marketing. He went to work as a bookkeeper for an agricultural products firm.

Then, a few years after graduating from college, he decided to go back to work for the Seven-Eleven division of the Southland Corporation.

It seemed a good choice. The Southland Corporation was a diversified company, into such fields as insurance, food processing and retailing. The Seven-Eleven division, particularly, had had a phenomenal growth while Michael Sedita had been growing up in Houston. The stores filled a definite and expanding market. They had good management, attractive advertising, and wide name recognition in the areas they served.

The management program Michael Sedita entered required initial service in an actual store, managing it. After learning the business fully from the inside, he could be moved—to the North Houston District Office of the Southland Corporation, for instance. That is why Michael Sedita was assigned to Seven-Eleven Store No. 12616, which was located in a shopping center between East Houston Road and Surry Road, to begin his management career at the Southland Corporation.

Working the night shift there, he had met Officers Hogg, Carmichael, Cormier and the others who stopped in regularly. For them as for many people who kept night hours, this store was the best place for quite a distance to shop or get coffee. The officers remembered Michael Sedita as a chunky man who had trouble keeping his weight down, but a hardworking, solid, friendly and cheerful fellow.

On May 21, 1974, Michael Sedita had been working the night shift there at Seven-Eleven Store No. 12616. That was the night, as chance would have it, that Kenneth Brock walked in and pointed his gun at the store manager.

And now, instead of progressing toward the North Houston District Office of the Southland Corporation, Michael Sedita was lying in the Harris County morgue on the autopsy table. He was no longer a human being. Doctors Green and Erickson did not stop to reflect on his life. Instead, they systematically removed his organs, sectioned them, and threw them one by one into a garbage can with a plastic lining as they finished examining them. Finally, they replaced his scalp and closed his chest with coarse stitches.

And when the gutted hull of the cadaver that had once been Michael Sedita was presentable enough to be picked up by the funeral home his family had engaged, Doctors Green and Erickson moved on to their next autopsy.

* * *

During the time that the dead body of Michael Sedita was

lying in the Harris Country morgue, Kenneth Brock was being taken before a magistrate at the Houston Municipal Courts Building.

There, a municipal judge read him, once again, the same rights that Officer Cormier had read to him a few hours before at the scene of his arrest. "You have the right to remain silent. If you give up that right, anything you say can and will be used against you. . .," the judge was saying. By now, the words were familiar to Kenneth Brock; in fact, they had already been familiar to him. The incident on Surry Road had been just a point of culmination for him, something his life had been building toward since childhood.

Kenneth Brock was now 25 years old. He had been born August 3, 1948, as the eldest child of Albert Jessie Brock and his wife, Dorothy, in the small town of Eggnonfield, Florida. While Kenneth was still a child, his mother had divorced his father, who was an alcoholic and did little to support the family.

Soon his mother remarried. But Kenneth Brock's stepfather was not easy to live with, either, and the second marriage also ended in divorce. Kenneth Brock's mother went to work in Texas as a maid, cleaning out model homes. Meanwhile, as a result of his family situation, young Kenneth repeatedly had trouble staying in school.

It was while he was still in school, apparently, that his dependence upon drugs began.

Kenneth Brock had six younger sisters, who had a real affection for him, and it was natural for them to look up to him. But he was unskilled, uneducated, and unintelligent, and he had difficulty holding a job. He fell in with companions whose conversations were about burglaries, drugs and crime. He tried to compensate for his inadequacies by becoming a regular user of drugs—first alcohol, then barbiturates and other pills, and then, apparently, heroin.

In 1967, Kenneth Brock was arrested for two burglaries. He was then 19 years old, but he was still trying to finish school. The prosecutor who was assigned to the burglary cases recognized them as ordinary economic offenses, probably drug-related, of the type that occurs dozens of times daily in a city like Houston. And in a plea-bargain that was standard for an offense of that severity, Kenneth Brock, with the advice of his court-appointed counsel, pled guilty in exchange for a recommendation to the judge by the prosecutor that the sentence be suspended.

That was six years ago. Since then, Brock had worked only sporadically. He had taken to selling drugs and to robbery to support his own use of drugs. Finally, in what seemed to be a last effort to salvage something worthwhile of his life, he enlisted in the Marine Corps and went to boot camp in North Carolina. But there, it quickly became evident that for Kenneth Brock, joining the Marines was a mistake, and so he deserted.

From that point on, his life went ever more steadily downhill. He lived in Houston with a girl named Cynthia Morales. She drove and he robbed. The murder of Michael Sedita was part of a series of offenses that included the other cases of attempted murder and robbery for which he was now wanted.

It was hard to say exactly how the events in his life had brought Kenneth Brock to the present. He had an intelligence in the low average range; that meant he was no genius, but it also meant there were many normal persons in the population with I.Q.'s far lower than his. And he was perfectly sane, with no debilitating psychoses. But heredity and environment had generated in him an aggressive, drug-dependent and impulsive personality. He was not a person who considered the future or its consequences before he decided to do anything.

And when he was surrounded by police officers after he robbed Seven-Eleven No. 12616, it probably seemed to Kenneth Brock that he had very little future to consider in any event.

Now, in the Municipal Courts Building, Kenneth Brock stood before the bench as a municipal judge finished explaining to him the charges he would face for the death of Michael Sedita. "Do you have any questions about these charges, or about the rights I have explained to you?" the judge asked him.

"No," said Kenneth Brock.

And with that, the defendant was taken to the city jail and held without bond.

* * *

Meanwhile, the police investigation moved into its follow-up phase.

At the jail, Officer Orlando inventoried articles taken from the arrested man's person. Orlando found that Kenneth Brock was virtually a walking cash register. In his pockets, Brock was carrying a large number of quarters, dimes and nickels. There was even loose change in his boot. In his pockets Orlando also found 3 ten-dollar bills, 8 fives, and 37 ones. There was, finally, a live .22 bullet identical to that removed from Michael Sedita's body, which Orlando found in Brock's pocket.

The murder weapon was conspicuously absent. Officer Cormier asked Brock where it was. "I dropped it in the ditch," said Brock. He had simply thrown the pistol away before he jumped the fence into the woods.

Under several inches of water, amid a clump of high weeds that had to be cleared away, the officers found the pistol—right where the killer had told Cormier it would be.

Once the physical evidence had been found and inventoried, the officers submitted it to experts for testing.

The shirt that Michael Sedita had been wearing went to the Houston Police Department chemistry laboratory with a request that a nitrite test be conducted. Since the firing of a gun expels nitrite salts in a cone from the muzzle, the spreading pattern of the particles on the shirt would allow an estimate of the distance the gun had been from Michael Sedita's chest when the trigger was pulled. After testing the shirt, Chemist J. A. Zotter concluded that the pattern showed a loose contact wound, or at most one in which the gun was only "inches away."

Next door to the chemistry laboratory, firearms expert G. E. Martinez used the recovered gun to fire a bullet similar to the one that killed Michael Sedita into a special target filled with packing material. Then he examined the two bullets under a comparison microscope. If the grooves produced by the barrel were the same on both bullets, Martinez would be able to identify this pistol as the murder weapon. If they were perceptibly different he would be able to say that it was not the gun that had killed Michael Sedita. In the end, the cheap manufacture of the "Saturday Night Special" Kenneth Brock had used defeated the analysis, because it lacked the stabilizing grooves of more accurate, expensive pistols. Martinez was forced to conclude that it produced "insufficient definite and consistent characteristics to effect an identification."

Kenneth Brock's lawyer would make much of this failure at the trial, when the case finally reached court.

Other officers followed out another important lead: the license number of the getaway car. Within hours of the murder, they were calling the owner of the car. The call ultimately prompted the getaway car driver to surrender. Her name was Cynthia Morales, and the car belonged to her father.

At her father's urging, Cynthia Morales gave homicide detectives a written statement saying that she had been in the car with Kenneth Brock on the night of the murder. She said that they had been drinking—"a few beers." But Cynthia Morales maintained that during the robbery she had been "half asleep" and therefore she "did not know where Kenneth Brock had parked the car or what he intended to do."

She said she thought Kenneth Brock had gone into the store because he "needed some cigarettes."

The grand jurors saw the case differently, and they indicted Cynthia Morales for the robbery.

When the case reached court, no one was surprised to see that Kenneth Brock's lawyer had subpoenaed Cynthia Morales as a defense witness; but the defense attorney rested his case without ever calling her to testify in front of the jury. Her story was hard to believe.

* * *

Everyone who could see the State's evidence at this point was certain that Kenneth Brock had murdered Michael Sedita in cold blood. The evidence was overwhelming. After all, not every case has six police officers who can testify that they saw the defendant pull the trigger.

But before anyone in the criminal justice system regarded the outcome as foreordained, it had to be remembered that Kenneth Brock would have a defense lawyer. It would be that lawyer's job to see that the state's evidence was not the only picture the jury saw.

Under the rules of procedure, the lawyer would have to be given all written statements of witnesses. In these, Ella

Garver had described the killer's hair as "blond," while Phil Ochsler had said it was "reddish brown." There were literally dozens of similar discrepancies. They were the type of small variations that are typical of honest witnesses to a dramatic event, but it would not be the lawyer's job to excuse them on that ground. Instead, it would be his job to magnify them as much as possible—and if a hole in the state's case resulted and caused Kenneth Brock's acquittal, well, that was the defense lawyer's job too.

The defense might conceivably be one of mistaken identity, for instance. After all, the defendant was not arrested in the tight circle of surrounding officers. The lighting had been poor. The witnesses' stories would conflict in the details. The story might be that Kenneth Brock was just passing through when he was arrested, totally unexpectedly. The defense was not, of course, bound by the state's evidence, and witnesses to substantiate such a story might be found.

This mistaken identity defense would not be highly credible, but then it did not have to be credible to be successful. All the defense had to do was to create a reasonable doubt in the minds of jurors to entitle Kenneth Brock to an acquittal. And the effectiveness of the defense might be enhanced by any number of unforeseeable occurrences. The jurors might turn out to be people who had an abiding animosity toward police officers, the judge might cripple the state's case by excluding crucial evidence, the defendant might cry in front of the jury and make a good witness. All of these things were quite possible, and they had certainly resulted in acquittals in "strong" cases before.

And actually, there was at least one defensive theory that would be much better than mistaken identity.

An experienced criminal lawyer could predict the best defense just from hearing the outlines of the state's case. To convict Kenneth Brock of capital murder, the state would have to prove that he killed Michael Sedita *intentionally*. If the discharge of the gun was an accident, the defendant could not be convicted of that offense.

So the best defense story might have the defendant tell the jury, "I didn't mean to shoot the store manager. The gun just went off. The police scared me, I was drunk out of my mind, there was a rock on the ground. I tripped over it, and that's why the gun discharged. Why would I shoot him? I had no reason to shoot him." The judge would instruct the jury that if they believed this accident defense, or even if it gave them a reasonable doubt, they must acquit Kenneth Brock of capital murder.

Ironically, the defendant's drug involvement—which the police had discovered in their search of his apartment—might even be used to bolster such an accident defense. He might contend that he was drunk and drugged and not conscious of what he was doing. In fact, the ingenious thing about an accident defense would be that it would turn all the prosecution's most devastating evidence to defense advantage. A theory of accident would actually be made more credible by the senselessness and brutality of the killing.

The prosecution's answer to this defense was also easy to predict, but it would be much harder to present to a jury. The defendant had fired at Sergeant Hogg, announced his intention to kill the victim, and escaped before the officers could shoot. His statements, actions and demeanor contradicted the defense of accident. But to *prove* that to a jury, beyond a reasonable doubt, would require exhaustive and convincing prosecution. It would also require intense concentration by twelve jurors willing and able to avoid emotional distraction by the biggest wild card in the case—the death penalty.

The state's case, to put it in the vernacular, was "pat." It was almost *too* "pat." And the apparent strength of the evidence just might turn out to be an illusion. The crime was clear to the police, but the outcome was no more clearly predictable than the end to a mystery novel. What would the *jury* do? That was the real question.

CHAPTER THREE
PRELIMINARY MANEUVERING: THE LAWYERS, THE JUDGE AND THE JURY

Assistant District Attorney Rex Emerson was the assistant in charge at the "intake" division the morning Kenneth Brock was arrested. "Intake" was a small cubicle on the first floor of the Houston police station, staffed most hours of the day by prosecutors who had the job of accepting or rejecting charges brought by police officers or citizens.

Intake is interesting for a prosecutor—but only the first time he or she does it. The majority of prosecutors do not regard it favorably. For one thing, it involves a lot of waiting. For another, it is necessary in some cases to tell a police officer "no"—to refuse to file charges. The reason for a refusal sometimes reflects directly upon the quality of the work the officer has done, and the result is then unpleasant. Citizen complaints, which have been through police channels and have already been refused, are even more unpleasant, because it is usually unrealistic to expect conviction; and the assistant in charge has to tell the citizen, with his beaten face flaring, that the criminal justice system will do nothing about it.

There are some compensations. Police officers who come into the office are usually in an expansive mood because they have just cleared a case and put an arrested person in jail, and the stories they have to tell are fascinating. And sometimes a lone state's attorney will get a challenging and esoteric question from officers: "Can I arrest this dude for flying his old Cessna while he was pilled up out of his mind?" (The answer: Yes, he can.)

More frequently, however, intake is just a job that has to be done.

As Emerson sat at intake, homicide detectives came in to file charges on Kenneth Brock. They were more somber than expansive this time.

Emerson talked to them for a few minutes and read the reports they presented. It was not just a murder, he realized, it was a capital murder, a death penalty case—and one of the first he had seen. Mentally he considered the types of killings that were capital: killing a police officer on duty, killing during an escape from prison, killing during a rape, a robbery, arson, burglary, kidnapping.... This was a killing during a robbery. That meant it was a capital murder.

After studying the facts and getting a second opinion from another prosecutor, Emerson was satisfied that a charge of capital murder was justified. And so he drafted a capital murder indictment, charging that Kenneth Brock had "unlawfully and intentionally caused the death of Michael Sedita" while "in the course of committing the offense of aggravated robbery." Then he sent the papers he had drawn, together with the officers' reports, witnesses' statements and scientific evidence, to the grand jury division of the District Attorney's Office.

A few weeks later, a grand jury heard the case and true-billed the papers Rex Emerson had drawn. Kenneth Brock was indicted for capital murder.

* * *

The indictment against Kenneth Brock went through the Harris County District Clerk's random filing procedure. There, it happened to be assigned to the 178th District Court.

That meant that it would be in the 178th District Court of Harris County that Kenneth Brock would be tried for capital murder.

The courtroom of the "178th," as it is called for short, is big and imposing. It is two stories tall, and it is covered with traditional dark oak paneling. Its heaviness, however, is softened by the wear and tear of a thousand past trials. An uneven row of discolorations on the elegant wall behind the jury box shows where hundreds of jurors, while listening to evidence over many years, have leaned back too far in their swivel chairs. Incongruously, there are also cheap modern details, such as a black plastic sign that proclaims in white letters: "Throwing cigarettes on the floor is prohibited by order of the court." The floor gives evidence that this prohibition, like many orders of the court, is not enforceable.

An intricate panel, towering from floor to ceiling, adds an impression of solidity to the elevated bench that is the judge's position in the courtroom.

The judge of the 178th, Judge Dan Walton, is a big man with a square jaw, ever-present pipe, and a mane of curly gray hair that makes him "look" like a judge. His powerful frame is a clue to the days when he played football at Vanderbilt College, where he was a consensus All-American end. Every criminal lawyer knows Judge Walton's judicial trademark: although he is, in the final analysis, a decisive man, he decides every question with painstaking care that is also painstakingly slow.

Judge Walton's mind does not run in channels that allow preliminary matters to be decided quickly. On a typical Monday morning, when the day's docket may be overflowing with administrative matters, a chance visitor might see the judge sitting at the bench while a standing crowd of lawyers, witnesses and defendants silently waits for him to read every word of an inch-thick court file covering one of the dozens of cases on the morning's docket. "I've seen him studying even the edges of the papers," says one lawyer. Even if it is a simple matter of administration, such as appointing an attorney or even scheduling a hearing in the future, Judge Walton may start reading the papers, and if he does, every other case will have to wait while he reads the arrest warrant, the bond, the indictment, the complaint, and every other paper in the individual file.

Because of this ponderous pace, Judge Walton has a significant backlog of serious felony cases. It numbers in the hundreds of rapes, robberies, burglaries, murders, thefts, and other assorted crimes.

But the very characteristics that make the judge so slow in dealing with his day-to-day docket make him the ideal judge to preside over a big case, a capital case. Prosecutors and defense attorneys agree: if capital cases were to be assigned to a single judge in Harris County (as some have proposed, to simplify docketing), no finer judge for the purpose could be selected than Judge Walton.

In addition to his painstaking care, Judge Walton is one of the brightest members of the Harris County judiciary. He was a member of a prestigious firm in civil practice before entering public life. Both sides get a fair hearing before him. The defense has a full opportunity to present its version of the facts, and the prosecution is held rigidly to the rules of procedure and its burden of proof. And there is one other thing about Judge Walton that is important: His intelligence and meticulousness make him among the least likely of Houston's felony judges to be reversed by an appellate court.

When the random docket placed the case against Kenneth Brock in the 178th District Court, this assignment of the case to Judge Walton meant that the case would be slowly, deliberately, and carefully tried.

* * *

As Kenneth Brock came before the bench for arraignment, Judge Walton asked whether he had a lawyer. Brock didn't. A lawyer for this case would come cheap if he charged less than five thousand dollars, and of course Brock was indigent. Judge Walton read the file. Then he had the clerk prepare an affidavit of indigency for Kenneth Brock to sign, adding to the file. Finally he turned to the court coordinator, whose job it is to expedite matters in the courtroom, and said, "Appoint Adrian Burk."

The most striking feature of the indictment, of course, was the gravity of the offense, and so the judge had wanted to appoint someone with experience, someone with old-fashioned toughness and nerve. The appointment of Adrian Burk meant that whatever else could be said at the end of the trial, there would be no one who would doubt that Kenneth Brock's counsel had given him the best kind of defense possible.

Adrian Burk is a close friend of Judge Walton's. Their backgrounds are even parallel: Burk was an All-American football quarterback at Baylor College years ago.

As a trial lawyer, Burk is a master of the unexpected. Before a jury, he is voluble and expansive. He is also a convincing persuader. He can draw laughter from the most unexpected sources or turn the most insignificant matter into a serious inquiry, if it advances his client's cause. Above all, he has some twenty years' experience in the use of credible arguments, both logical and emotional, in front of a jury.

Burk is a Baptist. He is devoted to his religion and teaches in Sunday School. It is therefore not surprising that his manner before the jury is that of a fundamentalist preacher. His halo of gray hair, his big frame and flamboyant joviality, his dress that is conservative to the point of drabness, and his willingness to quote scripture and prayer before the jury would, unquestionably, mark his representation of Kenneth Brock as something out of the ordinary.

It was perhaps inevitable that the Big Baptist lawyer and the antisocial dropout murderer would form a closer relationship than is usual between lawyer and client. As time went by, Burk began to feel sympathy, friendship and finally love for this man whom the state was seeking to put to death. He brought Kenneth Brock supplies in the jail. Under his influence, Brock began reading the Bible.

It was Burk's aim, above all, to save Kenneth Brock's life.

Before trial, he would file a blizzard of motions. He would exploit them to discover the State's case and to pick and pull at it.

Throughout the trial, he would use allegations that the prosecution was engaging in misconduct to try to blunt the damage of the state's case. This is today a standard defensive tactic, but Burk would employ it skillfully.

As the prosecutor struggled to get his evidence admitted, piece by piece, before the jury, Burk would struggle with equal zeal to exclude as much as he could.

He would fight over every part of the court's instructions to the jury. He would cross examine every witness vigorously. He would choose jurors that gave him the best chance at acquittal. Most of all, he would structure every part of the case, from jury selection to argument, so as to make his defense a coherent, comprehensible, and above all believable one.

* * *

The assignment of the case to Judge Walton and the appointment of Adrian Burk meant that there would be an able judge, and an able defender, to see that the Brock case was fairly tried from the defendant's standpoint.

Who would represent the point of view of the people of Texas?

The assignment went to Assistant District Attorney George Jacobs.

And since Jacobs is one of the authors of this book, perhaps this would be a good time for him to step forward and introduce himself.

"When I got the Kenneth Brock case to try," Jacobs says, "I had been at the District Attorney's Office for about five years. I had tried plenty of cases—all kinds of cases; everything from minor misdemeanors, traffic-court-type cases, all the way up to some pretty bad murders—but I'd never handled a capital case. I'd never even seen one.

"I figured that put me at a little bit of a disadvantage, in a way, with a lawyer like Adrian Burk. Adrian's been around for a long time.

"In fact, it made me nervous enough so that I can assure you, the *defendant* looked a lot more cool and collected than *I* usually felt whenever I walked into court—but, he was that way.

"I went to law school because I wanted to handle cases that were important. I wanted to have a chance to stand up for what I thought was justice in a particular situation. The law school I went to had its reputation mainly as a night law school, and it wasn't the fanciest school to go to, and I had to work to put myself through. I really had to want it. And I did.

"When I got out, I got lucky. I got a job with a judge, Judge Douglas, who is a judge on the Court of Criminal Appeals, which is the highest court in Texas for criminal cases. The judges on that court each have a recent law graduate as a 'law clerk,' which means a research assistant and legal advisor. It was a one-year position, and he was a great man to work for, and I learned a lot.

"One thing I learned was that the ideas I had had about the criminal justice system weren't really the way it was.

"I saw that it was *hard* to prosecute someone who was really guilty, even if you had all the evidence, and make it stick. I was impressed with the fact that an assistant district attorney needs to be skillful at what he does, just like a criminal defense lawyer. That wasn't the impression I had before.

"When I got through with my year, I was really happy when I got a job with Carol Vance, who is the District Attorney in Harris County, which covers Houston."

During his five years, Jacobs settled down in Houston. He met and married his wife, Sharon, and moved to a house at the outskirts of the metropolitan area, where it fades into the Texas countryside, so that he could have plenty of room.

And he started out prosecuting misdemeanors.

The misdemeanor courts in Houston are truly bargain-basement justice, just as they are most places. The cases are thefts of less than $200, driving-while-intoxicated, assaults and the like. It was not unusual, at the time Jacobs started, for a team of three prosecutors to have to handle a docket of 100 to 150 cases a day. The next day, that meant, the same three would get another 100 to 150. There was obviously no way anyone could handle each case conscientiously; the workload put a premium on the ability to dismiss cases, even solidly prosecutable ones, to concentrate on those cases in which the evidence and the need to prosecute was most clear.

"The method you learned right away was 'when in doubt, throw it out,'" Jacobs says. "It meant that there were a lot of cases where the people of this county didn't get justice—there might be a real bad assault, for instance, and it would be dismissed first thing out of the chute if the defense made noises that even sounded like self-defense. Not to mention the fact we plea-bargained everything cheap, just to move the docket. But looking back, I think it's a good thing for a prosecutor to go through. Since then, the first thing I think of if there's a substantial doubt in the case is to dismiss it, or at least I try to think that way."

After a year and a half of misdemeanor court, Jacobs "graduated" to prosecuting felonies—first burglary cases, then robberies, then murders. And now a capital murder.

"As far as prosecuting Kenneth Brock, I figured I did have some things going for me," Jacobs says. "I had a pretty good foundation in procedural rules from being with Judge Douglas, and I could usually stay calm in hot situations—usually—and in this case, I really had evidence I could believe in. I knew I couldn't out-orate Adrian Burk in front of the jury. So I was as meticulous as I could be in preparing my evidence. I made a notebook covering the testimony of every witness—that kind of thing. I didn't want to foul up and then see this guy get acquitted just because I, individually, fouled up."

Jacobs would need every asset he had, and more, just to stay even with Adrian Burk in the Kenneth Brock case.

* * *

Now the stage was set for the kind of pre-trial skirmishing that marks the beginning of nearly every serious criminal case.

Burk would try to get Jacobs' evidence thrown out, and to get advantages in selecting the jury, and so forth. He would use the legal rules about admissibility of evidence, the constitution, technical statutes, and any other legal principle he could that would serve his purpose, because that was his job—to attack the prosecution's case. The pre-trial stage offered an excellent opportunity.

Pre-trial is mainly the defense lawyer's show. The defense lawyer files legal papers, called "motions," in an attempt to get rulings from the judge giving the defense advantages at trial. For the most part, Jacobs could do nothing—other than try to prevent his case from getting hurt too badly by rulings on Burk's motions.

The filing of the motions was like throwing darts at a board. Some hit their mark and some did not. The best strategy was to throw plenty of darts, so Burk did. Sometimes, the strategy was apparent from the nature of the motion itself, but others had purposes that were far more subtle—to test the state's case, to put state witnesses on record in an unfavorable position, and the like.

For example, there was a "Motion for Discovery," in which Burk sought to inspect all the state's significant evidence (this motion was granted in part by the court, so it may be counted as having hit the mark). There was a "Motion to Produce Exculpatory and Mitigating Evidence," by which Burk sought to have the State and all its agencies search their files completely and turn over any information that might be useful to the defense (granted in full by the court). There was a "Motion with Reference to the Arraignment of the Accused," a "Motion for the Record of the Deceased," and a "Motion to Sequester Jurors." There were motions to have the prosecution produce criminal records of all witnesses (there were none, but Burk wanted to find out), and motions to stop the prosecution from going into all sorts of different types of evidence. Every motion had to be heard, and many of them added to Burk's store of useful information or gave him advantages at trial.

One of the most interesting motions Burk filed was called, simply enough, "Motion to Suppress Evidence."

By this motion, Burk sought to have all the defendant's confessions, admissions or statements of any kind hidden from the jury. That included the "I shot the store owner" remark, and it included the statement in which Kenneth Brock admitted where he had thrown the gun.

Burk knew the importance of these items of evidence, and he did not want the jury to hear them.

The Motion to Suppress contained standard claims. For instance, it alleged that the statements had been "forced" and "coerced" from the defendant in violation of the "Fifth, Sixth and Fourteenth Amendments to the United States Constitution." These allegations, of course, were euphemisms for a charge of police brutality. And the Motion to Suppress also contained another claim: it charged that Officer Lilley had violated the constitution in that the defendant "was not advised he had the right to seek legal counsel" or to "have legal counsel present at the time defendant made any statement to the police."

Here it was: the predictable charge of wrongdoing by Officer Lilley. Presumably, the charge meant that Lilley should have stopped his arrest and interrupted the defendant's blurted admission until he could warn the defendant of his rights. It was an extravagant claim; but Burk, of course, was only doing his job. He had to make these allegations, because it was not up to him to see that Lilley was treated fairly. His job was to get Brock acquitted.

Judge Walton held a lengthy hearing on the Motion to Suppress. Most of the important witnesses who would testify at the trial were called to the witness stand; the hearing turned into a little "trial before the real trial." Finally, Judge Walton rejected Burk's claims. Jacobs' evidence would not be thrown out; it could be heard by the jury. There had been no police brutality in this case. And the police had acted properly with reference to warning Kenneth Brock of his rights.

Of course, Adrian Burk had still gained a great deal from the pre-trial phase of the proceedings. For one thing, some of his motions *had* hit the mark, and some of the evidence had been thrown out. For another thing, he gained a great deal from the Motion to Suppress itself, even though Judge Walton had rejected it. How had he gained? In a very important way: It is always advantageous to a criminal lawyer to have the opposition's case spread out and revealed so that he can begin to pick it apart. As a result of the Motion to Suppress, Adrian Burk got a chance to cross examine most of the State's main witnesses at length during the hearing—to discover and pick apart their stories. Now he knew, for instance, that if he were to present a defense of accident, the admission by Kenneth Brock—the "I shot the store owner" remark—would not be all that devastating, because there was no admission that the shooting had been intentional. Furthermore, during the hearing, Burk had collected bits and pieces of testimony from various witnesses that would help him argue to the jury that the killing was accidental. The hearing, in other words, helped Burk decide on the defense strategy he would employ at trial and gave him ammunition to execute that strategy.

And so, as the day of trial approached, Burk knew more and more about what he was up against and what he could use to combat it. His pretrial motions had occupied much of the months of November and December, 1974. They had been exhaustively thorough.

On January 6, 1975, the first working day of the new year, the final pre-trial process—the arduous process of selecting a jury—began. It was a little over seven months after the murder of Michael Sedita.

* * *

Jury selection did not actually get under way until the afternoon of the 6th.

Judge Walton was seated at the impressive wooden judge's bench in the 178th courtroom. At counsel table, Jacobs sat on one side, Burk and his client on the other. The judge had ordered that a supply of jurors be brought over and seated in the jury room. One by one, the "venirepersons"—as potential jurors are called—would be led into the courtroom by the bailiff and individually questioned first by Judge Walton, then by prosecutor Jacobs, then by defender Burk. The process, everyone knew, would take several weeks of hard work. It had now just begun. The bailiff had brought out a young man named Gerald Cline and seated him in the witness chair for examination.

". . .Mr. Cline," Judge Walton asked the first potential juror when he had been seated in the witness chair, "Do you have any conscientious scruples or conscientious objections against the imposition of death as a punishment for crime in a capital case?"

The juror, Mr.Cline, looked as though he had been asked to explain the general theory of relativity. He looked up at the judge quizzically. "Now what was that you were telling me?" he asked. "Say that again."

Judge Walton tried again. He knew that the question was tortuous in its wording, but that wording had to be used in questioning the juror—because these words were used by the Supreme Court in specifying how death penalty jurors were chosen.

"I say, do you have any conscientious scruples or conscientious objections against the imposition or infliction of death as a punishment for crime in a proper case?"

The lawyers looked at the juror intently and waited for his answer.

"I would say yes," said Mr. Cline. "It would depend on the case."

The judge, still not satisfied, tried to nail the answer down for the record. "Well, that's the reason I qualified the matter—'in a proper case,' " he told the potential juror. He explained that the decision was entirely up to the jurors what verdict they would render in the case. "I am simply trying at this time to ascertain whether you are conscientiously opposed to the law of the State that authorizes a jury to return a verdict that would result in imposition of the death penalty for a person found guilty of the offense of capital murder."

Now Mr. Cline understood. Promptly, he answered: "No, I'm not opposed to that."

Jury selection in a capital case is tedious. The potential

jurors are questioned endlessly, one at a time, with the same questions repeated in little variation for each. But the tedium is that of an intricate contest, like the opening moves of a game of chess. Jurors are psychologically conditioned by this subtle opening process of adversary questioning; they can be influenced, persuaded or antagonized. More importantly, depending upon the way they answer the slow and deliberate questions put to them, they will be accepted or excused by lawyers who stake a good deal of the case upon a guess about their reactions to the evidence.

Examination of this first potential juror, Mr. Cline, was a typical example.

Gerald Cline was a truck driver for a gas company, unmarried and nineteen years of age. The lawyers knew this information from glancing at a form that Mr. Cline, and every other venireperson, had had to fill out before arriving in the courtroom. From a glance at the form, and from seeing Cline's short hair and work clothes, the lawyers already knew a great deal about him that was useful.

For example, it was significant that he was a young person. It was also important that he was in a work position that did not require him to make difficult decisions. These factors favored the defense, because they indicated that he might be hesitant to make unpleasant decisions in a capital case. On the other hand, he was a working man who would not sympathize with a robber and who would do his duty if he saw it clearly, and that favored the prosecution. The lawyers knew that they would have to listen to Mr. Cline's answers carefully to know which of these tendencies to consider most likely.

From listening to the venireman's answers to Judge Walton's questions, the lawyers could see that this Mr. Cline was cautious. He would not stick his neck out until he understood everything. He might be suspicious of the prosecution's case if it left any stone unturned. But he was decisive once he understood, and he was unequivocal in saying that he was not opposed to the death penalty.

As Judge Walton finished qualifying the potential juror, Mr. Cline began to shape up as a man in the middle—a person who might be acceptable to both sides and who might be selected on the jury.

Jacobs started his questions slowly, recognizing Mr. Cline's potential importance.

The prosecutor was concerned, first of all, that Gerald Cline might be so cautious that he would not consider any evidence sufficient to prove a case beyond a reasonable doubt. So he started his questioning of the juror by explaining that the State had the burden of proof—but it was a proof beyond "reasonable" doubt, not beyond "all" doubt. "What it does *not* mean," Jacobs said to Cline, "and what is strictly *not* required, is that the State prove to you beyond *all* doubt, every single *iota* of a doubt, of a defendant's guilt, and I am sure you can see the reason for that, because it would be impossible."

Then Jacobs asked, "Can you agree with that and abide by it?"

"No, not really," said Gerald Cline.

"Why?" What's the problem there?"

The venireman was not able to articulate his objection immediately. He began, "Well. . .you should have all the evidence." Then he hesitated. "You know, like you say—" Then he hesitated again. "I can't really answer that without hearing the case. . .I would have to hear it, but—"

"You understand I'm not trying to pre-commit you to any verdict one way or another," Jacobs said, trying again. He explained, once more, that the burden of proof was "beyond a *reasonable* doubt." "Now it is impossible," he continued, "and the State cannot prove anything to you beyond *all* doubt. Do you agree with that? Or do you have a question about that?"

"I agree after you restated that," said Mr. Cline, now willing to commit himself. "You are saying up to a reasonable doubt, right? Okay. I agree with that, because you can't give a jury everything. That's impossible."

Strategically, Jacobs had reached his first objective with this venireman. It was essential to make sure that he would consider the witnesses in the light of reason, because the witnesses would not be Supermen—they would be ordinary human beings with ordinary memories and perceptions. Without this kind of questioning, there are some jurors who will reject overwhelming proof in the most surprising way, because of some minor conflict. At the same time, Jacobs had been careful to handle Mr. Cline with courtesy—in fact, with kid gloves. Examination of a potential juror, who, after all, will be deciding the case for or against the person who is doing the examining, is quite different in this respect from the examination of witnesses.

Finally Jacobs said, "Your honor, we pass the juror."

Now it would be Adrian Burk's turn.

Burk, like Jacobs, started slowly. But when he got deeply into his examination, his own technique surfaced. It was a style different from Jacobs' style. It was neither better nor worse, neither more nor less effective—but it was distinctly different.

For one thing, Burk did not shrink from meaty subjects or from graphic terminology. He told Gerald Cline that the State of Texas "will ask you to vote to send this man to the electric chair, take his life."

That explanation got the juror's attention in a way that nothing else had yet.

With this elementary beginning, Burk asked, now, "Mr. Cline, do you know what a capital murder case is?"

"No, I don't."

Burk began to explain what a capital murder case was. "And do you understand how a person is put to death if he's adjudged guilty and the jury answers questions that cause him to be sentenced to death?"

"No, I don't really."

Burk was willing to tell him. "Well, it's through the electric chair. That's our method of electrocution. I want you to understand all the ramifications of your verdict as a juror in this case," Burk said helpfully. "Are you with me?"

"Yes."

Burk went on, trying to engender in the juror a repulsion to the death penalty. "And do you believe it is just and fair punishment?" he asked finally.

"If proven guilty," said Mr. Cline.

The examination of Gerald Cline took the better part of an hour. Later, when the record was prepared, it occupied more than forty pages of type. But it had transformed Mr. Cline from a name on paper to a human being whose broad characteristics were now known to the attorneys. Ultimately, it was a picture the State could live with but the defense could not.

"What says the State?" Judge Walton asked.

"The State will accept Mr. Cline, your honor."

"What says the defense?"

Burk had a difficult decision to make. He could have the venireman removed from the jury by using one of his "peremptory challenges." He had fifteen such challenges, but the state also had fifteen, and he did not want to squander them. Finally, Burk decided that although the juror's caution made him somewhat attractive to the defense, if he heard the evidence in this case the odds were unacceptably high that he would vote in favor of the death penalty.

"We will exercise our peremptory challenge, your honor," he said.

Gerald Cline was excused.

* * *

Jury selection droned on, and on, and on. Throughout this exhausting process, the lawyers struggled to stay at peak mental acuity.

They were assisted in this endeavor by occasional acrimony and occasional humor. For example:

"...All right," Adrian Burk was saying to one juror after several days of jury selection had passed. "What do you do when you're not working?"

"Sleep, mostly."

"What else?"

"When I'm not doing that, I'm chasing women."

"When you're not sleeping or chasing women, do you have anything else that you do?"

"Well, I dance, play ball."

"Have you ever tried marijuana?"

"No,—I don't think so."

"Have you ever been around people that have tried it?"

"I don't know what marijuana is."

. . .

"Do you know what 'conscientious scruples' means?"

"No, I do not."

This time it was Jacobs, not Burk, who used a peremptory challenge. Jacobs figured that a juror who bantered with the defense lawyer during a capital murder case, claimed not to know what marijuana was and answered questions about conscientious scruples without knowing what "conscientious scruples" meant, was not to be trusted to say whether the case had been proved beyond a reasonable doubt. Burk's ostensibly playful questioning of this venireman had in fact been quite skillful.

As the hours went by and stretched into days, and the days grew into weeks, each side's peremptory challenges were gradually exhausted. The attorneys were forced, to an ever increasing degree, to take chances in accepting jurors. The case inched into its third calendar week.

And then, suddenly, in the middle of the third week, there were twelve people who had been accepted by both sides.

The jury that would try Kenneth Brock had been selected.

There were six men and six women. They were a conglomerate mix of races, ages and occupations. A few were blue-collar workers and a few were housewives and there were some white-collar workers among the twelve. Jury selection had educated all of them to have a keen sense of the concepts that they would have to use to decide the case. Jury selection had also removed those who said they could not, for one reason or another, be fair to the defendant, and it had removed those who said they could not, under any circumstances, sit as jurors in the trial of a capital case. What was left was a jury that was not perceptibly favorable either to one side or the other.*

---

*The following name in this chapter was changed, without alteration of the incident in which the person was involved: Gerald Cline.

CHAPTER FOUR
THE TRIAL

On January 23, the twelve persons remaining from the process of elimination that is called jury selection stood, all in a group, and raised their hands. They swore the traditional oath required of all jurors in criminal cases: that they would "a true verdict render, according to the law and the evidence." The trial was about to begin.

"All right," said Judge Walton. "You may be seated, members of the jury. Mr. Jacobs, you may read the indictment."

Jacobs stood, faced the jury, and started to read. "In the name and by authority of the State of Texas, the Grand Jury of Harris County...do present that in the County of Harris and State of Texas, one Kenneth Albert Brock"—the jurors looked at the defendant—"on or about May 21, 1974, did then and there unlawfully, and intentionally, cause the death of Michael Sedita..."

Jacobs read on. The indictment was the all-important document that set forth the elements of the State's case, the facts that had to be proved. It was technically worded, dry and dull, but it was the first statement to the jury of the charge against Kenneth Brock in positive language. Jacobs read it slowly and distinctly.

"...against the peace and dignity of the state," Jacobs said, reading the final words of the indictment. These archaic words were required, by law, to be at the end of every indictment in Texas. They were completely superfluous to the charge, and nobody knew what had prompted the Texas legislature in some long-forgotten session to require that they be there, but the indictment would be absolutely defective (and any conviction would be reversed) without them. Jacobs was careful to include them, even though they did sound a little out of place.

On the other side of the table, Kenneth Brock sat beside Adrian Burk. He did not have the matted beard, long hair or unkempt appearance of the time of his arrest. Instead, he wore spotlessly clean clothes, his face was clean-shaven, and his hair curled softly about his ears. At the beginning of his trial, for understandable reasons, he looked clean-cut and innocent.

Adrian Burk stood and entered Kenneth Brock's plea to the indictment: "Not guilty."

* * *

One of the first witnesses Jacobs called was Sergeant Hogg. He was unquestionably the State's most important witness. He had been the man in charge the night of the murder, and he was the only witness who had seen the entire event from start to finish.

That meant that Sergeant Hogg was also important for Adrian Burk, but in a different way: Burk desperately needed to exclude or discredit the sergeant's testimony.

And so some of the most vigorous lawyering of the entire trial came near the beginning, while this crucial witness testified.

"I grabbed my shotgun," Sergeant Hogg was saying, "and I proceeded to run around the corner, and when I reached the corner here, the defendant fired a shot at me."

Burk was on his feet, with a lengthy objection that concluded, ". . .the witness has testified to an extraneous offense for which the defendant does not stand indicted. It's prejudicial to the defense of the defendant and I object and ask that it be stricken from the record and that the jury be instructed to disregard it."

"That's overruled," said Judge Walton.

"I move for a mistrial, your honor."

"That's overruled."

"Please note our exception, your honor."

This would be the pattern that most of the trial would follow. Jacobs would struggle to get the facts before the jury in accordance with the rules of evidence, and Burk, who had no interest in having the jury receive evidence that incriminated his client, would struggle equally to have it excluded from the jury. He would cite to the judge as many legal theories as he could. And then he would make sure that his objections were fully reflected in the record, so that if an appeal was necessary he could hope that the Texas Court of Criminal Appeals would disagree with one of Judge Walton's rulings.

Burk even objected to evidence that did not directly incriminate his client. It had started with a diagram, marked as State's Exhibit 3, a diagram of the scene of the homicide. Jacobs wanted to show the diagram to the jury simply to facilitate the jury's understanding of the evidence; it would be easier if the jurors understood first where the Seven-Eleven was, where Surry Road was in relation to the woods, and so forth. But Burk, as might be expected, did not share the objective of simplifying the evidence for the jury; that would make it easier for the jurors to understand evidence that was incriminating. He objected when Sergeant Hogg tried to explain the diagram. "It has not been proved by this witness," he argued. "There is no testimony by him other than the fact that this looks like it, and we object because there is no showing by this witness that he is familiar with the distances indicated on it or the area as generally depicted by it. Further, there are statements on the exhibit that are prejudicial, and conclusions of law. . .and we object to the admission of State's Exhibit 3 into evidence."

Burk's objection covered all the bases. But Jacobs had covered all the bases, too. Before calling Sergeant Hogg, he had had three other witnesses testify. The first, Investigator Mark Argo, had testified about the way he had measured the distances on the diagram; the second, Deputy Sheriff Sherman Bradshaw, had taken aerial photographs from a helicopter so that the exact details of the crime scene could be compared with the diagram, State's Exhibit 3.

Judge Walton was ready to decide on Burk's objection. "That's overruled," he said. Jacobs' meticulous planning was beginning to pay off; the diagram was admitted into evidence.

"Note our exception," said Adrian Burk.

With the jurors finally able to look at the scene diagram,

Jacobs was now ready to move on to the meatiest part of the evidence. After objections from Burk to various questions, on the ground that they were about "extraneous offenses," were "repetitious," were improper "bolstering" of the State's own witnesses, were "hearsay," were "prejudicial," were "leading" the witness, suggested a "conclusion" to the witness, and several others, Jacobs moved Sergeant Hogg through the story of the killing. The problem with these objections was that every one of them had some arguable basis in the complicated law of evidence, and it took judgment to decide that they were inapplicable to the specific questions Jacobs was asking. The evidence moved slowly. Finally, Jacobs reached the point of the actual shooting.

"Had any officer attempted to approach Mr. Brock at that time, or had anybody fired, when he shot Mr. Sedita?"

"No, sir, they had not."

"Was anyone advancing toward him at this time?"

"No, sir, they were not."

"Did you yourself, or were you able to, observe *any* reason that would have caused the defendant, Kenneth Brock, to shoot Mr. Sedita?"

"No, sir, I did not."

"All right. Did you hear a shot fired?"

"Yes, sir, I did."

"Did you see a flash, or not?"

"No, sir."

"Exactly how far were the defendant and Mr. Sedita positioned from each other when the shot was fired?"

"They were sideways in the alley with the defendant behind Mr. Sedita."

This was the first time the jury had heard the details of the killing. They were listening carefully. Hogg was an excellent witness, with an attitude of quiet competence. But were the deliberateness and brutality of the offense really being conveyed to the jury? Jacobs, keenly aware that he had the burden of proof on all the issues, repeatedly underlined the details of that crucial instant. He started, again, with the taking of the hostage down the alley to Surry Road, and went through the story once more, in depth.

"So, then, if I understand you correctly, you had the defendant positioned between you, is that right?"

"Yes, sir, that's correct."

"All right. Did you make any statements, or say anything, to the defendant Kenneth Brock at this time?"

"No, sir, I did not."

"Did you hear other officers say anything to him?"

"I could hear muffled words, but I couldn't understand the words."

"All right. Now, after you had positioned him between you there on the road, tell the jury what happened next."

"We stopped there to avoid getting him into any kind of panic, and he walked on to approximately this position here, and a little farther down here to approximately here." The sergeant was indicating the movements on the diagram. "And there were words exchanged but I couldn't make them out. It was too far away from me then. And I heard a shot and saw Mr. Sedita fall."

"All right. Now, what had the other officers down at the other end of the road done, at that time, or what had you observed them do?"

"I observed them—they were at this point, when Mr. Sedita and the defendant were approaching them, and they had started backing up when the defendant shot Mr. Sedita."

Jacobs went on with the questioning, trying to make the jury see each part of the event with as much clarity as was humanly possible. For although the public image of the courtroom lawyer is that of a slashing cross-examiner, the fact is that direct examination of one's own witnesses is far more difficult than cross examination—and, most of the time, more important. At one point, Jacobs had Sergeant Hogg physically demonstrate, using the actual pistol that had been recovered from the ditch, how Kenneth Brock had killed his victim. Jacobs used his own body to play the part of Michael Sedita. Like actors on a stage, the prosecutor and policeman played the crucial moment for the jury to see. Jacobs had the burden of proof, but he also had overwhelming evidence, and he wanted to get all of it that he could through to the jury.

Finally, when he was sure that everything in the sergeant's testimony was clear, Jacobs passed the witness. Now it would be Adrian Burk's turn.

* * *

Burk's cross examination was apparently premised on the

theory that the killing was precipitated not by any voluntary act by Kenneth Brock, but rather by the actions of Hogg and the other police officers.

"All right," he was saying. "Now, Mr. Hogg, what I'm getting at is that you gentlemen there obviously were intent on pressuring the suspect and prevailing on him to surrender, weren't you?"

"If at all possible, yes, sir."

"If at all possible, you wanted him to surrender?"

"Yes, sir."

"If at all possible, but what if it was not possible for him to surrender? Supposing his mind was too warped or crazy that he would not yield—"

Jacobs interrupted. "We object to the form of the question, your honor. Counsel is stating facts that are not in evidence."

"He's probably right, judge," said Burk. "I withdraw it."

Burk continued. "Mr. Hogg, do you think that you were putting too much pressure on whoever was in the alley with Mr. Sedita? Do you think you put too much pressure on him, whoever it was with Sedita, by pressuring him?"

"No, sir, I do not."

"Why?" Burk wanted to know. "You see, whoever this fellow was, he said, 'back up, back up.' He said that more than once, didn't he?"

"Yes, sir, he did."

"And as a matter of fact, the deceased told you to back up, this man was crazy, didn't he?"

"Yes, sir."

"The deceased, Mr. Sedita, told you, back up, this man was crazy?"

"Yes, sir."

"But still, Mr. Hogg, you all pressed on, didn't you?"

Hogg's answer was firm. "No, sir, we did not."

Now Burk saw the need to extricate himself gracefully, but his momentum carried him on. "I understand you were trying to do your duty as you saw it under the circumstances that you should do it, but—"

"No, sir, we did not press on. That's my answer to your question." Burk had pushed the matter too far, and it was now evident to everyone that the sergeant's first priority had been Michael Sedita's life.

But in spite of this gaffe, Burk had planted the seed of this idea that the police officers had produced the murder. It was a theme to which he would return, time and again, during the course of the trial.

And Burk scored a number of other points.

For one thing, he gave material assistance to his accident defense during the cross examination of Sergeant Hogg. He brought out a description of the scene as "full of chug holes and uneven terrain and a lot of things in it." This depiction of the road surface might help him make it more credible that his client could have tripped and pulled the trigger accidentally. Burk also emphasized the flimsiness of the gun: "Do you know anything about guns? Is that normal, for that to act like that?" He had Sergeant Hogg handle the weapon, demonstrating the light trigger pull and haphazard chamber action. When the sergeant replied, "Yes, sir, that's what's dangerous about those Saturday Night Specials," he had made his point—although he requested, and got, an instruction from Judge Walton that the jury was not to consider the derogatory "Saturday Night Special" characterization of the gun.

Burk also went over the details of the offense with Hogg, laying groundwork for the possibility that he could get later witnesses to contradict those details. He got Hogg to admit, at one point, that his testimony about the place he first observed the defendant was "wrong." He asked questions about whether anybody had threatened to shoot Kenneth Brock or whether Brock had "received any abusive treatment at the hands of any officers that night." He laid groundwork for his theory that intoxication had added to the accident: "Did his eyes look like they were a little blank, a little glazed over, fixed?" When Sergeant Hogg replied that they did not, Burk asked, "And you wouldn't say anything here that would deprive him of a fair trial, would you?" in a tone that all but said Hogg was a liar.

It was a vigorous cross examination.

* * *

The case would not have been complete without at least one serious charge of prosecution misconduct. Burk supplied it.

The charge arose over photographs that Jacobs began to

introduce into evidence through Sergeant Hogg, photographs showing the scene of the murder. Burk complained that he had not had sufficient time before trial to see them. Further, Burk charged that Jacobs' failure to make them available for inspection, as he saw it, was a violation of the court's order on the defense motion for discovery.

"I would like to make this objection into the record, your honor," Burk began, "and point out to the court that heretofore, during preliminary matters that have been conducted outside the presence of the jury, the court has instructed the state's attorney, Mr. Jacobs, to make available to me on behalf of the defendant all of the photographs that the state intended to introduce into evidence here before the jury and before the court, and with that in mind, on the day of the court's ruling, I went to Mr. Jacob's office where I was shown approximately four photographs. . . ."

Jacobs interrupted. "Excuse me, your honor," he said as calmly as he could. "I don't know what Mr. Burk is going into, but since this happened outside the presence of the jury, I would ask that we approach the bench to see what his point is so that I can answer it at the bench."

It turned out that what Burk wanted was a dismissal of the entire murder case and the acquittal of Kenneth Brock on the ground that Jacobs had violated his client's right to discovery.

The judge had the jury taken from the courtroom. This was not going to be something that could be resolved by a whispered conference at the bench. In fact, it was becoming increasingly evident that it was going to take some time to unravel Burk's charge.

Before Burk could argue his motion, he had to produce evidence of the prosecution misconduct he was charging. The witness he called was, of course, himself. While it is unusual for attorneys to testify in a case that they are trying, the practice is becoming increasingly common today since allegations of prosecution misconduct have become a standard defensive technique.

Burk testified about the judge's order on his Motion for Discovery. The judge had ordered the prosecution to allow his inspection of all photographs related to the case. "At the close of trial proceedings on that day," he testified, "I went to Mr. Jacobs' office, whereupon he showed me, as I recall, four

8x10 photographs." The photographs that were now in issue had not been among those four.

When Burk had finished, the judge turned to Jacobs and said, "Any questions from the state?"

"Mr. Burk," Jacobs asked, "so that the record will reflect exactly what the situation is here, what time did you arrive in the courtroom this morning?"

Burk told him.

Then Jacobs got to the point. "And do you recall when you approached counsel table that I presented you with two packets of photographs and presented them to you for your examination and perusal, and I said to you, 'Mr. Burk, here are photographs we intend to offer in the trial of the case and pursuant to the court's order I am giving them to you at this time so that you may have an opportunity to examine them,' and I did present you with the photographs at that time, did I not?"

"Mr. Jacobs," Burk answered, "You handed me two packets of photographs with the statement that here are some additional photographs that I intend to introduce. I would correct you, sir: I do not recall and I do not intentionally dispute your word, Mr. Jacobs, if you said this . . . . That was the first time I had ever seen the exhibits."

Jacobs examined Burk further. The court's order covering the photographs had been entered in the afternoon, only two working days earlier, and Jacobs had furnished Burk the pictures he then had, immediately. The other pictures, which Jacobs had had to receive from the custody of the police, had been shown to Burk early this morning. In other words, it had taken Jacobs something between one and two actual working days to show Burk the pictures he did not have immediately available. Jacobs had not really violated the order of the court.

"All right," Jacobs went on. "Further, Mr. Burk, this morning before the jury was called in, you did return those pictures to me in the envelope that I had given to you, did you not?"

"I made certain, Mr. Jacobs, that the pictures you handed me were not mutilated, damaged, mishandled, marked or desecrated in any way. . .," Burk replied in an ironic tone.

But that was not Jacobs' point at all. "And at the time you

returned them to me, you made no request of me for additional time to examine them, did you, sir?"

"No, I did not, Mr. Jacobs."

In the end, Judge Walton overruled Burk's motions for dismissal of the charges, for a mistrial, and for exclusion of all pictures from evidence.

The jury was brought back in, approximately two hours after they had been removed at the start of the controversy over the pictures. The court reporter's notes, by this time, were so lengthy that the end of the pictures controversy appeared on page 3,417 of the transcript. The judge instructed the jury that the pictures at issue had been admitted into evidence.

As the trial progressed, Burk continued to use novel technical theories to exclude evidence. In one instance, he tried to get the testimony of a witness suppressed in its entirety because the witness had talked to the investigator, Mark Argo, in violation—as Burk saw it—of an order of the court. In another instance, he insisted on the right to see the original handwritten statement of a witness, and this demand led to a hearing at which seven witnesses were called outside the presence of the jury. The hearing only confirmed what had been apparent from the start—that the witness' statement had been typed from the handwritten form, then the handwritten original thrown away—and the judge overruled Burk's motion to stop the prosecution on this ground, since the typed copy of the original was available to the defense throughout the witness' testimony.

* * *

"Would you state your name for the members of the jury, please?" Jacobs was saying to a new witness.

"Joe Bill Walker," said the witness.

The calling of Joe Bill Walker represented something of a minor triumph for the prosecution. He was the truck driver who had seen Brock crawling across the road, out of the woods, and had shined his spotlight on him. If Sergeant Hogg was, figuratively speaking, the Samuel Johnson of this story, Joe Bill Walker was its Boswell. But the officers on the scene had failed to get his name, not realizing how essential his testimony would be. It had taken Mark Argo days of work and not inconsiderable ingenuity to locate him. The offense report that the officers had prepared had, mistakenly, identified the man in the truck as a wrecker driver, and through this slender lead, by contacting the officers and contacting, in turn, a number of wrecker drivers, he found one that was able to tell him the name of the man he was looking for.

Now, Joe Bill Walker sat on the witness stand and told the jury, "I got my spotlight and shined my spotlight on the road, and I seen this man"—he identified the defendant—"was crossing the road on his stomach."

The irony was not lost on the jury. Here was the amateur crime-fighter, lured to the scene because he heard a report on a CB radio that promised excitement, catching a desperate and dangerous criminal who had eluded a posse surrounding him with dogs and horses. It was a scene straight from the movies. And Walker, with his salt-of-the-earth mannerisms, did not let the jurors down, as he went on to describe Brock "easing along on his stomach like they do in the army."

It was important testimony. Without it, there would have been a hole in the state's story as Brock went from the woods into the residential area where he was arrested. Without it, Burk might have had a shot at a defense of mistaken identity. And the obvious attempt to escape the consequences of his crime that Walker's testimony so graphically showed would not assist Brock's defense of accident.

How would Burk deal with this testimony?

The approach Burk used was simplicity itself, but ingenious simplicity. Burk looked at Walker, with his faded blue jeans, his pearl buttoned shirt, his boots and his short-sided haircut, and decided that an ounce of humor was worth a pound of exculpatory evidence. After establishing that Warren's truck was a half-ton pickup, he moved on to the heart of the matter:

"All right. I guess that you are one of those people that has got a KIKK sticker on the back?" (KIKK is a Houston radio station that caters to country tastes).

"Yes, sir," said Walker.

"And 'Drink Budweiser,' on the back, too?".

"No, Sir," said Walker happily, because although he didn't necessarily like Budweiser enough to put an ad for it on his bumper, he did like to talk about his truck.

"And a gun rack?"

Of course it had a gun rack. "Yes, sir," said Joe Bill Walker.

"And curtains?"

"No, sir, no curtains," said Walker, looking like he was thinking about putting them in, though.

"A Wallace for President sticker on the bumper?"

"No, sir."

"But that's the kind of truck you are talking about?"

"Yes, sir," said Walker, because Burk had, indeed, really hit on exactly the kind of truck it was. Walker was smiling because he liked to talk about his truck. The jurors were smiling, too, because they liked to listen to a man talk about his truck who so obviously enjoyed it.

Burk went on, following the assumption that a laughing jury is seldom hanging one.

After five or six more questions, Jacobs began to wonder whether Burk and Walker were ever going to stop talking pickup trucks. Finally, Burk began asking about Walker's stepmother's pickup truck—did it have a spotlight on it, too?—and this was too much for Jacobs, who objected that the question was "immaterial." But the judge, who was not going to stop Burk from defending his client even if the defense was a little unorthodox, said: "Overruled."

Burk got some advice from Walker on the best place to buy a good spotlight for a truck ("You can buy them at Western Auto or K-Mart,") and then stopped talking pickup trucks. He talked with Walker a few minutes about whether he belonged to a union. Then he asked Warren whether he had "ever seen anybody who was drinking beer and popping pills who did or said things that they ordinarily would not do or say?" (yes, he had, Walker replied), and whether on those occasions Walker had "seen the glassy look in their eyes?" ("Yes, sir"). Then Burk got Walker to describe what the eyes of the man he saw crawling across the road that night were like. It was the intoxication theory again; since Sergeant Hogg had said Brock's eyes looked normal, if Burk could get Warren to contradict that, he would not only impeach Hogg's testimony but shore up his accident defense at the same time.

"He had a glassy-eyed look and they were also bloodshot," the witness answered. Burk had scored.

It was almost an anticlimax when, after Walker, Jacobs

called Officers Jalomo, Phillips and Orlando to testify about the murder they had seen that night.

* * *

The state's evidence continued to build. Jacobs called the other officers, Ella and Jim Garver, Phil Ochsler, Andy Hart, and finally his technical witnesses: Martinez, the firearms expert; Zotter, the chemist; and, to end on a note of strength, Green, the medical examiner. Patiently, Jacobs brought out the details from each in the same way that he had from Sergeant Hogg.

But the more colorful testimony, in most instances, was elicited by Burk. His defensive theories began to gel, built on a foundation of folksy but at times brilliant cross examination. Basically, he had six themes that he developed throughout the case: (1) that the shooting was an accident; (2) that it had happened because the defendant was intoxicated to the point of being glassy-eyed; (3) that the investigation had been incomplete and incompetent; (4) that the police officers had beaten, abused and threatened Kenneth Brock; (5) that the police officers had pressured Kenneth Brock so intensely that they put him "in a box," "in a vise," or "in a bind" and thereby produced the killing themselves; and (6) that nobody could tell just what had happened that night, or even whether the man with the gun had been Kenneth Brock, because the lighting was too poor and there were too many discrepancies between the witnesses.

Finally, Jacobs got all his evidence in. He had been working carefully, slowly, without attracting attention. It all depended upon the jury. Would they respond to Burk's six themes, or to Jacob's one?

* * *

Jacobs rested his case.

Shortly after that, Burk rested too.

And with that, the jurors had heard all they were going to hear on the issue of Kenneth Brock's guilt or innocence.

There was one person, of course, who had been present the night of the homicide who was not called to the witness stand. That person was Kenneth Brock himself. The decision not to testify was Brock's own choice; it was a right he had under the fifth amendment to the constitution, the privilege against self-incrimination. The jurors would be instructed that they could not hold it against him. For in a very literal sense, Kenneth Brock owed nothing to the State of Texas in his trial—and he did not have to testify if he did not want to.

CHAPTER FIVE
THE ARGUMENTS AND THE VERDICT

"...but if you do not so believe, or if you have a reasonable doubt thereof, you will acquit the defendant and say by your verdict not guilty."

Judge Walton was reading his instructions to the jury. Texas law required the judge to give the jury a written copy of the instructions to take to the jury deliberation room. But first, the judge had to read them out loud with the jurors present in the courtroom. This repetition gave a special emphasis to the instructions, and so did the fact that the judge was the most influential person in the courtroom.

Judge Walton had earlier recessed the trial for a day to prepare the instructions he was now reading. He knew that it was common for convictions to be reversed on appeal in Texas if so much as one sentence in the jury instructions was improperly given. Adrian Burk had known that too, and he had filed written objections to every significant part of the instructions the judge was now reading. Those objections would be the basis for a major part of his appeal, if one was needed.

Now, as Judge Walton read the law that would control the case, the jurors were listening to every word. The judge explained the three possible verdicts carefully: first, capital murder; then, murder; then "not guilty."

The end of the instructions was the part with the greatest psychological impact. The judge had written the last paragraphs of the instructions to protect the rights of the defendant to a fair trial. "In all criminal cases," Judge Walton told the jurors firmly, "the burden of proof is on the state to prove the defendant's guilt beyond a reasonable doubt, and such burden remains on the state throughout the trial of the case.

"The defendant is presumed to be innocent until his guilt is established by legally admissible evidence, beyond a reasonable doubt; and in case you have a reasonable doubt as to the defendant's guilt, you will acquit the defendant and say by your verdict not guilty."

Jacobs listened to these words, which he had heard literally hundreds of times before, and he thought once again how difficult they made it sound for the state to make its required proof. No matter how horrible the crime was, no matter if it was committed before six policemen—those words applied to this case just as they did to any other. The judge had told the jury no less than five different times throughout the instructions that the state had the burden of proof "beyond a reasonable doubt." The jurors had been hearing those words since the beginning of the case, and in fact these were things the jurors had no doubt heard all their lives. Of course, the jury instructions contained plenty of elements that the prosecution wanted in them, too, but none had anything like the impact of these simple, eloquent words: "And if you have a reasonable doubt, you will acquit the defendant."

Was it possible? In the face of all the evidence, could the jury really acquit this defendant?

Jacobs knew the answer to that. Certainly, the jury could acquit the defendant. Jacobs knew better than to take anything for granted. Some jurors, he knew, hear the words "beyond a reasonable doubt" and expect a proof of near-magical perfection. Some jurors come into a case from the beginning with a cast of mind that makes no evidence convincing enough. The odds seemed against it in this case, but the chances of acquittal were real and sobering.

The judge finished reading the instructions.

It was time now for jury argument.

* * *

"I believe in our system of justice," Adrian Burk told the jurors as he started his argument.

Then, almost immediately, the big defense lawyer began

to tell the jurors why they should acquit Kenneth Brock.

"This case, like a lot of other cases, kind of reminds me of an iceberg," he said. "An iceberg is out there in the water and you see some of it above the water and some of it you can't see, because it's underneath the surface of the water. And some things that transpired here in this trial can be discussed and others can't." Burk gave the jurors an example of what he meant: cash had supposedly been found in the pockets of the defendant, but "this may be one of the things that's under the water, I don't know. You didn't see any cash brought in here."

Burk was arguing the case exactly the right way. When all else fails, a defense lawyer can always make points by thinking of something the prosecution could have done but didn't and then arguing that the omission creates a reasonable doubt as to the defendant's guilt. Here, since the cash hadn't been brought in and put into evidence, it might not exist; and who could be sure, the inference went, that the entire prosecution case wasn't the same way? Of course, the argument was fatuous—there always has to be some item of evidence somewhere that the prosecution did not produce, otherwise the trial would never end—but neither Burk nor Jacobs was foolish enough to ignore it. In a criminal case, especially a capital one, anything can happen.

And Burk had plenty of other reasons why the jury should acquit Kenneth Brock, in case they didn't like his first one.

"I think and I submit to you that they are wrong in their identification," he told the jury. "They have no earthly idea whether that's the gun or not.... When they came in and told you that they identified him from what they saw out there in that alley, I think they are asking you to believe a fairy tale. I don't think they could."

In other words, the officers had arrested the wrong man and let the real killer get away. Reasonable doubt.

And even if Kenneth Brock had been on the scene of the crime, the killing had not been intentional, said Burk. It was an accident.

"If he intended to take a life, would he have done it in front of six police officers?" Burk asked the jury in an impassioned voice. That just did not make sense; why would Kenneth Brock throw away his "ticket to freedom?" And now, Burk's words began to tumble faster and faster as he supported this theory of accidental homicide by jumping from one piece of evidence to another:

". . .Did they rush this man in a way that caused him to move suddenly, that caused Mr. Sedita to move?. . ."

". . .It occurred at night, a lot of it transpired down a dark alley. . ."

". . .The chemist told you that people that take those barbiturates and wash them down with beer and get loose—or 'stoned,' as one of the young men said—they get a glassy look in their eyes. . ."

Kenneth Brock had been jostled. He was intoxicated to the point of stumbling, moving on unfamiliar terrain, carrying a cheap flimsy weapon, frightened by police officers who were pressuring him beyond endurance, and he had been jostled and the gun had gone off. That was Burk's theory of the case. And as the big defense lawyer went on with the reasons for it, his argument became disjunctive, almost kaleidoscopic, to accommodate every bit of testimony he could remember: "The size of the two people. . .The light pull on the trigger. . .Maybe they rushed. . .Such an apprehension in this man's mind. . .that the gun discharged. . . ."

All the argument had to do to succeed was to create a reasonable doubt. When one listened to it, it seemed irresistibly persuasive.

And then, in his conclusion, the impassioned defense attorney pulled out all the stops.

"I have appreciated this opportunity to speak on behalf of Kenneth. I love him. I love him. You don't know him as I do, and I say that to you from the bottom of my heart."

There was not a trace of insincerity in Burk's voice.

"You are going to be asked to return a verdict that could take this man's life from him," he went on. "I ask you to do one thing. . .that when you go back and you reach your verdict, that you speak for divine guidance and you ask His help in arriving at your verdict. And when you do that, I will be satisfied and grateful.

"Thank you."

With that, Adrian Burk ended his argument. He was emotionally drained. He sat down, heavily, and stared forward.

* * *

This argument had been exactly the type that was most

likely to save Kenneth Brock from a capital murder conviction.

There was much in the argument that was questionable, even extravagant. It had rambled for the better part of an hour, and it was not likely to win any prizes in a debating society. But no one could fail to appreciate that a human being with protected legal rights was on trial after Burk's summation. And no one could avoid doubt on the crucial question of intentional-killing-versus-accident.

Jacobs stood up and held the sides of the podium, and he looked at the jury. Now it was his turn to speak.

"Mr. Burk has protected the rights of this defendant," he said. "I don't think there's any question about that.... And I think that's good.... Because I think we all know that nobody is going to be dragged into court and have any of their rights taken from them."

And then Jacobs started telling the jurors why the homicide was not an accident.

He argued the point the same way he had put in his evidence: by a painstaking and complete recitation of all the facts in the case. He reminded the jurors what Kenneth Brock had done. And when he had finished, the deliberateness of the killing stood out in bold relief.

Kenneth Brock had circled the store, looking. "I wonder how many times he drove around that store, planning his opportunity," Jacobs said. Brock had had his girl friend, Cynthia Morales, prepared for the escape. "He's got his getaway car out there. He's got somebody to drive it, and the motor is running and the lights are on and it's ready to go." Brock had pointed a gun at the people in the store and told them to lie down on the floor. That was "so nobody would think anything was wrong."

Kenneth Brock had planned the robbery and he had planned to escape.

Brock had not even left the manager in the store when the robbery was completed. Instead, he had deliberately kidnapped the manager and calculatedly held him hostage. And then the killer had done something that spelled out his intent clearly. "Sergeant Hogg drove up in his car and got out, and he saw that it was a Houston policeman," Jacobs said. "And we knew right then that he was willing to do anything to get away, he would do anything to get away. Because he shot at

Sergeant Hogg, a Houston policeman in full uniform coming toward him with a gun."

And what had Kenneth Brock done next, coldly and intentionally? Jacobs reminded the jurors that he had put Michael Sedita in a position where he was likely to be killed by shoving him directly into the line of fire.

Deliberate act was piled on deliberate act as Jacobs recounted the evidence. The defendant had pulled the trigger with the gun squarely against Michael Sedita's chest, because the wound was a contact wound. It had gone through Sedita's main heart artery. Kenneth Brock had held the pistol almost exactly perpendicular to Sedita's chest, because the trajectory through the thoracic cavity was nearly perfectly horizontal. The police officers had been taken by surprise by the killing, but Kenneth Brock had not, because he had crossed a ditch, scaled a six-foot chain-link fence, and disappeared in the woods before the officers could gather their wits to shoot. And the killer had nearly gotten away. Because it was by chance that a man in a truck had spotted him crawling on his stomach across the road.

Jacobs digressed a moment to express the indignation he felt such a deliberate crime should evoke. For Michael Sedita, he reminded the jurors, had been a human being. Sedita "had some rights too, and he never got a chance to have a trial."

Before murdering the storekeeper, Kenneth Brock had even announced his intentions for the whole world to hear. "He told them, 'get out of my way or I'll kill him.' " Then, standing there where his getaway car driver had left him, without any transportation, knowing that he could not escape—there were "helicopters, cars, officers all over the place"—Kenneth Brock knew what he had to do. And what he tried almost worked, Jacobs reminded the jury. "Because all the officers knew Mr. Sedita, and what do they do? They went running over to Mr. Sedita to help him, and that gave this man over here a few seconds, the time he needed to jump into those woods."

"He killed him for the time he needed," Jacobs said. "And Mr. Burk talked about that—he stood there a minute, and why would he throw away his ticket to freedom? Well, he did it with this gun here." Jacobs even used Burk's own metaphor as he drove the point about Kenneth Brock home: "He cashed his ticket in."

* * *

At 3:38 p.m., the jury retired to deliberate.

At 5:15 p.m., one hour and thirty-seven minutes later, the jury foreman sounded a buzzer and signaled that the deliberations had reached an end.

"Mr. Foreman," said the judge when the jurors had been assembled in the courtroom, "Have you reached a verdict?"

"We have, your honor," replied the foreman.

He handed the verdict sheet and instructions to the bailiff, who handed it to the judge.

True to form, Judge Walton was slow and contemplative. He inspected the verdict sheet carefully, holding it with both hands directly in front of his eyes. Everyone in the courtroom sat on the edge of his chair—except the jurors, who looked tired, frustrated, aged years by the process. Then, at last, the judge read the blank the foreman had signed. It said, "We, the jury, find the defendant, Kenneth Albert Brock, guilty of the offense of capital murder, as charged in the indictment."

CHAPTER SIX
THE PENALTY HEARING

Adrian Burk's client had been convicted of capital murder.

That meant that Kenneth Brock was facing the death penalty.

The next step was the penalty hearing. The jurors would hear additional evidence, receive additional instructions from the judge, and hear jury arguments from the lawyers about the sentence. It was, in effect, a new and separate trial—a trial about whether Kenneth Brock should get the death penalty.

At the end of the penalty hearing, the jury would have to answer the questions required by the Texas capital murder statute. Was the killing deliberate or premeditated? Was there a probability that the killer, Kenneth Brock, would be so violent in the future as to be a continuing threat to society? Those were the life-or-death questions.

If the jurors answered "No" to either question, Kenneth Brock would be sentenced to life imprisonment. Adrian Burk would have saved him from the death penalty.

But if the jurors were satisfied beyond a reasonable doubt that the answer to both questions was "yes," Kenneth Brock would be sentenced to death.

The case was a long way from being over, in other words. The hardest part was just beginning.

For Adrian Burk, it meant tremendous pressure. He had felt pressure, of course, during the trial on guilt or innocence, but it was nothing like the pressure now that the penalty hearing was about to begin. He knew that Jacobs would argue that the death penalty was the only proper and just sentence in the case. With equal conviction, Burk believed that Kenneth Brock's life deserved saving, and he intended to save it. He started fighting toward that goal with a primitive kind of energy.

Burk knew that his best chance to prevent a sentence of death would be to stop the prosecutor from proving that Kenneth Brock would be prone to future violence. That was the most difficult question the jury would have to decide.

Jacobs was certainly ready to go forward with his proof on that issue. He had his witnesses present, sitting outside the courtroom. There was Jean Pace, whom Brock had robbed the day before the murder of Michael Sedita. There was Warren Nettles, whom Brock had stabbed and nearly killed, senselessly, nine days before killing Sedita. And there were others: a probation officer and a deputy district clerk, to testify about Kenneth Brock's criminal record.

Adrian Burk knew that if the jury heard this evidence, their reaction would be to find that Kenneth Brock was a violent man, if they were sensible. He knew, therefore, that he had to prevent the jury from hearing this evidence.

And so Burk called upon the tool that he had used so well during the guilt-innocence phase of trial: the rules of evidence, which could be used to exclude testimony from the jury.

One of the rules of evidence in Texas was a rule against "extraneous offenses." Previous offenses had to be kept hidden from the jury, this rule said, unless they were directly relevant to an issue the jury would have to answer. This "extraneous offense" rule was the obvious one for Burk to use to object to Jacobs' evidence. Of course, Jacobs would argue that the previous offenses were directly relevant to the defendant's propensity to violence and therefore admissible. Burk would simply have to persuade the judge otherwise.

Knowing what was coming, Burk acted quickly. Before the jury was even brought into the courtroom to hear the penalty evidence, Burk made a motion to the court to exclude Jacobs' evidence. No witness should be permitted to testify about "extraneous offenses," he argued. In fact, the prosecutor should be ordered not even to ask questions about them in the presence of the jury.

Judge Walton listened to Burk's motion and was frankly

uncertain how to rule on it. The capital murder statute was brand-new. There were no court decisions interpreting it. If he let the jury hear Jacobs' evidence, Judge Walton knew he would be courting a reversal of the conviction if the Texas Court of Criminal Appeals disagreed with him; and a reversal would mean that the entire process, from jury selection on, would have to be done all over again. But if the judge excluded the evidence, he would be hiding from the jurors information that they needed to reach an intelligent decision on the crucial issue.

Finally, the judge decided to hear all the evidence by himself before making a ruling. He would conduct a dry run of the whole penalty hearing before he let the jury hear anything.

* * *

"Would you state your name for the court, please, ma'am?" Jacobs asked his first witness in this unusual hearing before Judge Walton.

"Jean Pace," said the witness.

Jean Pace had been a clerk at a Seven-Eleven store—a different one from the one where Michael Sedita had worked. She told the judge how Kenneth Brock had robbed her, the day before Sedita's murder.

"I looked up and this guy was coming around the counter at me with a gun," she said. "He came around the counter and grabbed me and pulled the money out of the register."

Kenneth Brock had gotten away with forty-seven dollars that time.

When Jacobs had finished examining Jean Pace, Burk cross-examined her. He asked her how many times she had been robbed.

"Three times," was the witness' answer. Understandably, she said she no longer worked for the Seven-Eleven store chain.

Brock had known exactly what he was doing and had been cold and deliberate. "He didn't say anything to anybody in the store and he had the gun to my neck," said Jean Pace.

The second witness was Warren Nettles.

"It happened real fast," Nettles said. "And unexpectedly. And he stabbed me in the right chest, and I shoved him, and he come back at me two or three other times. I don't remember if I had four or five stab wounds."

Nettles described how it had come to pass that Kenneth Brock had attemped to murder him. Brock had been "hanging around several people and trying to sell quaalude." Quaaludes were "downers;" they were pills similar to barbiturates. The assault was unprovoked, Nettles explained. Even Burk's cross examination brought out no reason for it. "Brock had been hounding me, more or less, and several other people in there," the witness said. "I even bought him a glass of wine to keep him off me. I had gone into the rest room and he followed me back there. I played him a game of pool just to satisfy him. He was too drunk to play, and I turned around from the pool table and had stepped over to the bar, and I just felt something behind me."

"All right," said Judge Walton to Jacobs. "In the interest of time, I will inquire of state's counsel, do you have any authority that you rely on in the proffer of this matter of extraneous offenses?"

From the way he asked the question, Jacobs sensed that the judge was going to exclude the evidence.

Jacobs told the judge his position: evidence of violence was directly relevant because violence was the issue that the capital murder statute required the jury to resolve.

Burk's answer to that was short. "And I would say to the court, your honor, that this man's rights would be violated if it was shown to the jury."

"Well," said Judge Walton, "the court is going to sustain the defense motion to suppress the matter of extraneous offenses."

This ruling cut the heart out of the prosecution's case. The jury would not know about Kenneth Brock's other crimes when they deliberated on his sentence. Once again, the life-or-death issue had been reduced to a game with abstract rules, like a game of chess, and Burk had won a significant point that might well be checkmate.

* * *

Jacobs went ahead with the evidence he had left.

The court's ruling only applied to offenses for which Kenneth Brock had not been tried and convicted. In other words, Jacobs could still show the jury about any instance in which Brock had actually been convicted. There was only one such conviction: Kenneth Brock had pled guilty in 1967 to the offense of burglary with intent to commit theft. Jacobs called the deputy district clerk to the witness stand and introduced the judgment and sentence into evidence before the jury. At Jacobs' request, the clerk told the jury what sentence the defendant had served: "He was given five years in the Texas Department of Corrections. And it was suspended, and he was given five years probation."

This was not very persuasive evidence of Kenneth Brock's propensity toward violence.

And it became even less persuasive when Adrian Burk cross-examined the deputy clerk about the meaning of the sentence.

Burk made sure the jury knew that the "suspending" of the sentence meant that Kenneth Brock was not actually sent to prison. And he made sure the jury knew that the probation had not been revoked. That meant that Brock had served the probationary period without incident. The conviction had been seven years ago, and during that seven years, Brock (according to Burk) had been a good citizen. At the end of the probationary period, the probation and the conviction had been dismissed, as Texas law required when the probation was not revoked. Burk made sure the jury knew the case had been dismissed. He even pointed out that the dismissal meant that Kenneth Brock "got all his civil rights back" and "could vote."

By the time he had finished, Burk had accomplished something almost unbelievable. He had turned this burglary conviction into the equivalent of a good-conduct medal for his client.

Jacobs went on to the next part of his evidence. He would be allowed to present "character" witnesses against Kenneth Brock.

And his first character witness was none other than Jean Pace, the Seven-Eleven storekeeper whom Brock had robbed.

The irony of the situation was obvious to everyone but the jurors, and it had been carefully hidden from them. It came down to this: Jean Pace would be allowed to testify that Kenneth Brock had a bad reputation, but she would not be allowed to testify to the facts that gave cause to that reputation—the fact that he had robbed her, for instance. Before calling Jean Pace to the witness chair, Jacobs had carefully "prepped" her, and he had cautioned her not to say anything about the robbery. If she did, the judge would have to grant a mistrial under the rules of evidence, and the case would have to be started all over again, because the jury would know the truth about Kenneth Brock.

Even the question Jacobs had to ask Jean Pace was almost comical. Its ludicrous wording was required by the complicated law of Texas evidence. Jacobs had prepped the witness about the questions he would ask, too, because he knew that they frequently caused witnesses to stare in confusion.

"Jean," Jacobs asked, "will you tell the jury, based upon your one meeting with the defendant, Kenneth Brock, do you know his reputation in the community in which he lives for being a peaceful and law abiding citizen?"

Yes, answered the witness, she did indeed know that reputation.

"Is that reputation good, or is it bad?"

"Bad."

That was as far as Jacobs could go. He hoped that the jurors could read between the lines. Jacobs called three other character witnesses, each of whom had been a victim of, or a witness to, a violent offense by Kenneth Brock. Each time he was limited to the sterile "reputation" question he had asked Jean Pace.

Then he rested his case in the penalty hearing.

It was not exactly overwhelming proof. All the jury had heard from the state in the penalty phase of trial was four witnesses who testified vaguely that Kenneth Brock had a bad character, plus a deputy clerk who told about a suspended sentence for a non-violent crime seven years ago.

And now it was time for the defense to present its case on the penalty issue. And the defense lawyer was ready to bury the State's evidence.

* * *

Unlike the prosecutor, Adrian Burk had plenty of evidence that he would be allowed to have the jury hear. He started by calling the defendant's sister, a girl named Linda Brock. She was a nice girl, who obviously cared about her brother, and she made a good appearance before the jury.

Burk started by having Linda Brock give the jurors a picture of Kenneth Brock's home life. It was a picture designed to elicit sympathy from the hardest of hearts.

"My daddy was an alcoholic and my mother had to support seven children by herself," Linda Brock told the jury.

Kenneth Brock, said Linda, was the product of a broken home. His mother had divorced her father, and had remarried, and that had not worked out either. Little Kenneth had at first been "attentive" to his school work, but his father had mistreated him and even ordered him to leave home, and that had made it hard for him to stay in school.

That was when Kenneth Brock had been driven to alcohol and drugs.

Drugs, Linda said, were something that made little Kenneth into "a different person." It was not really his fault, either. "When he is smoking joints and he takes a pill, it takes over him and he doesn't know what he's doing."

Burk was making points, and he was not about to stop here. What he did next was nearly unbelievable.

"I'm going to ask that the bailiff please bring in Mr. Brock's five sisters," said the defense attorney. "The five Brock sisters, Nancy, Alma, Debra, Elizabeth, and Rhonda."

What Burk wanted to do was to line up the five little girls, dressed in their Sunday best, to show the jury what a nice family Kenneth Brock had and how much they loved him.

Jacobs objected to this unusual procedure. In the first place, it was not evidence; and in the second place, it was not relevant to anything but sympathy, and the jury was supposed to decide the case "without bias or sympathy." But Judge Walton, mindful of what was at stake, overruled the objection. He was not going to stand in the way of Kenneth Brock's defense, even if it took on the dimensions of a dog-and-pony show.

When the five sisters, looking innocent and demure, had been exhibited to the jury, Burk turned to Linda Brock, who was still on the witness stand. "Do all these five girls work?" he asked her.

"All but the two youngest ones," replied Linda Brock.

Linda Brock set the tone for the entire defense in the penalty hearing. Burk also called as witnesses Kenneth Brock's mother, a lady with whom Kenneth Brock had lived as a youth ("Kenneth always puts his arms around me and kisses me," she said), and a friend of Brock's who described his appearance on the day of the murder ("He was messed up on tuinals. . . . His eyes were glassy and he was kind of stumbling around and he just wasn't himself. . . .").

* * *

The courtroom filled rapidly after Burk rested his case. Now would come the explosive moment that the entire trial had been inching toward from the beginning.

The attorneys would pull out all the stops as they gave their jury arguments for and against the sentence of death.

A few of the spectators knew what to expect, because they had seen capital cases before—long ago, before the Supreme Court had struck down the death penalty. They knew that the defense lawyer would not dwell on the evidence in the case very heavily; instead, he would spend most of his time denouncing the death penalty as capricious, unfair, discriminatory, brutal, totalitarian, irrevocable, final, and ungodly. In fact, the defense lawyer would refer to the act of "burning" or "frying" or "pulling the switch on" his client instead of just calling it the "death penalty." The prosecutor would counter all this by eulogizing the victim, invoking the rights of law-abiding citizens, characterizing the death penalty as a form of societal self-defense, and talking about "saving the life" of the defendant's "next victim."

These kinds of arguments were to be expected, because experience showed they were effective in capital cases.

Burk stepped before the jury. And he did not disappoint any of the spectators, as he stepped almost immediately into his role.

"You have got to approach this with a serious, prayerful manner," he told the jurors, "because you are going to be asked by the State of Texas to pull the electric switch on this man."

He even gave the jurors a step-by-step chronology of an execution. "What takes place when a man is condemned?. . . First he is given a shower. . . . [They] strap him in the electric chair, shave your head, and run twenty-five hundred volts or however many volts of electricity through your body until a doctor comes in there. And after your body has cooled off, he places a stethoscope and determines you are dead, and you are taken out another door."

Warming to his subject, Burk had a great deal more to say about the death penalty.

"...It's unfair. And it's unfair from this standpoint:...you don't see any rich people getting the electric chair."

"...Two thousand years ago, they were throwing Christians to the lions."

"...Five hundred years ago, pickpockets were hanged in public, just drug out and hung from any sapling or tree that would hold them."

"...There is a thin veneer that separates you and me and us and this man here and everybody in this world from being savages, and we call that thin veneer civilization and Christianity."

"...I'm not concerned with your acting like a lynching mob, but I'm pointing out for you...if you give him the death penalty, there can be no appeal from the fact that he got the death sentence."

It was going to be a difficult summation for Jacobs to follow.

But the prosecutor, too, stepped into his expected role.

"I guess I should have brought the family of Michael Sedita in here and let them cry for you," said Jacobs. "But I knew that wasn't necessary. And he had friends and loved ones, too, but we don't get to see them. We don't get to hear about them. But they have to live with the fact that Michael Sedita had his life taken from him by this defendant over here without a trial, without a jury. Taken from him by this defendant over here without cause."

Jacobs was well aware that the main question the jury would have to answer was the one concerning the "probability" of the defendant's future violence. Was that probability such that it would make the defendant a "continuing threat to society?" A great deal of Jacobs' evidence on this issue had been hidden from the jury. But as Jacobs began to argue on the point, it became clear that there was also a great deal of evidence about violence that the jury had in fact heard.

And as his argument progressed, Jacobs built a convincing case based on that evidence.

First, there was the burglary offense. The defendant had broken into someone's house with intent to steal. It showed a contempt for the law and created a situation with high potential for violence. Kenneth Brock had been put on probation, given another chance, but he did not reform. That was clear, because it was after the burglary offense that the character witnesses had known him.

The character witnesses were a second indication. Not a single person had had anything good to say about Kenneth Brock. Every one of them knew him, and every one had said he was a violent person. One of them, Jean Pace, had met him in a Seven-Eleven, where she worked, on one occasion, and she said that he was not a "peaceful, law-abiding citizen." And the defendant's own sister had said that he was a regular user of drugs, and that they changed him into "a different person," a violent one. Given the pervasive availability of drugs, did that not make him a threat to society?

The killing of Michael Sedita had been deliberate, execution-style murder. It had started with the endangering of the lives of several innocent people. Kenneth Brock had pointed a gun at them and told them to lie on the floor. Then he had shot at, and tried to kill, a Houston police officer just because he was trying to stop a robbery and kidnapping. Finally, rather than surrender, Kenneth Brock had exploded Michael Sedita's aorta and left him to bleed to death in the middle of the road, for no other reason than to create a momentary diversion. What more did it take to show a man who was a "continuing threat to society?" What other kind of person would do that?

The answer to the penalty questions was yes, Jacobs said. The penalty hearing evidence, taken together with the evidence about the offense, justified the death penalty. "Vote it. Not only the testimony cries out for it, the facts cry out for it and that wasted life cries out for it. Let me leave you with one thought and then I will let you get on with your verdict. I don't read the Bible much, but when you get to the first chapter in the Bible, it says there: 'Whomsoever sheddeth man's blood, by man shall his blood be shed.' . . . I don't know what else we can do, but I do know this: if we don't live up to the laws and rules of society, then there's no hope at all for this society. And one of those rules is, 'Thou shalt not kill.' Tell them, people on the jury. Tell everybody out there that in Houston from this day forward, 'thou shalt not kill.' "

The atmosphere in the courtroom was tight and strained when, at 4:22 in the afternoon, the jury retired to deliberate on Kenneth Brock's life or death.

* * *

At 6:15 p.m. a note came out of the jury room, signed by the foreman: "What would be the ruling or result if we cannot reach agreement on one of the issues?"

Jacobs read this note and his heart sank. It meant that the jury was divided. It was the prelude to a hung jury. The case would have to be tried all over again from the beginning. A retrial might well cost the State more than $100,000, counting everything, and it was frustrating to think of the positive things such an amount could be used for; but the cost was the least of Jacobs' worries. When there is a horrible murder case, it should be resolved. Whether the resolution is a sentence of life imprisonment, or the death penalty, or whatever, this case should not have to wait another year or two before another trial could be held. But the jury could not be told, of course. Under the law, the judge could not answer the jury's question at all.

All the judge could do was to have the jury brought into the courtroom and give them a written order saying, "You are directed to continue your deliberations in accordance with the court's original charge." (Burk, ever mindful of his possible appeal, filed a written objection to even this innocuous communication, on the ground that it was "coercive of a verdict.")

The minutes stretched by and became hours.

At 8:00 p.m., the buzzer sounded. The jurors had reconciled their differences. They had reached a verdict.

A few of those watching had left. But the room was still full of spectators.

They tried to guess at the verdict as the jurors filed in. It was a life imprisonment verdict, most of them thought. The note they had sent out could only mean that several of the jurors had strong doubts, and it would be easier for those jurors to persuade the others that their view was reasonable than to be persuaded, themselves, toward the harsher verdict. But a veteran probation officer saw the jury come in, and he offered a different insight. "They had their faces down and their chins on the ground," he said. "I knew they had given him the death penalty."

The judge studied the verdict for what seemed an eternity.

Then he read the questions and the jurors' answers.

"Do you find from the evidence beyond a reasonable doubt that the conduct of the defendant, Kenneth Albert Brock, that caused the death of the deceased was committed deliberately and with the reasonable expectation that the death of the deceased or another would result?

"To which the jury answered, 'Yes.' "

Everyone waited. That was the "deliberateness" question, the easier of the two to answer affirmatively. The next question, the "violence" question, would tell the story.

The judge read it. "Do you find from the evidence beyond a reasonable doubt that there is a probability that the defendant, Kenneth Albert Brock, would commit criminal acts of violence that would constitute a continuing threat to society?

"To which the jury answered, 'Yes.' "

The jurors looked straight ahead, soberly, or at the judge, or down at their feet. They were exhausted. Once the judge released them, several of them wept.

On February 19, 1975, in accordance with the jury's verdict, Judge Walton pronounced sentence of death on Kenneth Albert Brock.*

*The following names in this chapter were changed, without alteration of the incidents in which the persons were involved: Jean Pace, Warren Nettles.

CHAPTER SEVEN
EPILOGUE

When the judge first announced that the jury had answered "Yes" to each of the penalty questions, Linda Brock had not understood what that meant. But when the judge pronounced the death sentence from the bench, she began to scream and had to be removed from the courtroom. It was, in fact, the second time that that had been necessary: the first had been when she had interrupted Jacob's final argument in the penalty hearing with cries of "Stop it! Stop it!" until a bailiff had had to take her by the arm and lead her to the hall. The Brock family had been miserable throughout the trial. Quite understandably, they were miserable over the sentence.

Adrian Burk, tough old fighter that he was, was shaken by it too. But Burk, with a courage that was in character with his conduct of the defense, walked over and shook Jacobs' hand. And he did not by any means give up after the verdict. He engaged another lawyer on the appeal, and he worked to get the sentence overturned.

For Burk's services during the trial, Judge Walton approved a fee in excess of $8,000, to be paid by Harris County since Brock was indigent. But lest it appear that he made money on the case, it should immediately be added that that sum was small in relation to the energy, skill and time that the big defense lawyer had devoted to the case. Today, Adrian Burk is general counsel to the Houston Oilers football team. He almost certainly lost time and treasure from his practice because of his representation of Kenneth Brock. In many ways, it was a thankless task; and certainly there was no adequate compensation for the pressure he went through over the trial and verdict.

George Jacobs continued his duties as a prosecutor in the District Attorney's Office. In a few months, he would try another capital case, another robbery-murder—the killing of an eighty-year-old woman who was bludgeoned to death in her own home with a pipe. As far as the Kenneth Brock case was concerned, Jacobs had felt throughout the trial that a sentence of death was the only just resolution. Now that the verdict had come in, he had a curious feeling: it was not an occasion for rejoicing, or for satisfaction, or for congratulation, but it was an event that did give a sense that some justice had been salvaged from a sorry situation. He spent the next day, and most of the next week, answering a flood of telephone calls from people who believed the restoration of capital punishment was necessary, and who complimented him on a job well done.

For Judge Walton, the trial of the Brock case had been a burden. It had been a long trial; his docket had done nothing but increase. If every case took as long, he would be able to handle only eight or ten of them a year. The judge went back to work, in earnest, on his docket.

For Kenneth Brock, the verdict meant the distinction of becoming the first person in Houston to be sentenced to death under the new capital murder statute.

A few weeks after the verdict, Brock was transferred to Huntsville, Texas, and incarcerated on death row. It would take years for the process of appeal to run its course, and during that time he would be held there. If the Texas Court of Criminal Appeals did not reverse his conviction and sentence, his lawyers would undoubtedly take the case to the Supreme Court; and all things considered, the question whether Kenneth Brock would die in the electric chair was still very much in doubt. Perhaps for that reason, he showed little emotion at the verdict and none at his sentencing. When someone suggested that he should invite George Jacobs to his execution, Kenneth Brock just nodded his head and smiled.

Kenneth Brock's victims did not fare nearly so well. Warren Nettles took nearly 200 stitches to close the stab wounds Brock had inflicted on him, not to mention the operations that were necessary to repair his internal damage. His ability to lift objects and to move his body was permanently impaired. As a result of his hospitalization and his infirmity, he lost his job, his marriage and most of what he had in the world. In the space of a few seconds, Kenneth Brock had ruined Warren Nettles' life.

And in the space of an even shorter instant of time, Michael Sedita's hopes and dreams had gone down the drain. The murdered storekeeper had worked his way through college, had graduated with a business degree, and had begun what appeared to be a promising career in management with the Southland Corporation. But instead, the life he had labored so hard to build had ended for no reason in this improbable place on Surry Road by a man who had nothing to live for and nothing to lose, and a gray stone with a spray of flowers marked the final resting place of Michael Sedita.

PART TWO

The Jury and the Life-or-Death Decision

WE DON'T WANT to leave the impression that the Kenneth Brock case was the only capital murder case tried in Houston, or even that it was a typical case.

There is no "typical" capital murder. The capital murder law was designed in the first place to apply only to murders of exceptional brutality, and nearly every case tried under it has been extraordinary in one way or another.

And since the cases defy easy categorization, it is difficult to predict the outcome in any given case. Will the jury opt for life or for death? That depends on the total picture the case presents—and it depends on the personalities of the jurors themselves.

In this part of the book, we will look at two capital murder cases and at the way the jurors handled the crucial life-or-death decision in each.

First, there is the case of John Stiles Griffin. Griffin escaped from a federal prison in California and committed a series of crimes in at least two states. In Houston, he committed two grisly murders—combination rape-robbery-murders. He was actually a five-time ex-convict, and his efforts to escape from the Houston jail where he was kept were unceasing as his trial approached. Would he be convicted on the circumstantial case the prosecution had built up? And if so, would he be sentenced to death—or to life in prison?

Ronald Clark O'Bryan's case was completely different in motive, in the method of murder, and in the personality of the killer. O'Bryan was a middle-class suburbanite who had a career as an optician. With financial troubles closing in on him, he took out a policy of life insurance on his son and then put cyanide in the boy's Halloween candy. During funeral services, O'Bryan sang a solo in the church for his son—after a crime in which, it seemed, he had sold his soul to the devil. The case became known as the Halloween Candy Murder case, and it received news coverage far and wide. Would the "Candy Man," as O'Bryan came to be called, be convicted of capital murder—or acquitted? And if convicted, would he be sentenced to life—or death?

These are two extraordinary capital murder cases, each quite different from the other.

The outcomes may not be what you would expect.

COUNSEL FOR THE PROSECUTION

The authors, David Crump (left) and George Jacobs, prosecuted Kenneth Brock, Gerald Bodde and Richard Vargas. "I don't read the Bible much," argued Jacobs to the jury in the Brock case, "but when you get to the first chapter in the Bible, it says there: 'Whosoever sheddeth man's blood, by man shall his blood be shed.'"

Stu Stewart "beats you fair and square, or not at all," as one lawyer put it. But even Stewart was non-plussed by the judge's pretrial rulings in the "Brady Bunch" case.

Ted Busch prosecuted John Stiles Griffin for committing "about as bad a murder as I've seen." The defendant left a fingerprint behind.

Doug Shaver, in the trial of Gerald Bodde, presented a witness who was so frightened she had to be dismissed. The witness was five years old.

Vic Driscoll told the jury that Ronald O'Bryan "sacrificed his son not on the altar of God as Abraham might have done, but on the altar of his own greed."

COUNSEL FOR THE DEFENSE

Stuart Kinard's client, Bernardino Sierra, confessed on television to six brutal murders—one of which he committed inside the county jail. "Is the death penalty a deterrent?" Kinard asked a defense witness.

"People are going to have a low regard for life if we take life," said Victor Blaine to the jury that decided Richard Vargas' fate. "...The only question is, if you don't burn him, would he do it again?"

Al Thomas (standing) and his co-counsel, Fred Heacock, defended John Stiles Griffin, who was accused of a bloody rape-robbery murder. "I tried to put the Bible where the jury would have to see it," said Thomas. "...it's a question of strategy."

"Does [Ronald O'Bryan] sound like a man who'd knock off his son for a few gold coins?" Marvin Teague asked the jury emotionally. (He also headed the defense team for Gerald Bodde.)

CHAPTER EIGHT
THE RICHMOND AVENUE MURDERS

It was two o'clock in the afternoon when Patricia Hixson got out of the car.

She waved goodbye as her tennis partner drove away, and she walked toward her apartment.

For pretty, 22-year-old Patricia, these April days were long and pleasant. She had been married to her husband, Walter, for just two months, and she was enjoying just being a housewife for a while. Today, for instance, was an especially beautiful, warm sunny day. She had plans to stay outdoors and make the most of it.

The plans included going bicycle riding with her good friend, Louise Ponder. Louise was going to come over this afternoon to visit. Patricia Hixson and Louise Ponder were very close. They had a lot in common: They were both newly married, they had worked together at the same job, and Louise had been a bridesmaid in Patricia's wedding.

Marriage had changed Patricia's life, but there were many parts of it that remained the same. Walter had moved into the apartment where she had lived while she was single—apartment number 144, at 5127 Richmond Avenue. There were advantages to living in the same place. For one thing, she knew her neighbors, and many of them were friends.

Now, as she climbed the steps toward her apartment, Patricia passed the window of one of her friends—a neighbor named Robin Couch. Robin looked out and saw Patricia for an instant. The two women's eyes met, and they smiled at each other.

Robin Couch had no way to know, at that moment, the significance of that brief glance.

There was nothing to direct her attention to the burly man in his late twenties who was watching, with curious interest, as Patricia climbed the stairs. And Robin could not have realized, then, that she would be the last witness to see Patricia alive.

* * *

That had been two o'clock, when Patricia Hixson had returned to her apartment.

It was now 6:30.

Detective Carolyn Stephenson was sitting at a desk in the homicide division office of the Houston Police Station, finishing her paperwork. Her shift was over. It had been over since 4 o'clock. She would finally be able to leave for home, she thought, two and a half hours late—as soon as she finished this report.

"Stephenson!" she heard a voice call. It was her supervisor, Lieutenant Crittenden.

She stepped into his office.

"You got one," Crittenden said. "Go make the D.O.A. at 5127 Richmond, apartment 144."

Stephenson's shift was not ending after all. It was a double murder, Crittenden explained.

Not much was known about the case yet. The husband of one of the victims, Walter Hixson, had reported it to the police. The dead women were Patricia Hixson and Louise Ponder. The lieutenant added that it appeared a rape might have been involved. The next shift with a rape investigator had not come on yet, and so Stephenson would have to go.

Detective Stephenson was used to shifts that didn't end on time. She was a veteran of fourteen years on the force. She had come up through the ranks the hard way, starting in juvenile and working in vice, narcotics and in the city lockup. She had been assigned to homicide in 1970, when police departments throughout the country had begun to realize the necessity of having female officers in traditional police positions. And that was also when she had earned the rank of detective. It was the highest rank a woman had ever held in the Houston Police Department.

Carolyn Stephenson certainly did not look like everyone's stereotype of a police detective. She was an attractive redheaded woman—well dressed, petite, and with delicate features. She was cheerful and feminine—so much so, in fact, that her male counterparts could address her with the words, "Hi, kid," and get away with it. But Stephenson also had something else. She had the stomach for police work.

"I like police work," she was fond of saying, "because it's not routine. Every day's a new situation." Sometimes the job got to her, but she could handle it.

And that was why she was leaving, now, for the Richmond Avenue address Lieutenant Crittenden had given her. She found herself in the company of two other veteran Houston officers, Detectives L. W. Henning and J. M. Roescher.

Carolyn Stephenson could sense it already. She had a feeling, she would later say, that the murders of Patricia Hixson and Louise Ponder were going to be "as bad a homicide scene as I've ever made."

* * *

Apartment number 144 at 5127 Richmond was moderately expensive and immaculately kept.

The floor was covered with a cheerful yellow shag rug.

It was 6:44 p.m. when Detectives Stephenson, Henning and Roescher walked in the door. They immediately saw the young man who was sitting on the floor in the living room, crying softly.

While Henning and Roescher went into the hallway and back toward the bedrooms, Carolyn Stephenson went to the young man on the floor and spoke to him. "I'm Carolyn Stephenson. I'm a detective with the Houston Police Department," she said. "What's your name?"

"Walter Hixson," the man answered, with difficulty.

Walter Hixson was holding a throw pillow in his hands. He was twisting it, wringing it, back and forth.

"I know this isn't a good time to talk to you, but I have to," Stephenson said. She paused. Then she said, "Can you help us? Can you tell us what you know?"

Walter Hixson said that he would try.

"Are you the one who reported this to the police?"

"Yes."

Haltingly, Walter Hixson told Carolyn Stephenson that he had come home from work and walked into the apartment. It had been unlocked. He had taken his coat and tie off and sat down. A moment later, when he still hadn't heard anything from Patricia, he had called her name. There had been no answer. And so he had walked back to the bedroom.

There, he had seen his wife and her friend Louise Ponder lying on the floor. There had been a lot of blood. He hadn't touched the bodies. Instead, he had come back to the living room and called the police.

"Do you know anything about who killed your wife?" Carolyn Stephenson asked quietly.

"No."

"Do you know of any reason why anyone would want to kill her?"

"No."

With that, Carolyn Stephenson went to join the other two detectives in the bedroom.

She was totally unprepared, even with all her experience, for what she saw. Patricia Hixson lay in the corner, her torso resting on a crumpled cardboard box. There was blood on the wall behind her. She was still wearing her tennis dress, but it was pulled up around her stomach.

Stephenson had her notebook out.

She wrote that the dead woman's bra "was completely soaked in blood, and detectives were unable to determine its color."

Patricia Hixson's right arm was "extended straight to the south, along and touching the west wall, palm up—hand in a fist." And Stephenson's notes went on to record a bizarre detail: "There were white shoe strings (2) tied around the right wrist and there was a defense wound on the right wrist."

The victim's wrists had been bound. There were constriction marks on the flesh under the strings. The attacker had been a powerful man who had tied his victims, hand and foot, while killing them. And he had kept stabbing them, and kept stabbing them, long after they were dead.

The "defense wounds" that Stephenson noted were slashes on the hands and wrists, characteristic of the wounds a person fending off a knife attack will receive. They were mute testimony to Patricia Hixson's pathetic attempts at self-preservation.

Patricia Hixson's fingernails were broken. She was riddled with red gaping holes in her arms, neck and chest.

A few feet away lay the other victim, Louise Ponder. And in the same businesslike jargon, Carolyn Stephenson described her body, too.

Louise Ponder, she wrote, "was face down, and a brown leather strap was around her neck. And what appeared to be a coat hanger was also visible around the complainant's neck."

It was not just brutal. It was incomprehensible. The attacker had circled the woman's throat with the leather strap. Then he had tightened it by twisting the coat hanger wire.

And the attacker had made sure Louise Ponder was unable to cry for help. "The complainant was gagged," Carolyn Stephenson wrote, "with ½ inch adhesive tape across her mouth, under her chin and up both sides of her face."

Evidently, death had come slowly for this victim. The crisscrossing straps of adhesive tape would not have been necessary otherwise.

Louise Ponder's hands were tied behind her back "with what appeared to be nylon hose at the wrists." Again, the bindings had been tightened with "a piece of what appeared to be coat hanger" wrapped around them.

And Louise Ponder had been raped.

Her attacker had left her nude from the waist down, and barefooted. Her bicycling shorts had been cut off her body. Her bra had been severed in two. Later, the medical examiner would report that there were remnants of spermatazoa in her vagina.

Her breasts were crisscrossed with rows of stab wounds, parted into ugly red semicircles.

There would never be any way to be sure exactly how it had happened, but Carolyn Stephenson thought she knew. The attacker had used some pretext to get Patricia Hixson to let him into the apartment. There had been a struggle, and he had tied her. Then, perhaps, Louise Ponder had knocked at the door.

In a frenzy, Stephenson thought, the man had killed Patricia when he heard Louise. Then he had overpowered the second woman. And, the detective thought, he had tortured and raped her. There were small, non-fatal "pick" wounds on Louise Ponder's extremities. There were burn marks on her elbows.

There was no way to know how long it had taken. Carolyn Stephenson fought to keep control of her stomach. It took three pages just to fill in the standard wound description, because Patricia Hixson had twenty-nine separate stab wounds and Louise Ponder had eleven.

Outside, the press was on the scene. The detectives stopped the photographers at the door, with cameras clicking. It took considerable effort to keep them and the reporters from entering the apartment.

Carolyn Stephenson was disgusted. "They don't care if justice gets done," she said later. "They like it better if it isn't. It makes a better story." Right now, she just wanted to be alone so she could do her job.

The photographers congregated outside the bedroom window. They tried to take pictures through the curtains.

Carolyn Stephenson kept writing. She described the hands of the two victims. Each of them had a gold watch, and a gold wedding band set, still in place undisturbed.

But the most surprising development in the case was yet to come.

* * *

Carolyn Stephenson was interviewing a witness—a man in uniform.

"I saw him walking around on the parking lot," the security guard said. "He looked like he was in a daze."

The security guard was talking about Walter Hixson. And what he was saying was that Hixson had been near the apartment, near the scene of the crime, during the time when the murders were probably committed. It was in conflict with Hixson's own statement, because he claimed to have been at work.

Carolyn Stephenson thought hard.

Could Walter Hixson have committed these murders?

It seemed almost inconceivable—a husband who could kill his wife, rape and kill her friend, tie them both and then pretend to know nothing after calling the police. Was it possible? But as soon as she asked herself that question, Stephenson knew the answer.

It was possible. Stranger things had happened. In more than seventy percent of homicides, the attacker and victim know each other, and a husband is often a logical suspect for the murder of his wife.

Detective Stephenson took Walter Hixson into custody.

Early the next morning, she released him. She had talked to Walter Hixson at length, and she was satisfied that he was telling the truth. Most of his afternoon could be accounted for by independent witnesses. And the officers had discovered, by now, that the killer had probably changed his own bloody clothes for clothes in the apartment, belonging to Walter Hixson. That might explain the security guard's error.

Walter Hixson was innocent.

But he had spent most of the night of his wife's murder in police custody, away from the solace of family and friends.

* * *

Carolyn Stephenson seemed to be a long way from a solution to the Richmond Avenue Murders.

There was no solid suspect and there were few leads. What was to be done?

There were at least two things the detectives knew to do immediately. They needed to cover the crime scene like a vacuum cleaner. And they needed to talk to everyone in the area who might know anything.

Shortly after the detectives had arrived, the crime scene had given up the first clue that might help to track down the killer. There was a pair of checked pants lying on the bed. Walter Hixson said they did not belong to him.

There was blood on the front of the trousers.

Maybe, Carolyn Stephenson thought, the killer had left these trousers. He would have known he could not wear them; the bloodstains were too conspicuous. He had probably exchanged them for a pair of trousers in the apartment.

And inside the trousers pocket was another lead.

It was a bus ticket—a ticket from San Diego, California, to Houston. The date was April 25, 1974. It was now April 27. It was a two-day bus ride from San Diego to Houston. The killer probably had been just passing through.

And there was something else in the pants pocket. It was a key—a key with a red tag that said "Astroworld Hotel." The Astroworld was a medium sized hotel near a giant amusement park in southeast Houston.

Perhaps the killer had been to the Astroworld, either to stay there or to break in. Perhaps someone could identify him. Detective Henning left immediately to go there, to the the Astroworld, leaving Stephenson and Roescher at Richmond Avenue.

For hours, Stephenson and Roescher worked on the physical evidence. They secured and described everything they could see.

Step two was to question everyone who might have seen anything—anything at all.

Carolyn Stephenson found that witnesses around the apartment complex could add relatively little. There was only one promising lead—and it was a strange one.

A neighbor named Paul Manteris told the detectives that he had been accosted at his door by a man with a U. S. Customs identification card. The man had asked to be admitted to Manteris' apartment, and Manteris had let him in. They had had a short conversation and the man had left. It was around 2 p.m. And the man had headed toward the Hixson apartment.

It sounded as though a Customs agent had been near the Hixson apartment. Or maybe it was someone posing as a Customs agent. That might explain how the killer had gotten inside the apartment without attracting attention.

Manteris said he thought he would be able to recognize the man if he saw him again.

Carolyn Stephenson spent six hours at the crime scene. Then she kept at work, for the rest of the night, trying to put together the parts of the puzzle. When the sun came up, and 8 o'clock rolled around, she started her next day's shift.

And she remained on the job, hour after hour, trying to solve the Richmond Avenue Murder Case. Could there be a lead to be found from the bus ticket, she wondered—the ticket from San Diego?

* * *

The San Diego Police Department gets hundreds of crime

reports a day.

One of them, Carolyn Stephenson thought, might provide a link between the clues she already had and the killer she was trying to find.

Detective work is hardly glamorous. It starts with the tedious step of collecting miscellaneous facts, and it progresses into the equally tedious step of making sense out of the clues those facts provide. And so detectives spend a great deal of their time plowing through crime reports in an effort to find a common thread.

Carolyn Stephenson got on the phone to San Diego.

Hours later, it paid off. On April 25th, the date of the bus ticket, San Diego had reported a burglary in a hotel room. The victim had been a businessman named Arnold Merrill. That was significant to Stephenson, because the name "Merrill" had been found on the register of the Astroworld Hotel, corresponding to the room number on the key found in the Hixson apartment.

The killer had apparently burglarized Merrill's room in San Diego. And then he had used Merrill's identity when he had gotten to Houston.

The bus ticket. The San Diego burglary. The Astroworld key. The name on the register. The trail of the Richmond Avenue Murderer led from California to Houston. But where did it go from there?

For two days, Carolyn Stephenson's leads varied with no recognizable pattern. The description of a Chicano man furnished a possible suspect for the San Diego burglary. Was he the Richmond Avenue Murderer? Was it a bellboy from the Astroworld, or one of Louise Ponder's old boyfriends who had given her some trouble, or a drifter from Pennsylvania who was arrested near the Hixson apartments? Each of these possibilities had to be considered. But each evaporated as quickly as it appeared.

The detectives needed a break in the case.

* * *

When the breaks finally came, in the week following the Richmond Avenue Murders, they came as a result of chance.

The first break involved a robbery in Galveston, Texas.

The homicide division got a call from a University of

Houston student who had been at a fraternity party in Galveston. He had been staying overnight at a hotel, and he and one of his friends, together with their dates, had been accosted by a man with a shotgun. The man had tied them up, he said, and robbed them. The man had been frightened off by a knock at the door. He had stolen a car, some clothes and a few dollars in cash.

Might it have been the same man, the caller wondered? Since he had fit the description that had been printed in the papers for the Richmond Avenue Murders, and he had tied up all these people and gagged them, could it be the same man?

Carolyn Stephenson shuddered when she heard it. That fortuitous knock on the door had left the intruder no time to kill his victims. The students had no idea how close to death they may have been. Stephenson put Galveston on an imaginary map in her mind; and she drew a mental line, representing the path of the killer, through that city.

That was a break in the case.

But the biggest break was yet to come. It would begin with a call to the police about a man who was acting strangely inside a motel in Port Arthur, Texas, and it would end with the man's arrest for impersonating a U.S. Customs official.

The man's name was John Stiles Griffin. And the events leading to the arrest were unusual. They began when Griffin stopped to go to the bathroom.

* * *

"Acid's worse than heroin when I come down off it," John Stiles Griffin said later. "So I was jumpy as hell.

"I was in the bathroom for about fifteen minutes. I was running like a horse—all jacked up."

Griffin was coming down from a very long trip. The LSD he had dropped was treated with "speed," and that gave a better high—but it also made him even more paranoid than usual. He fought, now, to keep his bearings.

He was inside a motel room in Port Arthur, Texas, going to the bathroom.

He had come here in the first place because he was in desperate need of money. He was nearly out of cash. Motels were the easiest places to get money, for Griffin, because the doors were easy to open and people from out of town generally had money lying around. But the odd thing was that he was too shaky, now, to pull it off. Besides, his bladder was bursting. The call of nature had taken precedence over his finances for the moment.

It was dangerous, he knew. The LSD was making him act strangely. The guest in this room was a woman who had opened her door in response to his knock and had let him in to use the bathroom. She was obviously frightened. What an inconvenient time to have to take a piss—!

Finally, he finished. Now, to get out of there.

But as he stepped out of the bathroom, John Stiles Griffin saw that there was a bellboy in the room with the woman. That was a bad sign. She had been frightened enough to call the motel office. That meant that she had probably been frightened enough to call the police.

John Stiles Griffin thought fast. He had not spent half his life in prisons without learning a few things. And one of those things was how to imitate police talk. He could do it so it sounded better than the cops themselves, at times.

He fingered the Customs I.D. in his pocket.

"Let me introduce myself," he said to the bellboy. "I'm with the U.S. Customs Service, and we're here on a stakeout."

He fished out the Customs I.D. and held it up. The bellboy gave a visible sigh of relief.

"You just took a load off my mind," said the bellboy. "Somebody just reported seeing somebody with a gun."

"Oh," Griffin said casually, "that was me." He had left his rifle in the bushes outside.

Almost apologetically, the woman said: "Well, I've already called the police."

That was going to mean trouble, Griffin knew. But he heard himself say, "No problem. I'll just call in and cancel it."

John Stiles Griffin had been free for a week. When he had gotten to Houston, he had been in a fog, blazing on LSD. He hardly remembered hitchhiking to Galveston, and his memory of the visit to his mother's home in Beaumont, where he had picked up the shotgun, was hazy. Now he was in Port Arthur, Texas—heading for Florida—and he needed money—

But he had to do something fast, or he was going to get arrested.

As soon as he finished retrieving his gun, he saw that the patrol car was there.

It was a good thing he had been thinking ahead.

Officer M. A. Hebert looked startled at this dishevelled man, carrying a rifle, who walked out of the bushes. He looked even more surprised when Griffin showed him the Customs I.D. and told him he was a federal agent working a narcotics case.

"Please," Griffin said with authentic confidentiality, "look. Let's get away, because you're in a marked car. And it'll blow our stakeout."

Officer Hebert believed him. Griffin bent down to get in the car. He urged the officer, again, to drive away. When they got far enough away, Griffin thought, he could turn the gun on the officer if he had to. His mind raced. He could take the car. And it might be necessary to kill the cop—

Hebert drove around the corner, with Griffin in the passenger's seat. He parked the car.

Moments later, a second patrol car arrived. Then there was a third. And suddenly it became clear that Griffin's cover wasn't going to work. The other officers had to be told what was happening. Griffin kept talking. But the officers began to realize something was wrong. It was an instinct, a sixth sense—the smell of danger in an otherwise innocuous situation, born of a thousand street encounters. The officers asked Griffin where he was stationed. Who else worked out of that location? Who was with him now?

Come to think of it, why hadn't he called in to alert the locals in the first place so the stakeout wouldn't get blown? That was what Customs always did when they had a deal going down in Port Arthur. Then it developed that Griffin had never heard of the D.E.A.—the newly-formed federal Drug Enforcement Agency.

The officers weren't sure what they had. But Officer Hebert was suspicious enough, by now, to arrest John Stiles Griffin.

A day later, Carolyn Stephenson sat in the homicide office in Houston. She went over the arrest report from Port Arthur P.D.

The charge was "impersonating a federal officer."

Carolyn Stephenson turned it around in her mind. It all fit, she knew. A forged Customs I.D. badge. A muscular young man. A description identical to the one Paul Manteris had given—of the man who had shown him the I.D. and then walked toward the Hixson apartments.

And there was something else that fit.

John Stiles Griffin was an escapee from the federal correctional facility in Los Angeles, California. That was only a short distance from the city of Anaheim, California. Griffin had escaped last Monday, April 23, just a few hours before an Anaheim hotel maid had been found tied up, raped and stabbed to death. And that crime had been a carbon copy of the Richmond Avenue murders.

Carolyn Stephenson needed more evidence, though. For example, if she could match the arrested man's fingerprint to one of those found in the Richmond Avenue apartment, it would do wonders for her case.

* * *

"With all that adhesive tape," Carolyn Stephenson said, "You know there has to be a print somewhere." She was counting on Leblanc to find it.

L. N. Leblanc was one of HPD's best identification experts. He was fond of saying, "Finding a usable fingerprint is the exception rather than the rule." What he meant was that when prints are lifted from a crime scene, the majority of them are not suitable for identification, and the odds are high that all that will turn up among those that *are* suitable is prints of the victims themselves.

Leblanc had gone to the Hixson apartment and laboriously dusted every surface that seemed promising. He had covered the bathroom countertops, the doors, the knobs, the walls.

Gingerly, with a set of forceps, he had picked up those items that were moveable and brought them back to his laboratory for testing with a variety of chemicals and powders. Laboriously, one by one, Leblanc tested each of the tiny smudges he had found against the known print of John Stiles Griffin.

None of them seemed to fit.

Leblanc could get prints from improbable places, if they were there. Using a substance called Ninhydrin, he could develop them on paper surfaces. Ninhydrin reacted with fingerprint oils to produce a bright orange color pattern. There were even new techniques for bringing out fingerprints from dead human bodies.

But nothing worked.

Leblanc covered every inch of the adhesive tape that was recovered from the body of Louise Ponder. As he pushed his brush delicately across the tape surface, oval shapes appeared and flickered before his eyes. But none of the prints was usable for an identification.

Failure.

Finally, Leblanc applied his chemicals to the tape dispenser, which he had collected in a sample bag from the Hixson apartment. A piece of a print appeared.

It arched slightly, and it looked, in its basic configuration, like one of the prints that had been taken from John Stiles Griffin's right thumb after his arrest.

Would it be large enough for a comparison? It was nothing more than a scrap.

Under a microscope, Leblanc looked at the two prints—the known one from John Stiles Griffin's arrest papers, and the unknown scrap from the tape dispenser. Leblanc was looking for "points," or fingerprint characteristics—the small similarities that would let him say that the two prints had, or had not, been made by the same person. Fingerprint experts do not look at the overall pattern for this purpose; that is an unreliable guide for matching single prints. Instead, they looked for what they call "forks," "ridge endings," "dots," and other tiny patterns. And if they find a sufficient number of these in the same positions in the two prints, they are able to say that the two came from the same person.

Leblanc looked at the arch of John Stiles Griffin's known thumbprint, and he compared it, point by point, with the scrap he had lifted. Here was a ridge ending on the unknown scrap that matched, exactly, with the same point on John Stiles Griffin's known print. Here was a fork, and there was another ridge ending.

The similarities mounted quickly.

And a few seconds after he had begun the comparison—for it does not take a professional print examiner long—Leblanc was certain.

John Stiles Griffin, who had been in prison in California until April 23, had left his fingerprint to be found in the Hixson apartment on April 25.

He had left in on the same tape dispenser that he had used to gag Louise Ponder. It was the best evidence that could possibly have been found. John Stiles Griffin was the killer.

* * *

The fingerprint left no doubt whatsoever to Carolyn Stephenson. But there was a great deal more, she knew, that needed to be done. There was a large number of witnesses to interview. And it would be important to test their identifications of the subject in a properly conducted lineup.

That was why Carolyn Stephenson panicked, the day after Griffin's arrest, when she saw the picture the *Houston Chronicle* had run.

There, prominently displayed in a major Houston newspaper, was a photograph of John Stiles Griffin. The story beside it was about the Richmond Avenue Murders.

There was good reason for Stephenson's panic. She had not yet had a chance to conduct a lineup to see whether her witnesses—Paul Manteris, the people from the Astroworld, and the Galveston victims—could identify John Stiles Griffin. The fingerprint, of course, had been a milestone in her case, but she needed these eyewitnesses too.

The problem with the picture was that a lineup had to be just like a laboratory procedure. It was as delicate a process, Carolyn Stephenson knew, as a chemical test or a fingerprint identification. The reason was simple: the decisions of the United States Supreme Court required it to be. Those decisions were directly to the point and quite explicit. If the testimony of any witness was tainted by "suggestion," the testimony of that witness could not be used in court.

That was the reason, for instance, that a suspect always had to be displayed to witnesses in a group. The group had to include other people with the same general appearance as the suspect's. There could be no individual features that set the suspect apart from the others in the lineup, whether they were age, weight, height, dress, hair color or something else.

And certainly, a lineup identification by a witness who had seen this *Chronicle* picture would create problems in court. It was more than "suggestive." It identified John Stiles Griffin as the suspect.

Stephenson got Paul Manteris on the telephone. She was

relieved to hear that he had not seen the photograph. "Don't even look at a newspaper today," she said emphatically.

Manteris, impressed by her insistence, agreed.

More phone calls told Stephenson that none of the witnesses had seen the picture. She breathed a sigh of relief. But she decided to hold the lineup immediately, to avoid further problems.

The lineup room was like a tiny theatre. The five men—one suspect and four stand-ins—mingled about on the stage. Ironically, several of the stand-ins were police officers wearing casual clothes; for with his husky build, short hair and clean-cut appearance, John Stiles Griffin looked more like a police officer than like anyone else available. It was customary to let the suspect choose his position in the row, and Griffin chose position number two.

The bright lights were on. An officer working the front gave commands to the five men behind the one-way glass: "Turn and face left." "Turn and face right." The process was repeated for each of the ten witnesses. And each was taken outside, individually, and asked whether he or she had seen any of the men before.

"I see him," said Paul Manteris. "It's the man in position number two."

The Galveston witnesses came out of the room, nodding their heads before Carolyn Stephenson could ask the question. Eight of the ten witnesses were positive in identifying John Stiles Griffin. They would make good witnesses in court.

But the lineup also provided examples of the fallibility of eyewitness testimony.

Two hotel workers were positive in their identifications of the men in positions 4 and 5, respectively, as the one who had rented the room under the name "Merrill." Actually, positions 4 and 5 were both filled by stand-ins—who happened to be vice officers with the Houston Police Department. The witnesses were simply mistaken. It happened sometimes.

* * *

Now came the hardest part: fitting all the details together and filling in the gaps.

Bit by bit, it all came together.

—Handwriting analysis showed that the register slip signed with the name "Merrill" at the Astroworld Hotel matched other writing by John Stiles Griffin.

—John Stiles Griffin had had a pocket knife in his possession when arrested. The medical examiner said that the murder weapon was a knife with a blade 3 to 3½ inches long. That fit the red-handled pocket knife Griffin had been caught with.

—A watch found on Griffin's person at his arrest had come from the San Diego burglary.

—Various items belonging to Walter Hixson were found in the hotel room rented by Griffin. And a pair of trousers belonging to Hixson were found in the car Griffin stole and abandoned in Galveston. They could only have gotten there because he had taken them with him from the Hixson apartment.

—The red shirt that Griffin had been wearing was identified by the Galveston victims. He had stolen it from them.

The assistant district attorney at the intake desk accepted two capital murder charges against John Stiles Griffin. One accused Griffin of the murder of Louise Ponder during the course of a rape. The other charged him with the murder of Patricia Hixson during the course of a robbery.

Carolyn Stephenson had made her case.

But she had only made it on paper, of course, and that could turn out to be illusory. What would the jury do? That was the real question.*

---

*The following names in this chapter were changed, without alteration of the incidents in which the persons were involved: Patricia Hixson, Walter Hixson, Louise Ponder, Robin Couch, Paul Manteris, Arnold Merrill.

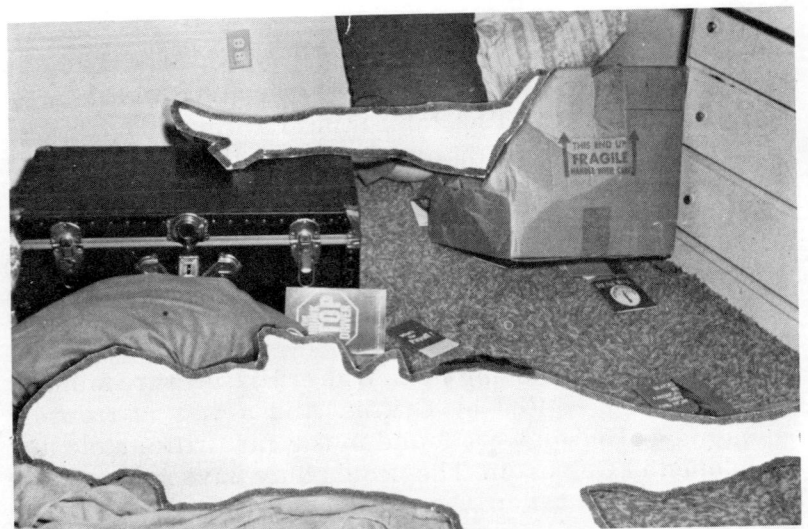

THE JOHN STILES GRIFFIN MURDER CASE—the homicide scene, according to Detective Carolyn Stephenson, was "as bad as I've ever made." The body of Louise Ponder is in the foreground, nude from the waist down. The body of the other victim, Patricia Hixson, is partially obscured by pillows and a crumpled cardboard box. The original photograph depicted the nature of this murder in a way that is conveyed only partially by this edited verson.

THE JOHN STILES GRIFFIN MURDER CASE—detail from original photograph of crime scene. This picture shows the bindings on the wrists of Louise Ponder (the body in the foreground). The killer tied her with nylon hose, then tightened that with a coat hanger. He also tied the victim's feet, circled her neck with a leather strap and coat hanger, gagged her with crisscrossed strips of tape, and raped her.

THE JOHN STILES GRIFFIN MURDER CASE—for every homicide, the Houston Police department fills out a wound chart, using either a male or a female standard figure. In this one, Carolyn Stephenson diagrammed the stab wounds on the body of Patricia Hixson. The wound descriptions took three pages.

THE JOHN STILES GRIFFIN MURDER CASE—this booking picture was taken in 1965, just before one of Griffin's earliest prison sentences. He was seventeen years old and on his way to the Texas Department of Corrections.

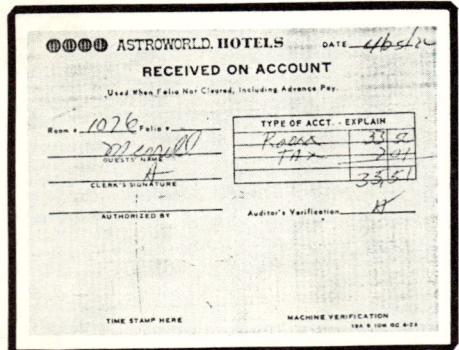

THE JOHN STILES GRIFFIN MURDER CASE—PART OF THE PHYSICAL EVIDENCE. Handwriting analysts matched this and other writing at the Astroworld Hotel to samples written by Griffin. This evidence helped to prove his guilt because (1) he had left his Astroworld Hotel key at the murder scene, (2) property stolen from the murder scene was found in the hotel room which he rented, and (3) the handwriting corroborated eyewitness identification of Griffin as the renter.

INKED FINGERPRINT   LATENT FINGERPRINT

THE JOHN STILES GRIFFIN MURDER CASE—PART OF THE PHYSICAL EVIDENCE. The inked fingerprint was taken after John Stiles Griffin was arrested, during the booking procedure. The latent fingerprint was developed by dusting the dispenser of the tape that was used to gag one of the victims, Louise Ponder, immediately before she was murdered. A fingerprint expert would analyze these prints by comparing "points," some of which are labelled in these photographs. Point number 1, for instance, is a "fork," point 3 is a "ridge ending," etc. Usable latent prints are hard to find. This one is smeared and overlaid with another print, but is sufficient for an identification.

THE JOHN STILES GRIFFIN MURDER CASE—Detective Carolyn Stephenson of the Houston Police Department Homicide Division, one of Houston's best police officers. "You can't do anything with Carolyn," said the lawyer who defended Griffin. "She knows what she's doing." Her peers in the police association agree; in 1976, they named her Police Officer of the Year. (Photograph courtesy Nancy Redding).

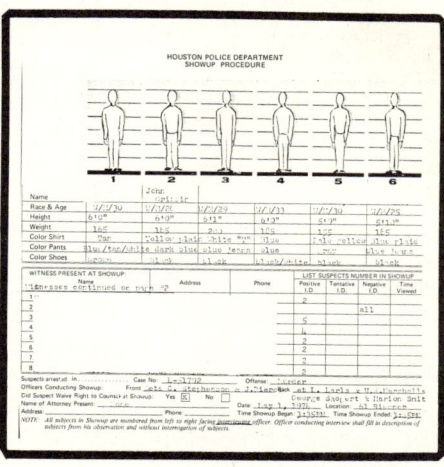

THE JOHN STILES GRIFFIN MURDER CASE—the lineup sheet. Each time that a lineup is conducted, the Houston Police Department fills in a form of this type. The names of all witnesses, and of all stand-ins other than the suspect, Griffin, are deleted from this copy. Notice that most witnesses identified Griffin—the man in position 2—but there were two witnesses who mistakenly identified stand-ins in positions 4 and 5.

THE JOHN STILES GRIFFIN MURDER CASE—The photographer took this remarkable picture through a small window in the courtroom door. Detective James Pierce testifies before a jury against John Stiles Griffin, who sits with the back of his head to the camera, behind his attorneys. (Photograph: Nancy Redding).

THE JOHN STILES GRIFFIN MURDER CASE—Officer M.A. Hebert of the Port Arthur Police Department arrested John Stiles Griffin. Griffin produced a U.S. Customs I.D. and told a story that "sounded convincing," but upon closer questioning Officer Hebert found that the suspect knew no other federal officers and had never heard of the newly formed D.E.A. (Drug Enforcement Agency). Griffin was carrying a knife that fit the measurements of the murder weapon used in the Richmond Avenue Murders, a shirt from a Galveston robbery and a watch from a California burglary. (Photograph courtesy Nancy Redding).

CHAPTER NINE
THE TRIAL OF JOHN STILES GRIFFIN

Homicide prosecutors get used to discussing the clinical details of murder cases in frank, professional terms.

They learn to suppress their revulsion because they have to, long enough to get the job done. But prosecutors are people too, and the revulsion is always there, under the surface.

You could see it now on Ted Busch's face, as he talked about the Richmond Avenue Murders.

"It was senseless, and it was horrible, and it was completely random," Busch said. "And you can make up just about any scene your mind can think of for those four hours, for what those two girls went through, and there's nobody who can call you a liar."

Busch is a veteran prosecutor. He came to Texas from his native Minnesota because "the army brought me here,'" and he stayed because he liked it. When he became a lawyer, he didn't like private practice. He became an assistant district attorney, he says, because "I wanted to be on the side of the angels," and he stayed "because I was satisfied.'

He had started prosecuting in misdemeanor court in 1960. Now, he was chief of the trial division. That made him responsible for most of the operations of the district attorney's office.

Busch is around forty, but he looks about twenty. His clean-cut, youthful appearance is at odds with his reputation as a courtroom fighter. When the Griffin case had come up for trial, the District Attorney, Carol Vance, had assigned Busch to handle it. "I'm just horrified at some of the cases we've had involving sadistic crimes of violence," Vance had said, sounding like an outraged citizen himself. He had wanted to try the case personally, the District Attorney had said, but other commitments would prevent him from doing so.

Now, a year later, Ted Busch looked down at the glass top on his desk and he began to talk about John Stiles Griffin: Griffin the man, Griffin the defendant, and Griffin the Richmond Avenue Murderer.

"It was about as bad a murder case as I've ever seen," Busch said.

"And just about as bad a defendant."

* * *

John Stiles Griffin was the eldest of four children born to a juvenile probation officer and his wife in Beaumont, Texas.

He once told a prison case worker, "My father is as honest as I am dishonest." And it was true: his parents were hard-working, middle-class, ordinary people.

There is nothing in Griffin's past to show exactly where he departed from his parents' example, but he was 13 years old at the time of his first arrest. That was in 1958. Three years later, in 1961, he had his first institutional commitment as a juvenile: he was sent to the State Reform School at Gatesville, Texas.

At the age of 17, Griffin earned his first prison sentence as an adult. It was on a conviction for burglary. He was paroled from that sentence; but within a year, he was back—again for burglary.

From that day forward, John Stiles Griffin spent all but a few months of his life inside prison walls. The time he spent on the outside consisted of brief interludes, created by paroles or escapes.

In 1965, he received a 6-year federal sentence for interstate car theft, and he was sent to the Federal Reformatory in El Reno, Nevada. From El Reno, he went to the Federal Corrections Institute in Seagoville, Texas. He failed on a work-release program there and was transferred to the higher security Federal Correctional Institute at Texarkana, Texas. From there, he went back to El Reno; and in 1970, he was paroled.

The parole did not last long. Within a matter of months, Griffin was on his fourth adult trip to prison, this time to serve a sentence for theft at Seagoville. In 1971, he escaped. During the time he was free, he committed a burglary in Las Vegas.

And that burglary was a preview of the Richmond Avenue murders. John Stiles Griffin tied up the woman he found inside the room he had entered, and left her while he stole her car.

Federal prison authorities failed to recognize this signal of Griffin's violent character. They thought of him as a burglar and a thief. He had not killed the victim that time.

For his most recent offenses, Griffin was given a sentence of 5 years. And in spite of his escape history, he was sent to a minimum security facility in Los Angeles.

A prison psychologist's report described Griffin's behavior as "classically antisocial," and a Bureau of Prisons staff report said, "He has been in repeated conflict with society and seems to have his own set of values. He is tremendously impulsive and irresponsible."

But John Stiles Griffin was intelligent. He boasted an I.Q. of 135. And he had learned, from being in prison most of his adult life, how to manipulate the system and the people who ran it. For instance, the same psychiatrist who called him "classically antisocial" believed Griffin's representations of good intentions. He wrote, "It is not anticipated that he will experience as much difficulty in the institutional setting as he previously had because of a desire to cease taking drugs, maximize chances for release, and live within the institution as comfortably as possible."

In addition to his manipulative abilities, Griffin had an accomplished expertise at obtaining drugs on the inside. At times during his prison terms, he supplied pills to other inmates. While in Los Angeles, he laid in a supply of LSD.

But he was a model prisoner there. He worked in the refrigeration shop, plumbing shop, group activities center, and electronics cable shop, and got excellent work reports everywhere. He even used his leisure time for self-improvement programs. After he had finished earning his high school degree, he began going to motivation classes. Soon he was running those classes. His caseworker wrote, "There have been definite noted positive changes in Griffin's character traits over the past 25 months."

Social work in prisons often has an Alice-in-Wonderland quality to it. That quality was certainly present in the reports Griffin received in December 1973, just four months before the Richmond Avenue Murders. His caseworker concluded, "Although Griffin has had five major periods of confinement, it is felt he has matured a great deal over the past 25 months. At this time, he definitely has the ability to remain in the community without violating the law."

It was a strange way of thinking. And Patricia Hixson and Louise Ponder would pay for it with their lives. On April 23, 1974, Griffin stopped "maturing," escaped from the minimum security facility, and took his LSD with him.

He apparently travelled to the city of Anaheim, just a few miles away, and murdered the hotel maid there.

That same afternoon, he travelled to San Diego, stole Arnold Merrill's identification, and bought a bus ticket to Texas.

He arrived in Houston on April 25th, took a room at the Astroworld Hotel, and had been in Houston only a few hours when he murdered Patricia Hixson and Louise Ponder.

On April 27th, he surfaced in Galveston. That was where he tied and gagged the people in the motel room. He did not have a chance to kill them, because a knock on the door frightened him away.

And on the 28th, just five days after his escape, he was arrested in Port Arthur—on the grounds of another motel.

* * *

A few days after charges had been filed against him, John Stiles Griffin agreed to talk to the Houston Police.

Carolyn Stephenson, together with Detective James Pierce, located him comfortably in an office, turned on a tape recorder and listened to him for the better part of an hour.

He remembered standing in the San Diego Bus Station—

"Where did you get a ticket to?" Pierce asked.

"I was going to go to Dallas," Griffin replied. "I reorganized my thoughts. And I decided, well, I'll go to Beaumont." He had gone to Beaumont by way of Houston and Galveston.

"I dropped two hits of acid in San Diego," Griffin went on, "which—one hit, or half a hit, will really get you wasted. So I blazed for the next 36 hours." By the time the bus trip ended, he said, "I might as well have been on a plane."

"You were on two trips, the bus trip and the other trip," Pierce said. Griffin laughed and agreed.

He admitted to the burglary of William Merrill's hotel room. And he described the robbery in Galveston.

"Oh, by the way," Pierce said, "what about that Customs identification? Where'd you get that?"

"I worked for Westlake Moving Company," Griffin answered. "We were movers for the FBI, Customs and so forth." This had been one of Griffin's jobs when he was on work-release in California.

During one of the moves, he explained, a box containing blank Customs identification cards and folders had dropped out and spilled. He had taken "two or three" of them. "I filled it out, and took a little picture, and put it on there," he said. "We all did it, you know. It was a joke. It was just a joke."

So that was where the Customs I.D. had come from.

But for all his talking, Griffin said he could neither confirm nor deny that he had murdered Patricia Hixson and Louise Ponder. He just couldn't recall. He had been on LSD the whole time, and he couldn't remember anything. "For me to sit here and actively tell y'all everything," he said, "would be impossible.

"Outside of Sunday, or outside of Wednesday, that was the only day I was straight; and I was just coming down then."

Pierce wanted to know what effect the LSD had had on Griffin. Did it make him belligerent? Did it make him feel strong?

"Did it make you feel like you could pick somebody up and throw 'em down?" Pierce asked.

"Oh, I could pick somebody up and throw 'em anyway," Griffin answered promptly. He had been a weightlifter in prison, he explained. "I've done over 1200 pounds in three lifts, three power lifts. I can bench press over 300, dead lift over 500, and squat over 400."

- That, the officers thought, explained a lot of things.

They thought about the riddled bodies of Patricia Hixson and Louise Ponder. And they shuddered.

* * *

The men who were appointed to defend John Stiles Griffin had no rapport with him as they began to build a case to save his life.

"I didn't like him at all," says defense lawyer Al Thomas. "And he didn't like us either."

That was a problem, Thomas knew. Theoretically, it might be possible to defend a man under these conditions. But it would be hard. As a practical matter, you can't defend a man very well if he won't talk to you; and you can't protect him if he won't follow your advice.

Thomas does criminal defense work almost exclusively. He is good at it. And there is no doubt he is one of Houston's more colorful defense lawyers. He has a revealing nickname: Everyone calls him "The Indian."

Just how The Indian came by his name is a matter of conjecture. Many of his friends believe he is called that because he *is* one, but that, Thomas says, is "an old wives' tale." The nickname may come from his Oklahoma origins. Or it may be because of his ruddy complexion and dark curly hair. Or it may, conceivably, be a result of his lifestyle. Thomas is unpretentious, erratic, and fiercely independent.

In any event, the name has stuck so tightly, says Thomas, that "Back home in Oklahoma, even the Indians call me 'The Indian.'"

He doesn't have a secretary.

He does have an office, but he avoids going to it except on Saturday ("That's when I collect my fees"). A person who asks to make an appointment with The Indian will be told, "I'm usually at the courthouse. You can catch me there."

When Thomas was appointed to defend John Stiles Griffin, his first official act was to try to get his client to remain silent. "He was running his mouth to anyone who'd listen," the lawyer says. This was the first confrontation between lawyer and client. Thomas kept insisting, and Griffin kept refusing, until, says Thomas, "we finally got him to dummy up."

But there was one subject Thomas was careful not to discuss with his client.

"I never did ask if he did it," The Indian says. "I didn't want to know." And he adds that all John Stiles Griffin told his lawyers about the crime itself "was that he was blazing on acid the whole time he was in Houston and he didn't remember anything."

* * *

It was not until jury selection was actually underway that John Stiles Griffin seemed to settle down and cooperate with his attorneys.

"I asked him one day, 'Are you right with the Lord?' " Al Thomas says.

"He answered, 'I don't know.' " Griffin seemed concerned enough to think about it.

That unusual exchange led to a visit by Thomas' mother, who delivered a Bible to John Stiles Griffin. The whole incident, for some reason, led to a greater degree of trust between this strange prisoner and his lawyers. "I tried to put the Bible where the jury would have to see it," Thomas adds. He regarded it as a way to enhance his client's defense.

"Y'all are playing poker with my life," John Stiles Griffin said to his lawyers during one hard-fought day of jury selection.

"I guess you could say that," Thomas answered. "It's all a question of strategy."

For the first time, Griffin seemed to sense that this was a game that could be won—and, more importantly to Thomas, he seemed to care about it. "Well," he said, "let's play cards."

* * *

Jury selection did not go well for the prosecutors.

Ted Busch felt uncomfortable with the jury that was finally selected. So did Alan McAshan, the prosecutor who was assisting him.

Jury selection is only loosely related to the law. It is actually an exercise in a kind of applied psychology. It depends, more than anything else, upon an understanding of people—and of how they are likely to vote when they become jurors.

And unfortunately, it has little to do with the romantic ideal of an "impartial" jury. Each side is trying to get a favorable jury, not an impartial one.

Much of it is founded on stereotypes, and the stereotypes, at times, seem to approach pure prejudice. Are white collar workers likely to vote for conviction in a given case? If so, the defendant's lawyers will strike them. Are women, as a class, more likely to acquit in a given type of case than men? Then prosecutors will follow the percentages—and strike them.

Polls show, for example, that women are far less likely to support capital punishment than men. A jury with a majority of women is far more likely, on the average, to acquit or assess a life sentence in a death penalty case than one composed of a majority of men. It is not quite that simple, of course, because the statistics do not apply to all women or to all men. But nevertheless, both Ted Busch and Al Thomas recognized the significance of the composition of the jury that would try John Stiles Griffin.

There were seven women and five men.

"All these women qualified," Ted Busch said. "It amazed me that they all did." In spite of the strength of his case, it made him uneasy.

And there was something else that troubled Busch. There had been a large proportion of potential jurors who had indicated adamant opposition to the death penalty, initially, but who had changed their answers and qualified under persistent questioning by the judge. When this would happen, Al Thomas would grin and punch his fist through the air like a cheerleader. "I knew Busch would have to strike all those people," he says. "I was just saying to myself, 'come on, baby, use up those strikes.''

The faster Busch used his peremptory challenges, Thomas knew, the faster he would run out of them, and the faster he would have to begin accepting jurors who were opposed to his case. And although it was an intangible thing, Busch had a sense that that had happened to him by the time jury selection was over. It was one of the reasons he was uncomfortable.

Across the table from Busch and McAshan, Thomas—and his co-counsel, Fred Heacock—were happy when jury selection ended.

"We won the battle of the strikes," Thomas says.

"We even snuck one past Busch," Thomas adds. "We had one lady who was a Pentecostal. One of their tenets says that we are in a state of grace here and now. They believe that any sin can be forgiven." The Pentecostal lady was going to be a problem for the prosecutors where the death penalty was concerned.

"Fred and I were extremely satisfied with that jury," Thomas says. "We even started getting downright friendly with John Stiles Griffin."

* * *

The State's first witness was Walter Hixson.

It was visibly hard for him to testify. He had to relive the day he had found his wife's body in his apartment. But that, by itself, was not the hardest part of his testimony. The hardest part came after Busch had finished questioning the witness, and the strategy that Al Thomas had mapped out for the case began to emerge.

Thomas had a simple theory of the case: John Stiles Griffin hadn't killed Hixson's wife. Hixson had.

Griffin had been there in the Hixson apartment. That had to be admitted, Thomas decided, because there was no way around the fingerprint on the tape dispenser. But Thomas had also concluded that there was no reason Griffin could not have left while the two women were still alive.

"Our theory was that John Stiles Griffin had got in there and tied 'em up," Thomas says. The fingerprint made that much undisputable. But the theory went on from there. "Walter Hixson came home, saw them tied up, and freaked out," Thomas says. "And he killed 'em both. It's a terrible thing to accuse him of," Thomas adds, "but his actions were strange."

It was not only terrible; it seemed ridiculous. And it was inconsistent with the physical evidence—the bloody pants with the bus ticket and Astroworld key in them, for one thing. But it was Thomas' defense. And he was skillful in developing it.

He was gentle, polite and restrained as he made the awful insinuation start with the first witness—Walter Hixson himself.

"What time did you go to lunch?" Thomas asked.

Hixson told him.

"What time did you leave lunch? And where did you go from there?"

Using this technique, The Indian pinned Hixson down on the details of his day. And he established that there was a period of time, during the mid-afternoon, that Hixson had been "running errands." No one else had been with him to say that he had not gone home to his apartment.

Thomas pointed out that Hixson had been taken into custody by the police. And he pointed out that the apartment security guard had seen someone whom he had identified as Walter Hixson, wandering around near the apartment "as if in a daze."

The defense lawyer did nothing to anger the jury. He simply left the monstrous accusation hanging, like a will-o'-the-wisp, in the air. When Walter Hixson was finally excused from the witness stand, it remained in the air—too vague and undefined for Busch to answer. Thomas wanted the jurors to flesh out the idea for themselves. And yet none of them could fail to grasp the point he had made.

Reasonable doubt.

Paul Manteris was one of the next witnesses Ted Busch called to the stand. As Busch puts it, Manteris was as "strong as horseradish."

Manteris told the jurors about the strange man who had come to his door, showed him a Customs I.D., and asked to come inside his apartment.

"Is this the man?" Ted Busch asked, indicating John Stiles Griffin.

"Yes," the witness replied without hesitation.

And Griffin had walked in the direction of the Hixson apartment afterward, Manteris added.

Al Thomas' cross examination, again, was careful and controlled. It was designed to raise questions, not to answer them. And it was designed to exonerate his client.

Thomas pointed out that the direction the man had taken could have led him to the freeway and out of the apartment complex just as easily as to the Hixson apartment.

"You didn't see where he actually went?"

"No."

"You didn't see him actually go *into* any apartment?"

"No."

"The last time you saw him, he was heading in this direction, which could have been toward the freeway?"

"Yes."

The questions and answers meant nothing, really, except that the witness had not continuously observed John Stiles Griffin. But once again, the cross examination invited the jurors to discover an alternative explanation. And it could seem, to some of them, to create a reasonable doubt.

Carolyn Stephenson was on the witness stand, testifying for the prosecution, for over two hours.

Ted Busch led her through a description of the bodies, the scene, the bloody pants, the Astroworld Hotel key, the bus ticket and every other feature of the apartment.

Before passing the witness, the prosecutor asked her: "And did you take copious notes?"

'Yes," she responded.

Al Thomas' first question on cross examination was, "What are 'copious notes?' "

Everyone smiled a little at the phrase. Thomas, secretly, was hoping the witness wouldn't know what the word "copious" meant. If she didn't, he could follow up with a question like, "Well, why'd you testify you took copious notes, then?" and perhaps it would make the whole prosecution case look a little foolish.

Carolyn Stephenson paused momentarily.

Then she said, "It means I took a lot of notes."

'You can't do anything with Carolyn," Thomas said afterwards. "Heck, she knows what she's doing. She knows what she's about.

"We just sort of ragged her around a little bit."

Thomas' cross-examination did considerably more than that. It uncovered every possible point one could have thought of to help his "Walter-Hixson-did-it" theory. Was there a laundry mark on the pants, he wanted to know? Had Stephenson looked to see whether there was any sort of mark, or anything else, that might have showed that the pants belonged to Hixson?

Thomas, says Carolyn Stephenson, was "completely professional" in front of the jury. He didn't take any "cheap shots." That was the mark of a good defense lawyer.

Carolyn Stephenson was on the witness stand for several hours more. She was re-called to testify on three separate occasions.

* * *

Thomas built his defense with consummate skill. But he was trying to build bricks without clay.

His points of doubt, viewed realistically, seemed only to underscore the case Ted Busch was building.

Through nearly two dozen witnesses, Busch fought to get all his evidence before the jury. Thomas fought to keep as much of it as he could from being heard. When Thomas objected to testimony Busch offered about "extraneous offenses," Busch showed the judge why the testimony was admissible. He got most of the pictures of the crime scene admitted, over Thomas' objections and motions for a mistrial. And he built a proof of John Stiles Griffin's guilt that was simply overwhelming.

Finally, the parade of witnesses fit together like a mosaic. Busch's talent was that he made the mosaic emerge, from the various bits of knowledge, like ragged stones, that each witness could contribute.

Manteris' identification of Griffin as the man with the Customs identification. Griffin's arrest with the I.D. in his possession, trying to use it. The hotel key in the Hixson apartment. The property belonging to Hixson that had been found in the Astroworld Hotel room. The identification of Griffin as the man who had rented that room. Griffin's handwriting on the hotel register. The name "Merrill" on the register. The California burglary of Arnold Merrill's room. The watch from the California burglary in Griffin's possession. The knife, which fit the wounds. The Galveston robbery, and the car Griffin had stolen. Hixson's trousers, which were found in that car after Griffin abandoned it.

And Griffin's fingerprint on the tape dispenser.

"My guess was that one or two of the jurors had a reasonable doubt," Thomas said later. But, he admitted, "with all that evidence, you just couldn't find him not guilty."

It was early the next morning that the jurors returned, with a verdict that bore out Thomas' prediction.

They had found John Stiles Griffin guilty of capital murder.

* * *

The penalty hearing was short.

The prosecutors introduced into evidence John Stiles

Griffin's prior criminal record. The five periods of confinement, and all the multiple convictions that supported each of them, were all set out before the jury.

And it was time for jury argument—on the issue of life or death.

Jury argument, especially on a volatile issue like the death penalty, is a strange thing. Sometimes juries respond to logical reasoning. But sometimes they do not. A jury is not, and it has never been intended to be, a mere factual computer. And it was Al Thomas' genius that he recognized this principle as he stood before this jury, for the last time.

His argument was unconventional.

"You've convicted the wrong man!" he all but shouted at the jury, with an expression of contempt on his face. "You should have found him not guilty.

"And since you shouldn't have convicted him in the first place," the defense lawyer went on, "I'm not going to plead for his life now!"

That, in substance, was Thomas' whole argument. It lasted about thirty seconds. But it was perhaps the single most effective thirty seconds of the trial. Thomas understood jury psychology; he knew that most human beings feel uncomfortable finding anyone guilty in a court of law. The whole process, he recognized, could subtly make the jurors themselves feel guilty for rendering a "guilty" verdict. Thomas knew the jurors' inner guilt. And he was using it against them.

From head to toe, the defense lawyer radiated disgust—disgust at the jurors' dereliction of duty in finding his client guilty.

Ted Busch, the veteran prosecutor, had the last word. He answered Thomas' argument: there was no question of guilt, none at all, and there was no question the sentencing questions should be answered "Yes." Logically and forcefully, he summarized the evidence.

And he concluded by saying, "If this isn't a death penalty case, then there's no such thing."

* * *

The jurors were out for two hours. Then it was three.

"I know I'm either going to die or spend the rest of my life in prison," John Stiles Griffin said to Al Thomas. "Maybe I can do something to help somebody.

"Maybe," he added, "I can help keep them from making my same stupid mistakes."

It was the same sort of thing he had said to manipulate his case workers in prison.

Silently, the fourth hour of deliberations passed.

"If the death penalty was ever called for, this is the time," Ted Busch thought to himself, as the time dragged by.

Five hours.

Suddenly, the buzzer sounded from inside the jury room.

The jurors had reached a verdict. They filed out and took their places in the jury box. The foreman handed the verdict sheet to the bailiff, who handed it to the judge.

Judge Joseph Guarino held the sheet in his hand. Two "yes" answers would mean a sentence of death, while one, or more, "no" answers would mean a sentence of life imprisonment. Everyone wondered what those two words were—the words that the jury had written, that made the life-or-death difference.

The judge read the first question, slowly and with emphasis. It asked the jury whether John Stiles Griffin had committed the murders deliberately.

"Yes," was the jury's answer.

Everyone in the courtroom sat forward in his chair.

The judge read the second question. Was there a probability that John Stiles Griffin would be a continuing threat to society?

The judge read the answer.

"No."

"No." The second answer was "no." It was a sentence of life imprisonment. That was the jury's verdict—that John Stiles Griffin was to get a sentence of life imprisonment for the murders of Patricia Hixson and Louise Ponder. Al Thomas had won the case for the defense.

* * *

Today, John Stiles Griffin is in prison in Huntsville. Law enforcement officers in California have tried to put together enough evidence to convict him of the Anaheim Hotel murder, but thus far they have been unsuccessful. They have linked his name to other crimes there, and they have seen his method of operation in at least one more grisly murder. But there is not enough evidence. And it is unlikely that John Stiles Griffin will ever be tried for any of those crimes.

Griffin did not stop breaking the law after his arrest. On one occasion, he got a hacksaw blade smuggled into his jail cell and cut nearly through a steel plate before guards caught him. On another occasion, he improvised a knife with a two-inch blade inside the cell, using a cigarette rolling machine to make it. Griffin is dangerous, in or out of prison.

Although it seems improbable, Al Thomas maintains that Griffin is sincere about his newfound interest in religion. And Griffin is improving himself, again, in prison; he is going to school. "He has just about a 4.0 average," says Thomas. "He's had two things he's written published, and he's working on a novel."

He will be eligible for parole after he has served 20 prison "years." But that time limit is misleading, because it is possible, with "good time," to serve 20 "years" in ten calendar years or fewer, in the Texas prison system. If that were to happen in John Stiles Griffin's case, he would emerge from prison at the age of 38—in the year 1984.

It is not likely that parole will come that early. But it is fair to expect that a parole for Griffin will someday be forthcoming. Patricia Hixson and Louise Ponder will have been in their graves somewhere between eight and fifteen years, it seems safe to guess, when the parole board first considers whether to release John Stiles Griffin.

* * *

Why did the Griffin case come out as it did?

Why, for example, did John Stiles Griffin get a sentence of life imprisonment when Kenneth Brock had been sentenced to death? What was the difference between the cases?

Ted Busch knows part of the answer. It lies in the twelve people who rendered the verdict. "Wishy-washy, pussycat jury," he says. 'We had a really weak jury."

But Busch is equally hard on himself. "Wishy-washy prosecutor, too," he says. "I didn't get down into the trenches and go through the horror of the crime with them again during final argument. I just, calmly and coolly, said, 'This is what the evidence shows, and this is what you have to find.' I didn't get wrought up. And they need that."

Busch's self-criticism is far too harsh. A good trial lawyer always, without fail, blames himself whenever anything goes wrong; it is a characteristic of the breed. Actually, the verdict was surprising precisely *because* Busch had tried the case so well. The jury just didn't respond to his proof.

It came down to this: Al Thomas' final argument (or rather, final non-argument) was more effective than Busch's analysis of the evidence. In a logical world, perhaps, it should not have been; but nevertheless it was.

Carolyn Stephenson agrees. "The defense did an A-number-one job," she says. "They didn't miss a single chance to bring out any incident that was in their favor."

And she adds, "It was the Indian. He did it."

Still, Stephenson was shocked by the verdict. "If you can't get the death penalty in this case, then you can't get it in any case," she said. And she would be right, if it were not for the jury system—a system that allowed twelve people to listen to the kind of evidence they heard in the Griffin case, and then return a verdict pronouncing that the defendant was not a threat to society.

But characteristically, it is Al Thomas who has the most unusual insights into the verdict.

In the first place, Thomas denies that the verdict was really in his favor. "We didn't win the case," he says. "A not-guilty verdict would have been what we would have gotten if we had won it."

The murders, Thomas concedes, were "as brutal as any I've ever seen, as sensational as any I've ever seen." But by his inferences that Walter Hixson could have done it, and by his spectacular argument technique, Thomas had succeeded in planting that seed of doubt that makes a juror hesitant. Not hesitant enough to acquit, perhaps—but hesitant enough to be unable to sentence the convict to death.

And so the jury did not return a death penalty verdict, Thomas says, because "the jurors had a reasonable doubt that John Stiles Griffin did it." Of course, to have that reasonable doubt after all the evidence they had heard, the jurors had to be a certain kind of people.

Thomas had chosen them carefully.

The last word in the case belonged to The Indian.

He collected his fee for John Stiles Griffin's defense from the county. It was a sizeable sum, and with his lack of overhead, it seemed even more substantial. The Indian left a note for Ted Busch as he walked from the courthouse. It was scrawled in a cramped hand that was hard, at first, to read; but on second glance, it left no doubt about what it was saying.

"Busch," the note said, "I just got $6300.00 for Griffin case. Thank you very much. Al Thomas."

* * *

The Griffin case, with that, was over.

Within a few months, the sensational publicity connected with the case would subside, and others would take its place. There was one case in particular, involving a murder committed seven months after Griffin's crime, that would sieze the public's attention in a way that seemed to eclipse even the Richmond Avenue Murders.

It was called the Halloween Candy Murder Case.

The Halloween Candy Murder bore no resemblance to John Stiles Griffin's crime. The motive, the victim and the method of commission were all different. And the final suspect in the case was the last person anyone would have suspected.

The story of that case begins on October 31, 1974, when Ronald Clark O'Bryan's son was murdered in Pasadena, Texas.

CHAPTER TEN

THE HALLOWEEN CANDY MURDER CASE

After his son's death, Ronald Clark O'Bryan wept.

"He was all boy," the grieving father said. "He loved baseball, football—anything. He never met a stranger.

"But I have my peace in knowing that Tim is in heaven now."

O'Bryan's fellow citizens in Pasadena, Texas, shared in his shock and outrage. So did the rest of the nation, because the case had attracted the attention of the national press. A small army of reporters was camped on the doorstep of the Pasadena Police Building.

But there was no one so spectacularly affected as the boy's father.

On the evening after the boy's death, a memorial service for Tim O'Bryan was held at the Second Baptist Church. Ronald O'Bryan sang a solo in the boy's honor. It was a Baptist hymn called "Blessed Assurance."

As the father's strong, clear singing voice filled the church, listeners realized that he had changed the hymn as a tribute to his son. The usual words went, "This is my story/—This is my song." Instead, O'Bryan sang, "This is Tim's story/—This is Tim's song."

The distraught father had tears in his eyes as he sang. So did many in the congregation. It was profoundly moving. But Ronald Clark O'Bryan obviously had the full strength of his religion sustaining him, because he told the congregation that his eight-year-old son had "given his life to Jesus."

* * *

The autopsy report was standard.

It began with a section called "History." Here, in succinct and unemotional terms, the report told of the unusual way in which Timothy Marc O'Bryan had met his death.

"This 8-year-old white boy," it said, "arrived at Southmore Hospital Emergency Room at 9:20 p.m., where he was pronounced dead at 10:30 p.m. on October 31, 1974.

"Earlier, the decedent had been out trick-or-treating. He became ill after ingesting some candy obtained earlier that afternoon."

October 31. Halloween. Timothy O'Bryan, a normal eight-year-old boy, had received and eaten some candy that made him sick. In fact, it had made him very sick; it had made him vomit violently. The autopsy report described the volume of "red-gray frothy material exuding from each of the external nares."

Inside the morgue, Dr. Joseph A. Jachimczyk took personal charge of the autopsy. He was the county's chief medical examiner, and he was known throughout Houston as "Dr. Joe"—because of his unpronounceable last name. Dr. Joe was not only a medical doctor; he also had a law degree and was a licensed attorney. He knew the difficulties a case such as this could present in court. And so he was handling it himself.

The abundance of frothy material—so thick that it clogged the boy's bronchial tubes—was not caused by any of the ordinary lethal agents that Dr. Joe and his cohorts saw every day. It was not caused by an infection. It was not caused by hemorrhaging. And it was not the result of blows or "trauma."

It was a case of poisoning.

Dr. Joe's immediate task was to find out what the poison was and how much of it had been used.

He used a small circular saw to cut through the bone of the skull, completely around it. Then he removed the severed portion of the scalp like a skull cap. This procedure allowed the medical examiner to remove, section and inspect the brain. It was called "reflecting" the head. There was nothing unusual about it; dissecting the brain was part of a standard autopsy.

But Dr. Joe's findings from the brain in this case were not ordinary. Instead, they were highly unusual.

Almost immediately, he noticed the bright, glistening network of blood vessels that crisscrossed the top of Tim O'Bryan's brain. He saw that they glowed with an abnormal color and intensity. Something, he knew, was very wrong. And he thought he knew what it was.

It was cyanide.

This deep, cherry color was characteristic of cyanide poisoning.

Dr. Joe paused to speak into the microphone that was recording his report. "The surface vessels of the brain," he dictated, "were strikingly hyperemic red."

Liquid taken from the boy's stomach had a bitter smell, like almonds. That, too, was characteristic of cyanide. And when Dr. Joe tested the stomach washings with a reagent called prussian blue, it gave the color change that was a positive indication of cyanide, before his eyes.

Next, the doctor needed to know how much cyanide there was.

Dr. Joe took a measured sample of the stomach washings. He carefully noted the fraction the sample represented of the whole. And then he "titrated" it with silver nitrate.

The "titration" technique is a familiar tool of analytical chemistry. Here, it consisted of pouring a measured amount of another chemical, silver nitrate, into the sample—drop by drop, with a special glass column equipped with a sensitive valve—and waiting for the milky color that indicated it had reacted with all the cyanide in the sample. The doctor knew the concentration of the silver nitrate solution; and from this concentration, together with the volume of reagent he had used, he would be able to calculate exactly how much potassium cyanide was present.

Now, he had the result. 16 milligrams of the deadly poison had been recovered.

That was a huge amount to find in stomach washings of this kind.

The autopsy report was now complete.

Of course, the autopsy did nothing to tell what sort of person had given the poison to Timothy Marc O'Bryan in the first place. The key to the killer's identity was not to be found in the lab. It would be discovered, if it was to be discovered at all, in the streets and homes of Pasadena itself.

Somewhere in Pasadena, there was someone on the loose who was willing to kill an eight year old boy by giving him a piece of Halloween candy laced with enough potassium cyanide to kill him several times over.

* * *

Within minutes of Timothy Marc O'Bryan's death, the Pasadena Police Department had located the murder weapon.

A lot of people in the larger city of Houston, frankly, look down their noses at suburban Pasadena. Although it is located only a few miles from one of the nation's most populous metropolitan centers, Pasadena has the atmosphere of a small town. It is a blue-collar, refinery-and-factory city.

But Pasadena certainly has at least one thing to boast of. It has one of the finest investigative police departments in the United States.

Now, as Pasadena's homicide detectives looked at the "weapon," they were struck by its innocuous appearance. It was a plastic tube of purple-and-white powdered confection. It had the trade name by which it was sold, "Pixy Stix," printed on the tube. It was brightly colored, to appeal to children.

But the tube was lethal.

Ronald O'Bryan told the detectives that he had permitted his son to eat part of the Pixy Stix before going to bed. Within minutes, Timothy had complained of abdominal pain. Soon he had convulsed, vomited and lost consciousness. O'Bryan had called an ambulance, but the boy had died within a short time.

With characteristic thoroughness, the Pasadena officers interviewed the ambulance driver and hospital personnel. The boy's father had been "pretty shook," they said. When an ambulance driver had told him, "The boy isn't going to make it," O'Bryan had beaten his arms on the hospital wall and screamed, "Oh, God! Don't let my boy die!"

In fact, the doctors added, it had seemed for a moment that O'Bryan himself might have been poisoned, too.

It had been strange. O'Bryan had complained of the same symptoms his son was exhibiting. He had even lain on a stretcher for a few minutes. But when the doctors had offered to pump his stomach as they were pumping Timothy's, O'Bryan had said he didn't feel that bad. He had seemed more secure in his refusal of this service than one would have expected him to be, after showing the same symptoms that had so spectacularly killed his son. Perhaps it could have come, somehow, from being near his son—?

In any event, it was a mystery.

But where had the Pixy Stix come from? That was the real question.

The events preceding the boy's eating of the candy were not nearly so easy to trace as the events at the hospital. It turned out that the entire O'Bryan family—O'Bryan, his wife Daynene, their son Tim and their daughter Lane—had gone over to the home of their friends, Andy and Michelle Rourke, to go trick-or-treating. The Rourkes' children, Philip and Anne, were also in on the trick-or-treating.

The O'Bryan children had been excited and happy. Tim had been dressed as a warrior from the Planet of the Apes. Lane had had on the costume of a female from the Planet of the Apes.

The two fathers, Ron and Andy, had accompanied the children as they made the rounds of the neighborhood. Some of the candy had been collected by the fathers, to be given to the children later. Some had been accepted by the children themselves.

When they had gotten back to the Rourke home, after trick-or-treating, Ron O'Bryan had passed out the candy he had collected. The children's eyes had lighted; it had included five giant Pixy Stix. One had gone to Tim, one to Lane, one to Philip, and one to Anne.

There had been a fifth one left over. Ron O'Bryan had joked with the children, saying, "I'll just keep it and eat it myself." It had been amusing then, but it was frightening now. For O'Bryan, by not eating the Pixy Stix, had narrowly averted death himself.

There had been a young boy, a friend of the Rourke children, who had come to the door, O'Bryan told the detectives; and he had given the fifth Pixy Stix to the boy.

The Pasadena officers were aghast. O'Bryan was telling

them, in essence, that there were four more Pixy Stix in circulation—one of which had gone to a boy whose name O'Bryan did not know.

Immediately, the police department made a public appeal: any parent whose child had received Halloween candy that seemed suspicious at all should turn it in. Worried parents responded by handing in dozens of pieces of candy. And this public appeal resulted in the finding of the four missing Pixy Stix.

These four Pixy Stix, the medical examiner reported, were as lethal as the one that had killed Tim O'Bryan. Each one was stuffed with potassium cyanide.

Now, the Pasadena Police recognized the need for a systematic investigation of the route the trick-or-treaters had taken. They used a helicopter to take aerial photographs of the neighborhood, showing every house on the blocks O'Bryan and Rourke said they had covered. It was typical of Pasadena P.D.'s thoroughness. These aerial photographs would enable the detectives to interview witnesses with more precision. They could have the witness point out exactly where he had been and what he had seen.

And so on November 1, the day after the murder, Andy Rourke took the Pasadena detectives through the steps that the trick-or-treaters had followed. One by one, he identified the residences where they had stopped. The critical passage, it seemed, was on Pasadena's Donerail Street—a horseshoe-shaped residential lane with neat, new houses on it, located in an expensive new development called Bowling Green.

The group had stopped at 4126 Donerail first, Rourke said.

Then 4124 Donerail, next door.

Then 4122 Donerail.

From there, Rourke thought, the party had crossed the street to 4119 Donerail. The lady who lived there made it an annual custom to dress as a witch and serve "witches' brew," which in reality was Kool-aid.

Witches' brew. The detectives found it all chilling in spite of themselves. It was only play-acting for children. But it made this case, which was macabre enough already, seem just a little spookier.

The children had had some of the witches' brew.

The trick-or-treaters had then crossed back to the even-numbered residences and continued west. 4114 Donerail; 4112 Donerail—

After that, Rourke was not sure. But apparently, there had been another crossing, to 4111. In any event, Andy Rourke was sure of one thing: Ron O'Bryan had had the Pixy Stix in his hand before they had gotten to 4111 Donerail. He thought it had been on the even-numbered side of the street.

Was it 4112? Or maybe 4114?

Silently, the officers wondered: Which house was it?

Which of Rourke's neighbors was the murderer?

* * *

The next day, November 2, the officers talked to the grief-stricken father, Ronald Clark O'Bryan.

They had waited an extra day to interview him thoroughly. Now, they apologized for disturbing him at such a tragic time. The investigation, they felt, had to get underway. They hoped he understood.

"I'll help in any way I can," Ron O'Bryan said earnestly.

They started in with the neighborhood aerial photographs. O'Bryan, as it happened, remembered the journey much the same as Andy Rourke had. But he could add something Rourke had been unable to.

He remembered the residence where he had gotten the Pixy Stix. And he described it for the detectives.

It had been brown in color, O'Bryan said, with a brown wooden door of lighter color. It had small plants and bushes and some sort of hanging ivy in front.

He had gone to the door of this house with the children, he said. But the children had run back to the sidewalk, leaving him alone at the door when it opened. It had been a man with giant Pixy Stix in his right hand who had opened it.

"How many of you are there?" the man with the Pixy Stix had asked.

"Four or five," had been O'Bryan's answer.

"Here!" the man had said. And he had handed O'Bryan five Pixy Stix. Immediately he had shut the door behind him.

O'Bryan, now, told the detectives he could describe the man's clothing, but he was vague about the man's face. "I only saw it for a moment," he said.

And so the next step, it seemed, was to go out and find the house.

With O'Bryan in the car, the Pasadena officers drove slowly down Donerail Street. When they neared the bend in the horseshoe, O'Bryan pointed. "That looks like it," he said.

It was 4112 Donerail.

They turned and passed the residence again. This time, said O'Bryan, he was positive. That was the house. 4112 Donerail.

Now the officers had a solid lead. It coincided with what Andy Rourke had said the day before.

As the police car passed the house for the second time, everyone looked at the group of people who were standing in the front yard. O'Bryan reacted suddenly. He pointed out one of the men in the yard.

That was the man who had given him the Pixy Stix.

"I'm almost positive," O'Bryan said.

Within the next few hours, the officers covered 4112 Donerail—and all its inhabitants—like a glove. The man O'Bryan had pointed out was their first concern. He was the prime suspect. His name, it happened, was William Hudspeth. It seemed likely that the case was solved, and all it would take was follow-up investigation.

But almost immediately, there were problems with this simple solution.

The officers found that the man O'Bryan had identified had not been home at all on Halloween night. He had been at work. William Hudspeth worked at the Houston Airport, and his job required special skills. A large number of people had seen him there, and his work records showed that he was there all night. There just wasn't any question about it; the man O'Bryan said had done it actually hadn't been there at all.

And then the officers discovered something else that surprised them.

The children didn't remember seeing a man at that house. They hadn't seen anyone come to the door of 4112 Donerail. And neither, when he thought about it, had Andy Rourke. The way they all remembered it, there had been no one at home.

Something, the detectives knew, was terribly wrong.

And in any event, the investigation was back to square one.

"What kind of person do you think the killer is?" Ronald O'Bryan asked Officer W. D. LaNier.

"Some kind of perverted, abnormal, sadistic maniac," LaNier responded. "He'll kill again if we don't catch him."

O'Bryan burst into tears.

* * *

It was Friday, November 4.

The Halloween Candy Murder investigation had occupied most of the resources of the Pasadena Police Department for four days.

Assistant District Attorney Michael Hinton was in charge of legal matters connected with the investigation. He was in constant touch with the officers, because there were new developments almost by the minute. But he was also trying to handle his usual duties. It wasn't easy.

This afternoon, Mike Hinton happened to be teaching a class in the Pasadena Police Academy. Every year about this time, he came here to lecture new police recruits on the Texas criminal code. Ironically, he had covered the law of homicide in his lecture this morning. The Halloween Candy Murder, of course, had been on everyone's mind.

This morning, in fact, Hinton had had half a dozen interruptions having to do with developments on the Halloween Candy Murder Case. Now, at 1 o'clock in the afternoon, he had just resumed his lecture, and he was launching into an explanation of the law of theft.

"The crime of theft consists of taking property from another person 'without his effective consent,' " he began.

Suddenly, the door to the classroom opened and the lecture was interrupted once again. It was one of the officers in charge of the murder investigation, Lieutenant Goad. He asked to see Hinton privately, outside the classroom.

"We just received information that Ronald Clark O'Bryan took out insurance on his son just before he died," Goad said. "I think you'd better come see what we have."

Hinton was numb with surprise. He could hardly hear his own voice as he dismissed the class.

* * *

From 1 p.m. until 5 p.m., Assistant District Attorney Mike Hinton studied the evidence the Pasadena Police Department had collected.

Finally, he concluded—as the officers had already concluded—that Ronald Clark O'Bryan must have killed his own son.

First, Hinton thought, there was the Pixy Stix itself. The Rourke children said one had been given to Timothy and one to each of them. Strangely, the Pixy Stix that had killed Timothy—like the others—had been stapled at one end of the tube. It was not sealed, as it would have been at the factory, but stapled.

Why had O'Bryan given stapled Pixy Stix to the children?

Then there had been O'Bryan's accusation of the man at 4112 Donerail. The accusation against William Hudspeth was false, Hinton saw. The children and Rourke said no one had come to the door. O'Bryan could be excused, of course, for mistaken identification. But how could it be a mistake, Hinton thought, if no one had come to the door at all?

Now something else had come up.

The insurance.

Mike Hinton read, once again, the affidavit that O'Bryan's insurance agent had given to the detectives. "To the best of my knowledge," the affidavit said, "Ron O'Bryan called me at the office and stated that he thought he needed some more insurance on his children."

O'Bryan had said, at first, that he wanted $20,000 worth of coverage on each of his children, but he bought even more than that. "To the best of my knowledge," said the affidavit, "he never asked what the premium would be."

O'Bryan had been in an unusual hurry, the affidavit said. "Ron paid me $108.00 in cash for both policies that day. I thought this method of payment was unusual because I've had Ron's insurance business since about 1971 and he always paid on a monthly draft basis."

The affidavit was signed by O'Bryan's insurance agent, Gilbert Cartwright. It also pointed out that O'Bryan had made a strange request: he had not wanted his wife told about the policies. He had been quite insistent.

It was five o'clock now. Hinton had been going over the

evidence for four hours. He and the officers decided that the next step would be to get Ronald and Daynene O'Bryan down to the police station and talk to them again.

* * *

When the O'Bryans arrived, the officers immediately separated them.

Daynene O'Bryan was questioned by Officers H. J. Nassif and Evelyn Lancaster. Ronald Clark O'Bryan was taken into another office and interrogated by Detective D. N. Mullican.

For her part, Daynene O'Bryan seemed almost relieved to be able to talk to the police. "This is the first time anyone has really talked to me since Timothy's death," she said.

She added, "God will eventually give the person who committed this crime the strength to come forward."

"Mrs. O'Bryan," Detective Nassif asked, "How much life insurance did you and your husband have on your children?"

Daynene O'Bryan answered that each member of the family was insured for $10,000. The insurance was provided through their bank for a token monthly payment. But she wasn't sure they had even that much, because Ron had told her that he was reducing the insurance on her and the children.

Gently, Nassif explained to her that Ronald Clark O'Bryan had indeed rewritten the policy on the children. But he had not reduced it. Instead, he had increased it—to a total of $65,000.

And he had paid for the coverage in cash.

"Oh, my God,—no," said Daynene O'Bryan softly.

She lowered her head.

It took a moment before she recovered her composure. But when Daynene O'Bryan was able to talk again, she told Detective Nassif everything she knew that might help the officers to convict her husband for the murder of her son.

Her husband, she said, had good qualities, but he was a chronic liar, a dreamer, an exaggerator. She told the officers that the O'Bryans had received an overdraft notice on their account at the First Pasadena State Bank a month ago. They were almost broke and their car was about to be repossessed.

Ronald O'Bryan was thirty years old. He was an optician by trade, employed by the Texas State Optical Company. It was a decent living, Daynene O'Bryan said, but her husband was a spendthrift. He had held and lost 21 jobs in the last few years, and the family had lived in five different cities. They had had constant financial worries. Even the necessities of life had been in doubt.

O'Bryan had done some strange things, and his wife had sought psychiatric help for him. She described one chilling incident to show what she meant. Her husband had been in bed, abnormally tense, and she had suddenly realized that he was holding a bayonet under his pillow—pushing it in and out of its scabbard. She had had a harrowing feeling that he might use it on himself or her. But she had not been able to find a "good Christian" psychiatrist, so she had given up on this venture and decided "to just seek the help of the Lord."

And Daynene O'Bryan told the detectives something that made the whole case a little clearer.

She explained how her husband had collected fire insurance on their furniture when they had lived in Baltimore years ago. She was sure he had set the fire or had knowledge of it. And there had been another insurance fire after they had moved to Texas.

So that was why it had happened, the officers thought.

The murder of Tim O'Bryan was brazen to the point of stupidity. But insurance frauds are often brazen to the point of stupidity, and most of them succeed. Ronald Clark O'Bryan was a habitual liar, and he was unbalanced enough to do it. He had probably said to himself, So what? The insurance company will pay. On two occasions in the past, he had filed claims so transparently fraudulent that his own wife had seen him for what he was and yet both insurance companies had paid like slot machines. Seen in this perspective, Ronald Clark O'Bryan's murder of his son was nothing but an extension of the pattern he had always used to deal with his finances when they became acute. It was nothing but another insurance fraud—of monstrous proportions.

Finally, the interview approached its end.

"I feel that he needs help," Daynene O'Bryan said of her husband. "I feel that he is dangerous. I feel that he cannot be allowed to walk out of this place for the sake of other children, for Lane's sake and for my sake."

Meanwhile, in a separate room, Detective Mullican was talking to the man who had killed Tim O'Bryan.

* * *

"Mr. O'Bryan," asked Detective Mullican, "how much insurance did you have on Timothy, and how long was it in effect prior to his death?"

O'Bryan looked startled. At the commencement of the interview, Detective Mullican had warned him of his constitutional rights: "You have the right to remain silent. . ." That had surprised him, but this startled him. The police weren't supposed to know about the insurance.

Mullican was using an effective interrogation technique. Textbooks on police interrogation stress the importance of making the subject realize that his statements are but an elaboration of what the investigator already knows.

Talk to the subject politely, sincerely and patiently, the textbooks say. Be understanding. But be firm. And let him know that you know the facts. That was the effect of Mullican's first question.

O'Bryan paused before answering.

"Well," he said nervously, "I had a $10,000 policy with the New Outlook Club at the bank. Then I had a small policy or two, worth a couple of thousand dollars or so. I don't remember exactly how much the small ones are worth."

Detective Mullican knew that this was a lie.

When the subject lies, the textbooks say, show him the facts that disprove the lie. And have him explain them.

"Mr. O'Bryan," said Mullican politely but firmly, "isn't it true that around the first of October, just a few weeks ago, that you took out a $20,000 policy on your son and daughter?"

O'Bryan flinched visibly.

Mullican pressed him. "Mr. O'Bryan, isn't it true that about four weeks ago you called a Mr. Gilbert Cartwright, an insurance agent in Galena Park, and asked him to come to your office at Meyerland, where you work, and told him that you wanted to take out $20,000 policies on both your children?"

Finally, O'Bryan capitulated.

"Yes," he said. "He came over, and we discussed what kind of policy was needed and decided that one was best."

Again, O'Bryan was lying.

"Mr. O'Bryan," said Mullican patiently, "according to Mr. Cartwright, there was no discussion at all."

O'Bryan, flustered, knew that the officer knew he was lying. "Well, yes, I decided this one was best. I didn't want the other one."

O'Bryan explained his cash payment: "I just happened to have enough money on me." He had kept the policies secret from his wife—even to the extent of insisting that they not be mailed to him. "Well, I make all the decisions," he said. "She was real busy with church work."

Mullican asked why O'Bryan had been in such a hurry to file his insurance claim. Before the funeral, before the autopsy, in fact, within eleven hours of his son's death, O'Bryan had been calling the bank to get benefit forms. That was at 9:15 a.m., just a few minutes after the bank opened on the day after his son's murder.

"Well, Mr. Mullican," said O'Bryan, "I am in a very poor financial condition. And I didn't have the money to pay for the funeral."

"You are in a very poor financial condition, yet you could afford to pull over a hundred dollars out of your wallet and institute an excessive amount of insurance coverage?" said Mullican incredulously.

O'Bryan said that didn't seem unusual to him.

Mullican began to concentrate on the details of the killing. He asked whether O'Bryan had ever bought any Pixy Stix. Yes, said O'Bryan, he had; he had bought some just before Halloween, in fact. Mullican next asked whether O'Bryan had poured the candy down Timothy's throat. Well, O'Bryan answered, he had just sort of held the tube for Tim "so he wouldn't spill it." He didn't recall whether the Pixy Stix was stapled or factory sealed. He just hadn't paid any attention to that. When he was asked whether he had purchased a stapler recently, O'Bryan said "Yes," then said, "Well, no," and then changed his mind again and admitted that he had.

The interview had started at 5:30. It was now nearly 8 o'clock.

"Mr. O'Bryan," said Mullican, "do you feel like Timmy is better off being dead, since you feel he already is in heaven?"

"Yes," said O'Bryan, "I do."

Detective Mullican's report concluded with the following words: "After talking to Mr. Ronald O'Bryan for some two and a half hours, noting that he remained almost completely calm during this time even when asked a direct question about taking his own son's life, and after noting several very obvious lies, it is my opinion that Mr. O'Bryan is the prime suspect in the murder, by cyanide, of his son Timothy Marc O'Bryan."

* * *

It was one thing for Detective Mullican to write those words in an internal police report. It would be quite another if Mike Hinton said the same thing in a criminal indictment.

Normally, Assistant District Attorney Mike Hinton is no shrinking violet. In fact, he is one of the most colorful, boisterous prosecutors the Houston District Attorney's Office has ever seen. His infectious laugh, his booming voice and his taste for good Scotch whiskey are legendary to those who know him. He is a decisive man, with plenty of experience to back him up.

Hinton had been a prosecutor since he got out of law school. His formative years were spent in Randall County, Texas, where he was the District Attorney's only assistant. It was like being a country doctor. "There, you did it all," Hinton says. "Everything from going with the officers to make a bust to arguing the case in the Court of Criminal Appeals."

But on this case, Mike Hinton didn't know quite what to do.

"I'm grown up enough to make my own decisions," he says, "But this thing was bizarre.

"I was so shocked, I called Carol."

Carol Vance is the elected Criminal District Attorney of Harris County. Although the position he holds makes him Houston's top prosecutor, he does not routinely participate in investigations. The reason is simple: It takes all of his time to make the policy decisions that run his office. The workload of the Houston office is huge, and Vance has over 100 lawyers working for him as assistant district attorneys.

But Carol Vance still tries cases, and he can make investigative decisions quickly when the case needs him.

Now, Mike Hinton had Carol Vance on the telephone.

He told the district attorney the strange turn the case had taken. It was the father, Ronald Clark O'Bryan. The evidence was circumstantial. O'Bryan was persistent in denying his guilt. There would have to be a great deal more investigation before the case would be ready for trial. There was no doubt in Hinton's mind O'Bryan was their man, but this was a case with national attention focused on it. All the wire services were there. A father who had killed his own son—

"Do you want me to come out, Mike?" Vance asked.

"Yes," said Hinton unequivocally.

It was near midnight when Carol Vance drove out to the Pasadena Police Building. Once again, the officers went over the evidence they had gathered—this time, with the district attorney himself. It was early in the morning when Vance had heard enough. He agreed with Hinton's assessment. The man was a murderer. He should be charged. And it should be done tonight.

Together, the prosecutors drew the indictment charging Ronald Clark O'Bryan with the capital murder of his son.

It was not just murder; it was capital murder. The capital murder statute said that murder for "remuneration" was a capital offense. Life insurance proceeds were remuneration. And so the money that had been Ronald Clark O'Bryan's motive was also the reason his crime was a capital one. He would face the death penalty because of it.

Later, Hinton drew up four more indictments. Each of them charged O'Bryan with an offense of attempted murder.

There was one for each of the Pixy Stix.

Stripped of their legalism, these last four indictments told an amazing story. Ronald Clark O'Bryan had tried to kill his own daughter. He had tried to kill the two Rourke children and a boy from the neighborhood who just happened to be at the door. Had he succeeded, it would have seemed a random, purposeless act, and that was precisely the purpose behind it. Ronald Clark O'Bryan, the indictments said, had been willing to kill all these children merely to obscure the trail that led to him through the insurance policies, the Pixy Stix and the body of his poisoned son.*

---

*The following names in this chapter were changed, without alteration of the incidents in which the persons were involved: Andy Rourke, Michelle Rourke, Philip Rourke, Anne Rourke, Gilbert Cartwright, William Hudspeth.

THE HALLOWEEN CANDY MURDER CASE—the funeral of Timothy O'Bryan. The murdered child's head is visible in the open coffin. His death was caused by a large dose of cyanide, which has the effect of accelerating breathing, rushing blood to the brain, and finally inducing vomiting, convulsions and death. His father, Ronald O'Bryan, sits in the front row; he commenced the process of collecting $20,000 worth of insurance on the child's life before the funeral was held. (Photograph courtesy Houston Post).

THE HALLOWEEN CANDY MURDER CASE—the murder weapon was a plastic tube filled with an innocuous-looking confection called a Pixy Stix. O'Bryan handed out five of them, one of which was eaten by his son Timothy. The candy tube had been slit open and partially filled with poison. Tags on each tube contain exhibit numbers.

THE HALLOWEEN CANDY MURDER CASE—Daynene O'Bryan testifies against her husband. At lower left, in front of the witness, sits court reporter Ann Rossberg. Photographers are not usually allowed to take pictures during a trial; this shot was taken during the entry of a spectator into the courtroom, while the door was ajar. The photographer had stationed himself outside for precisely that purpose, and snapped the shutter before the door closed again (Photograph courtesy Houston Post).

THE HALLOWEEN CANDY MURDER CASE—booking photograph of Ronald Clark O'Bryan, taken shortly after his arrest for the capital murder of his son. Part of the evidence against him was his false accusation against an innocent stranger, whom he was willing to blame for the crime in order to avert suspicion from himself. On death row today, he still proclaims his innocence.

THE HALLOWEEN CANDY MURDER CASE—Assistant District Attorney Michael Hinton walks toward the Grand Jury Room holding the hand of one of the trick-or-treating children (Photograph courtesy Houston Post). Ronald Clark O'Bryan not only murdered his son, he attempted to murder his daughter and three other children by giving each a piece of Halloween candy containing cyanide.

CHAPTER ELEVEN
THE TRIAL OF RONALD O'BRYAN

Richard Harrison must have emerged from that three-hour conference with an awareness that his client's future was bleak.

But the veteran defense lawyer did not show it.

He met with the press and made a statement: O'Bryan was not a murderer. Instead, said Harrison, his client was "heartbroken over the boy's death."

He had been hired by relatives, Harrison explained, and the family might hire other counsel later. "But in the meantime," he said, "I am trying to protect this man's rights."

And Richard Harrison proceeded vigorously to do just that.

One of the first steps Harrison took was to file a request for an examining trial. An examining trial, in Texas, is a preliminary hearing; it is a procedure designed to determine whether there is sufficient evidence to warrant grand jury action on the case.

Why an examining trial demand in this case, since it seemed clear the prosecution could put on enough evidence to secure an indictment? The reason was simple. The prosecutors might be able to show probable cause, but they would have to put on their case to do it. And they would have to expose their witnesses to cross examination. That would give a good defense lawyer a chance to pick apart their testimony.

Harrison also filed a petition for habeas corpus. It requested the release of his client on a small bond.

As matters developed, only a single hearing was held—on

the habeas corpus petition. The State's case was complicated. Hinton called witness after witness. As Harrison cross-examined them, he began to learn what he needed to defend his client.

It became painfully obvious that the complexity of the case would require more than one lawyer for the defense. And Ronald Clark O'Bryan was indigent. He would not be able to pay the cost of a defense even by a single attorney.

And so Judge Frank Price, to whom the case had been assigned, appointed Harrison to represent Ronald Clark O'Bryan at county expense. He also appointed a second lawyer, to assist Harrison. Marvin Teague, a criminal lawyer with a reputation for excellence in getting convictions reversed by appellate courts as well as for vigorous defense at trial, joined the defense team.

Teague brought a distinctive flavor to the case. He had a crew cut and eyes that twinkled behind rimless glasses. He looked like what some courthouse practitioners call a "book lawyer," and in fact he was good with the books; but that wasn't all he was. He could be alternately scholarly and folksy. And he was a veteran of the rough-and-tumble trial ring. His experience included the defense of hundreds of serious criminal cases.

Mike Hinton was going to have a difficult time of it.

Hinton had secured the indictment he had sought from the grand jury, and he had succeeded in getting the judge to order Ronald Clark O'Bryan held without bond. But there was a great deal more he needed to do before he took his case to trial. And a lot of it would be unglamorous, plain hard work. It would involve digging for more evidence. Mindful of the circumstantial nature of his case, Mike Hinton wanted to be sure he had found all the evidence there was to find.

* * *

Assistant District Attorney Vic Driscoll is the perfect foil to Mike Hinton.

Hinton is boisterous; Driscoll is quiet. Hinton is the fiery orator before a jury, while Driscoll is the calm voice of reason.

Early in the case, Hinton recruited Driscoll as co-counsel for the state. The two prosecutors formed the core of the team. Together, they kept in close touch with the Pasadena detectives. Together, they reviewed the evidence and looked for new leads.

The investigation had continued without a pause after O'Bryan's arrest. The Pasadena detectives, very early, had searched the O'Bryan house and car. They had asked for, and gotten, the permission of Daynene O'Bryan, who had signed a standard consent-to-search form.

The search of the O'Bryan car had not turned anything up. But the search of the house had.

Officer Evelyn Lancaster had found a knife belonging to O'Bryan that had minute traces of purplish substance on it. There was also a pair of scissors in the house with the same traces.

The Pixy Stix had contained powdered candy that was about the same color.

Lancaster submitted the knife and scissors to the medical examiner's office for identification of the substance. If it matched the Pixy Stix candy, Hinton and Driscoll thought they would have some useful evidence.

The defense lawyers would probably attack the evidence on fourth amendment grounds, claiming that it was the result of an illegal search and seizure. They would try to get it suppressed. But they probably would not succeed, Hinton thought; a wife could lawfully consent to the search of a home jointly possessed by her and her husband. The Supreme Court had said so.

Meanwhile, a surprising development was beginning. The Pasadena Police Department was beginning to get calls from citizens who had something to add to the investigation. And quite a number of people, as it happened, had something to say about Ronald Clark O'Bryan's curious interest in cyanide.

Arthur Don Moseley was a typical example. A 42-year-old chemist with an oil company, he had known Ronald O'Bryan for four years. When he had read in the newspapers about the Halloween Candy Case, he had wondered about a conversation he had had with O'Bryan a few days earlier. Now that O'Bryan had been arrested, he called the police department to tell what he knew.

Now he was dictating an affidavit to the detectives.

"Some time in the early part of September, 1974—I think

it was on a Tuesday night—Ron called me about 9:00 p.m.," he said.

"He indicated that he was taking a chemistry course at San Jacinto College and had a discussion with his instructor about cyanide compounds."

O'Bryan had wanted to test his instructor's knowledge, Moseley said. At least, that was why he had told Moseley he was calling. The conversation had been lengthy, and O'Bryan had wanted to know how many cyanide compounds there were, what the most common ones were, whether cyanide was detectable in the body, and where it could be purchased. Moseley had told him that The Curtin Company, an industrial chemical sales company, was one of the biggest suppliers in the area.

"He then asked me how much cyanide it would take to be fatal," Moseley said. "I asked him why he wanted to know all this. It ran through my mind that his was not the kind of question that a grown man would ask."

Within hours, the Pasadena detectives were calling on the Curtin Company.

"He asked me if we carried potassium cyanide," said Curtin employee Sam Ricks, after identifying a photograph of O'Bryan. "I told him yes. I think the man wanted the one pound size, but we were out. And he asked about the five pound size."

Apparently O'Bryan had not bought the five pound bag because it cost too much. The price had been fifty dollars. He had gotten the name of another company, a company that sold cyanide in smaller lots, and he had walked out of the store.

The detectives got several other calls linking O'Bryan with cyanide.

Fred Hinman had been a patient of O'Bryan's at Texas State Optical Company. O'Bryan had been carrying a new pocket stapler with him. And after he had explained to Hinman what the visit was going to cost him, he had asked Hinman an odd question: "Say, what do you know about cyanide?" Hinman had told him that a small amount could be fatal.

Hinman had not realized the significance of the conversation until he had seen film clips of O'Bryan's arrest on television.

At about the same time Fred Hinman came forward, a coworker of O'Bryan's gave an affidavit that said: "Approximately the last two and a half weeks in October, 1974, Ronald approached me on different occasions when we were not too busy at work and asked me questions about potassium cyanide such as the lethal effects, and was it the most deadly poison.

"Also somewhere in the conversations he brought up the effect of arsenic, and was it as powerful as cyanide," the affidavit went on. "He seemed to be trying to decide which was the most powerful."

As Mike Hinton and Vic Driscoll read these affidavits, they marveled at Ronald O'Bryan's awesome cold-bloodedness.

There was one more thing.

The medical examiner's office had written a report about the substance on the knife and scissors. It was identical to the substance in the Pixy Stix. These two items, found in O'Bryan's home, were the implements that had been used to open the candy and to remove enough of it to put the cyanide inside.

* * *

The investigation was over.
The trial had finally begun.

As they plodded through jury selection, Hinton and Driscoll used extreme care to see that every juror could accept their case if they proved it. The case was circumstantial; would the jurors be able to believe circumstantial evidence? Could they decide in favor of the prosecution if that evidence was strong enough to overcome all reasonable doubt?

Jury selection had been going on, now, for over two weeks. Ten jurors had been selected. It was clear the process could not last much longer. There were only two more positions to fill, and besides, both sides were running out of challenges.

The man who might be the eleventh juror walked into the courtroom.

Hinton read his name from the jury list. "Dan Kirktrane," it said. Hinton knew that these last two jurors were crucial. When it got down to both sides' last challenges, and both sides were taking risks in accepting jurors for fear someone less acceptable might be the alternative, the case could quickly be won or lost on the choices that were made.

Hinton and Driscoll looked intently at Dan Kirktrane. He was carrying a motorcycle helmet. He had gold jewelry around his neck. His appearance radiated an anti-establishment attitude, a countercultural bias, that seemed sure to go deeper than the clothes he was wearing. Hinton and Driscoll knew that such nuances as this were the very essence of jury selection. And Dan Kirktrane did not look like the sort of man who would be comfortable voting as the prosecution wanted him to.

The examination was brisk. Dan Kirktrane answered the questions and was qualified. His answers were short and to the point.

Hinton whispered to Driscoll, "Do you think we ought to keep him?"

Paradoxically, Driscoll thought so. "He's a risk," Driscoll admitted. "We're taking a chance." But the prosecutors did not have enough challenges to remove everyone they might want to.

Finally, Driscoll—who had been examining this juror—stood. "The State will accept Mr. Kirktrane, your honor," he said.

Across the table, the defense lawyers reacted with surprise. But they were happy to agree. With satisfaction, they accepted the juror, too.

Dan Kirktrane became juror number eleven.

The drama of the moment overshadowed the strategy that had gone before it. Hinton and Driscoll had examined Dan Kirktrane with care. Could he accept circumstantial evidence? In asking the question, the prosecutors had brought out all the uncertainties that circumstantial evidence evokes, just to test the potential juror's reaction. Could the juror accept circumstantial evidence in a death penalty case, provided it was strong enough?

Kirktrane had said that he could accept the prosecutor's case if they proved it to him. He could also find in favor of the defense if there was a reasonable doubt. All four of the lawyers in the courtroom had believed him. Now, each of them watched as juror number eleven walked from the courtroom with instructions to return when the jury was complete.

Across the table from the prosecutors, Marvin Teague permitted himself a nervous chuckle. "He's one for the defense, I hope," he said softly to the prosecutors.

* * *

Andy Rourke was one of the State's first witnesses.

"He said he wanted to buy a home in the Bowling Green addition, where I live," Rourke said of O'Bryan.

O'Bryan had been nearly broke at the time. "He said, 'I've got some money, but I'll have some more coming in before the end of this year,' " Rourke told the jury.

Rourke took the jury through the route the trick-or-treaters had followed that Halloween night. And he described how O'Bryan had waited at the dark door of 4112 Donerail—a door that never opened.

Rourke's son, Philip, was simple and childlike. "We rang the doorbell, and yelled 'Trick or treat!' " he said, "but nobody answered the door, so me and Tim ran on to the next house."

The defense lawyers tried to cross-examine Philip, but they were singularly unsuccessful. As often happens with children, it only showed that he lacked the age and sophistication to lie.

The chemical salesman, Sam Ricks, told how O'Bryan had tried to buy cyanide from him.

The ambulance driver recounted O'Bryan's mysterious illness and miraculous recovery at the hospital.

Dramatically, the man O'Bryan had framed—William Hudspeth—told the jury where he had been Halloween night: at work, at the Houston airport. His co-workers corroborated his testimony.

A succession of Pasadena detectives told of O'Bryan's statements, half-truths, and falsehoods during the investigation. The interview with Detective Mullican, with its damning lies and evasions, was not admissible, because an oral statement of a suspect in custody cannot be told to the jury in Texas. But the previous statements of the defendant, before he was a suspect, were damning enough in themselves.

A vice-president of the company that manufactured Pixy

Stix testified that the candy was heat sealed at the factory. "We do not use staples," he said, "because it would be too easy for a staple to get into the candy and be eaten by a child."

The funeral director who handled the services for Timothy O'Bryan told of the grieving father's strange request: O'Bryan had wanted not one, but six, certified copies of the death certificate—for use, he said, in collecting insurance.

Officer Evelyn Lancaster told about the knife and scissors she found in O'Bryan's home.

The insurance agent, Gilbert Cartwright, testified about O'Bryan's cash payment, his strange secrecy, and his insistence upon buying straight life policies rather than the more logical juvenile policies.

O'Bryan's banker testified that the defendant's bank account was nearly empty. O'Bryan was about to have his car repossessed.

Daynene O'Bryan related to the jury how she had discovered the existence of the policies: from Detective Nassif. And she told how O'Bryan had held the Pixy Stix and poured it down Timothy's throat.

Arthur Don Moseley, the chemist, and Fred Hinman, the Optical patient, described their conversations with O'Bryan —and his unusual interest in cyanide.

But the best witnesses of all were the children. Their testimony made it clear that no one but O'Bryan had been responsible for the Pixy Stix. He had not gotten them from 4112 Donerail. That house had been empty, with no lights on and no one at the door. Ronald Clark O'Bryan had had the Pixy Stix all along. And he had given them out, one by one, to each of the children. The Pixy Stix had come from Ronald Clark O'Bryan's own hand.

A prosecutor who rests his case always feels some anxiety. It is easy to make a mistake and to leave something out. But this was one time when Mike Hinton did not hesitate to stand and say, "Your honor, the state rests."

* * *

If the defendant chooses to testify, it is always the high point of a criminal trial.

So it was in Ronald Clark O'Bryan's case.

The courtroom in Judge Price's 209th District Court was not large anyway, and today it was packed to the rafters. The reporters had all gotten there early and had the best seats. People from Pasadena ran them a close second. All the aisles were crowded with lawyers. No one could move. It was hard even to breathe.

The defense lawyers questioned their client for nearly three hours. They drew from him the story of his life, from his birth to the present moment. They had him describe how someone—an "unknown" person," he now said— had given him the Pixy Stix. Ronald Clark O'Bryan insisted that he had no idea who had given him the candy, and he denied that he had ever told the detectives it was the man at 4112 Donerail. "It could have been a man, woman, boy or girl," he said. He didn't know.

As the examination neared its end, Richard Harrison spoke earnestly to his client. The points he was about to make now were crucial.

"Did you ever put cyanide in a Pixy Stix and give it to your son, Mr. O'Bryan?" he asked.

"No, sir, I did not," the defendant replied firmly from the witness stand.

"And did you know that the Pixy Stix you gave that child had poison in it?"

"Good God," said O'Bryan emphatically. "If I had, I'd never have given it to him."

Finally Harrison passed the witness.

Mike Hinton's cross examination would come next.

Why had O'Bryan needed that much life insurance on his children, Hinton wanted to know?

"The two $20,000 policies were not taken out as life insurance, but to build up a cash value on them," O'Bryan said. When Hinton pointed out that the juvenile policies would have had a better cash value for the money, O'Bryan said he thought the ones he bought were just a better buy.

And then Hinton pointed out that O'Bryan, who had overinsured his children, had no such insurance on his own life.

As to the cyanide conversation with Hinman, O'Bryan said, it probably did not occur—because "we're not supposed to talk to patients." He had talked to his friend Arthur Don Moseley about cyanide, but it was just out of curiosity.

O'Bryan admitted that he had not been taking a chemistry course at the time, as he had told Moseley.

"Isn't it true," Hinton asked finally, "that from the very beginning of your marriage you lived beyond your income?"

"Yes, I have lived beyond my income," O'Bryan said. "I always wanted my wife and children to live well."

"Yes, I dream. I dream of the very best for me and my family."

* * *

The case was almost over, but not quite.

Mike Hinton had some rebuttal witnesses.

Robert Parkinson had attended the funeral. He had spoken with O'Bryan there. "I told him that Timothy looked so peaceful and so good that he might open his eyes and say something to me," Parkinson testified.

"O'Bryan replied that he, himself, had committed Timothy to the care of the Lord."

Parkinson also quoted O'Bryan as saying he envied Tim because he would not have to "go through the trials and tribulations" that his father had had to face. "That was the first time," Parkinson said with evident revulsion, "I have ever heard anyone say they envied someone who was a corpse."

The jurors listened to arguments and heard the judge's instructions. Then they left to deliberate.

Ninety minutes after the jury retired, it was back with a verdict. The judge read it with a clear voice: "We, the jury, find the defendant, Ronald Clark O'Bryan, guilty of the offense of capital murder, as charged in the indictment."

O'Bryan had been convicted of the murder of his son.

* * *

The penalty hearing was short.

The defense called a string of character witnesses for Ronald Clark O'Bryan. One by one, they testified that O'Bryan would not be a threat to society if given a life sentence. And one after another, they said they thought he was innocent in this case.

"If a person has been incarcerated," said one of the

defense witnesses, "it is the state's job to rehabilitate him—not to take a life."

The prosecutors had no additional evidence in the penalty hearing. The reason was that they had put all of the evidence they needed into the trial on guilt or innocence.

The crime spoke for itself.

When it came time for jury argument, Vic Driscoll stood for the prosecution. And it quickly became clear that for this case, at least, Driscoll was not going to be scholarly.

O'Bryan, said Driscoll, "did not have the truth in him, even when the truth would do him better."

"He has used his friends, his family and his church," the prosecutor went on. "He has sacrificed his only son—not on the altar of God as Abraham might have done, but on the altar of his own greed."

Marvin Teague saw the case differently.

"Sure, they lived high on the hog," the defense lawyer said. "Sure, they lived beyond their means—just like you and me.

"Maybe it's a crime if you don't have tears flowing like the Brazos in a flood," Teague went on, answering charges that his client had been cold and unemotional when accused of his son's death. "But does that sound like a man who'd knock off his son for a few gold coins?"

In the second defense argument, Richard Harrison told the jury not to lose sight of the "real" issues in the case. As he saw it, the real issue was that the prosecution hadn't proved anything. Not only had the prosecutors failed in their burden to prove the issues in the punishment phase of the trial; they hadn't even proved that Ronald Clark O'Bryan was guilty.

"Has the State proved that he ever bought cyanide?" Harrison asked emotionally. "No. Has the State proved that he bought Pixy Stix on or about October 31, 1974? No."

"And that's what this case is all about."

Harrison sat down.

Now Mike Hinton would give the final argument, the closing argument for the prosecution.

"It is the most despicable crime I ever heard of, to take the life of your own flesh and blood for money—to kill a kid for money," he shouted.

And Hinton did not hold anything back. He told the jurors that O'Bryan "ought to be damned for what he did."

Was O'Bryan dangerous? Was he a threat to society? Hinton's answer to that was an emphatic "yes." He reminded the jurors of the defendant's willingness to see another human being, William Hudspeth, falsely accused for his own crime. And he told them "not to forget for one minute" that O'Bryan had been perfectly ready to poison a group of other children "to cover up his tracks."

The courtroom was hushed as the jury filed out for the last time.

* * *

Dan Kirktrane's motorcycle helmet looked like a big plastic bowl. It was propped up on a chair in the jury deliberation room.

Kirktrane was colorful. The other jurors liked him. He was a man of judgment, and he had some influence with them. Now that they had discussed the evidence, they were ready to vote.

One by one, they filed by—and they dropped their slips of paper into Dan Kirktrane's motorcycle helmet.

It was an unorthodox ballot box, but it was the most functional one the jurors could find. Furthermore, they were not an orthodox jury. There were young people and old, blacks and whites—liberal and conservative. And there was Dan Kirktrane. It was a jury—and as juries always are, it was unorthodox. It was different from any other collection of twelve people.

On the first ballot, the jurors were unanimous.

They filed into the courtroom and handed the verdict sheet to Judge Price. The judge read it; then he announced that it was in order.

The jury's answer to the first question, he read, was "Yes."

Ronald Clark O'Bryan had killed his son deliberately.

The courtroom was hushed.

The answer to the second question, too, was "Yes."

There was a probability that Ronald Clark O'Bryan would commit future crimes of violence, and he would be a continuing threat to society. That was what the jury had found.

Judge Price, in accordance with the jury's verdict, assessed the defendant's sentence at death.

At his cell on Huntsville's death row, O'Bryan continued to protest his innocence. Marvin Teague, his lawyer, visited him in jail, and later said, "He told me he hopes the actual killer is caught before next Halloween, so this doesn't happen again."

And the minister of the Second Baptist Church said, "His religious faith is probably the only thing" carrying O'Bryan through the ordeal.

O'Bryan's fellow prisoners on death row seemed to like and accept him; none had a harsh word to say about this man who had used church and family to shield his act of murder. But in their cynicism, they gave O'Bryan a nickname that fit his case.

They call him The Candy Man.

* * *

What had produced the death sentence for Ronald Clark O'Bryan?

Why did O'Bryan receive a sentence of death when John Stiles Griffin, for example, had been sentenced to life imprisonment?

What was the difference between the two cases?

The O'Bryan prosecutors had selected the jury with painstaking care. They had done a superb job—not just in the jurors they had selected, for that is largely guesswork, but in the way they had questioned them.

And the case that Hinton and Driscoll put on was compelling. They, and the Pasadena detectives, had left no stone unturned. There had been fifty-one prosecution witnesses in all. Each one had told a small piece of the story, but the prosecutors had made them into a mosaic whole—and the pieces had come to life. Certainly the jurors had thought so; they had been completely convinced. As the foreman said, after the case, "The evidence of guilt was just overwhelming."

But it was more than that; the prosecutors had successfully made the jury feel the full horror of the crime. The helpless dependence of the victim on his father, the remorseless hypocrisy of the defendant, and his willingness to kill four other children made the offense stand out in any person's mind.

But even that was not all of it.

Ronald Clark O'Bryan had done more than commit murder. His was an act of desecration.

Ever since the dawn of time, the world's greatest literature has said it clearly: murder within the family is the worst kind of homicide. The ancient Viking legends condemn it as the most heinous of all possible offenses. The song of Beowulf glorifies violence, but it heaps contempt upon the "killing of kin." The Bible's strongest condemnation is reserved for Cain, who murdered his brother.

But there is another ancient story that fits Ronald Clark O'Bryan's case even better. It is the Faustian legend.

The Faustian legend has taken many forms, and it appears in different guises in different civilizations. For English-speaking peoples, the most famous version is Christopher Marlowe's play—in which Doctor Faustus bargains for earthly riches with Mephistopheles and Beezlebub, using his own soul as currency.

Ronald Clark O'Bryan was a modern Doctor Faustus. He invoked the name of Jesus and wept at the memorial service for his son. But his death sentence was a recognition of the fact that he also came as close as mortal man can come to selling his soul to the devil.*

---

*The following names in this chapter were changed, without alteration of the incidents in which the persons were involved: Arthur Don Moseley, Fred Hinman, Sam Ricks, Dan Kirktrane, Robert Parkinson.

PART THREE

The Evidence and the Life or Death Decision

THERE ARE SOME CAPITAL MURDER CASES IN WHICH the result is determined by the jury.

But there are other capital murder cases, too, in which the outcome is determined by knotty, technical rules of law, or by the availability of the evidence. In such a case, the question may come down to this: how much can the jury hear? What can the jury be told? What facts are there that remain hidden from the jury, either because they are not obtainable or because they are kept out of the trial by technical rules?

In this part of the book, we will look at two extraordinary cases.

The case of Gerald Bodde was a capital murder in which the prosecution had an unusual problem. As the trial got underway, the prosecution's evidence slowly began to disappear. The question was whether there would be enough left for the jury to see what had happened. Would Gerald Bodde be convicted of beating an elderly woman to death? And if he was, what would his sentence be?

And there was another extraordinary case that had serious problems about evidence—the cases of a bizarre group of men who called themselves the Brady Bunch. These four men seemed to have overwhelming cases against them—they confessed to a group of television news reporters, who filmed the confession and broadcast it on the six o'clock news. The members of the Brady Bunch were credited with six brutal murders, and their confessions described most of their crimes in detail. But would they be convicted? That depended upon whether the confessions would stand up in court.

Again, as with Ronald Clark O'Bryan's case or John Stiles Griffin's case, the results may not be what you would expect.

CHAPTER TWELVE
THE MURDER OF AN OLD WOMAN

The people who were involved:

Gerald Bodde... The defendant. He was accused of murdering his landlady with a pipe.

Jean Dodd... The defendant's former live-in girlfriend. When she discovered what he was like, she moved out as quickly as she could.

Roberta (Bobbie) Dodd... She was five years old and she called Gerald Bodde "Jerry," until she saw what he had done to Bernice Hartsfield.

Bernice Hartsfield... The victim. She was eighty-one years old.

Lieutenant Hiram Contreras... The Houston police officer who arrested the defendant and helped rescue the kidnap victim unharmed. The murder came as a complete surprise to him.

The Houston Police Department Property Room...	It, in addition to Gerald Bodde, was the villain of the piece.
The Hon. Dan Walton...	The judge. He finally decided that Bobbie Dodd couldn't be allowed to testify.
Marvin Teague, Donald Rogers and Frank Shepherd...	Counsel for the defense. One of their arguments was that Bernice Hartsfield might have loaned her diamond rings, silverware and bond certificates to the defendant.
George Jacobs, Doug Shaver and David Crump...	The prosecutors. They started the case with plenty of evidence, but during the trial it started, mysteriously, to disappear.
The jurors...	At times they must have seen the case as a modern-day Whodunit, but their final decision was about a brutal murder.

* * *

Jean Dodd walked from room to room in her apartment. There had been no word from the kidnaper for two days, and she couldn't stop looking at the telephone.

Her daughter, Bobbie, was five years old. But Bobbie had been missing since Friday, and no one knew whether she was still alive.

The last thing Jean Dodd had heard had been on Saturday, January 4. That was when Jerry Bodde, the man she had once lived with, had called to tell her that he had taken Bobbie and wanted a thousand dollars' ransom. He had said he would call again. But now it was nearly seven o'clock on January 6, and no word had come yet.

Suddenly, the telephone rang.

The two police officers who were in the room with Jean Dodd were immediately alert. One of them turned on the tape recorder. The electronic device that would attempt to trace the call was already operational. Jean Dodd's heart was pounding as she picked up the telephone.

"Hello?" she said.

The kidnaper's voice was relaxed and casual. "Do you want Bobbie back?" Jerry Bodde asked.

The tape reel was turning. Jean Dodd paid no attention to it as she answered, eagerly, "I got your money. I had it since Saturday."

"One thousand dollars?" the kidnaper asked.

"Where is my baby?" asked Mrs. Dodd desperately.

The kidnaper, though, was insistent. "You got a thousand dollars?"

"Yes," Mrs. Dodd answered. "I've had it since Saturday."

The kidnaper was still not satisfied. "Have you done called the law on me?" he asked. "Did you call the law?" With the two police officers standing beside her, Jean Dodd earnestly denied that she had. She tried to convince him, to reassure him.

"Well," said Jerry Bodde, "I'm going to send Bobbie back in a pine box if you called the law on me."

The officers watched as the tape turned on its reel. The conversation, they reflected, would have been humorous had it not concerned the child's life or death. "I'll send her back in a pine box?" It sounded like something straight out of the movies.

Actually, the whole kidnaping was hard to understand. Why would anyone hold a child for ransom and then make a demand for one thousand dollars? And why would anyone take the child of a woman whom he knew—especially when he also knew, as Gerald Bodde surely knew, that Jean Dodd didn't have a thousand dollars?

Mrs. Dodd was at the edge of poverty, and the ransom demand might as well have been for a million dollars. But she reassured the kidnaper—and hoped that if she met him at the payoff place, he would lead the police to her daughter.

The officers shook their heads. But they were hearing it with their own ears. And there was no question that the man's threats had to be taken seriously.

"Jerry, please," Mrs. Dodd breathed into the telephone. "I want my baby. I got you the money."

"Listen," said Gerald Bodde. "I'm taking care of Bobbie. I'm feeding her three meals a day and I'm taking good care of her. But I want a thousand dollars. I'm hard up."

And he gave her the instructions that told her where, and how, to make the payoff.

* * *

Three hours later, Mrs. Dodd took a seat in a crowded restaurant on Houston's west side. It was more crowded than usual, because it was filled with plainclothes police officers.

Mrs. Dodd had been seated only a short time when she was paged for a telephone call—a call she was expecting.

It was the kidnaper, Gerald Bodde. He had some new directions for her. There was a set of apartments up the hill from the restaurant, he said. Yes, Jean Dodd answered, she could see them.

"Go to apartment number 53 in those apartments," Bodde said. There would be someone there to take the money. And, the kidnaper reminded the distraught mother, if she didn't bring the money, he would send Bobbie home "in a box."

"I've already killed an old lady," the kidnaper added casually, as if in passing. "It was easy. And I'll kill Bobbie too." Jean Dodd, concerned about the child above all else, reassured him. The remark about "killing an old lady" didn't catch her attention.

She spoke to the officer in charge, Lieutenant Hiram Contreras. Then she left for the apartment complex. And within minutes, the police contingent had left the restaurant and had regrouped at unit number 53. Lieutenant Contreras stationed himself, along with two others, inside the apartment.

A few minutes later, Gerald Bodde arrived. He evidently planned to collect the ransom personally.

Jean Dodd saw him first. "Where's my baby?" she asked urgently.

"Where's the money?" Bodde answered.

Lieutenant Contreras stepped out of the door. "You're under arrest," he said. Another officer handcuffed Bodde and took the pistol that was in his pocket. The kidnaper had his hand on the pistol, and there were five live rounds in it.

"Where's the little girl?" Contreras asked.

"In San Antonio," Bodde answered. "And she's safe."

Within hours, the little girl was rescued from the boarding house in San Antonio where the kidnaper had left her. It seemed that the work of the police on the case was nearly over. The victim was reunited with her mother. And there was little further investigation needed to solidify the kidnaping case, because the suspect's voice was on tape, he was known to the victim, and he had been arrested in the very act of collecting the ransom.

But the case was not solved yet.

And the reason it was not solved was that the kidnaping was only the tip of the iceberg.

When Gerald Bodde had been arrested, there had been a set of keys in his pocket. One of them fit the car he was driving: a green Chevrolet, which was parked near the apartments. The car was filled with a curious set of items, including clothing, a radio, a set of silverware—and other personal property. There was a name on some of the articles: "Bernice Hartsfield."

"I've already killed an old lady," the kidnaper had said to Jean Dodd. But Jean Dodd had been so concerned about getting her daughter back that she had attached no significance to it. The course of the investigation might have been different if she had.

* * *

A few hours later, Bobbie Dodd was telling her story.

"Then we got on a freeway and drove a long ways," the child said. She was describing the trip to San Antonio. "Jerry never did play nasty with me or take my clothes off," she added.

Officer Mary Tobar was listening to the little girl and taking down her statement. Throughout the interview, Tobar asked the child questions to guide her through the kidnaping. For the most part, the story seemed simple and coherent. But there was one thing that Bobbie had said that came as a surprise, and it needed to be investigated right away.

"Before we left to get on the freeway," the little girl said, "Jerry went to some apartments. And Jerry told me to get in the closet because he was going to kill somebody."

That got Tobar's attention. He was going to kill somebody?

"There was an old lady there," Bobbie went on. "And Jerry got an iron rod from under the bed. And I heard him hit the old lady on the head. When I came out of the closet she was down on the floor and her head was bleeding."

Tobar wondered at it. The little girl did not seem to be inventing the incident. She could talk about it in detail. She even told Tobar how the kidnaper had wrapped the body in a blanket, locked it in a closet, and covered the blood on the floor with two small rugs.

Could there have been another crime involved in this kidnaping? Could there have been a murder too?

Mary Tobar asked Jean Dodd about it.

Something stirred in Mrs. Dodd's memory. "Jerry told me over the phone that he had killed an old lady," she said. And she added, "Bobbie doesn't lie." The child was not in the habit of making up stories.

Tobar thought about it. The car that Gerald Bodde had been driving at the time of his arrest was registered to a Mrs. Bernice Hartsfield. And some of her property had been found in the car.

Earlier, the Houston Police Department had run a "make" on the car, routinely. But the NCIC—the National Crime Information Center—had reported no "stolen or wanted" on it. Now, suddenly, it dawned on the officers that there would not have been any stolen-or-wanted on the car if the owner had been killed before it was taken.

Someone looked up Bernice Hartsfield's number in the telephone book, dialed it and listened to the ring for several minutes. There was no answer.

Within minutes, a team of detectives was knocking at the door of the modest white frame house that was the Hartsfield residence. The door was locked, and there was no answer. The officers took it from its hinges and went inside. They searched each room, one by one. The master bedroom, they saw, had a safe in it. The safe had been opened and ransacked.

Finally, the officers struggled to open the hall closet.

"Jerry wrapped this old lady up in a blanket that he killed," Bobbie Dodd had said. "And locked her up in a hall closet."

Now the closet door was open. There, on the floor, was a rolled patchwork blanket. It was rolled around something bulky and soft, and the ends of it were tied—tied with electrical cords. Immediately, the officers knew what it was.

There was blood oozing from one end of the blanket.

Inside, there was an elderly lady. Her name was Bernice Hartsfield. But a friend who came to identify the body found that Bernice Hartsfield was hardly recognizable, because her face had been misshapen by a severe beating with a blunt instrument. It was blackened on both sides. Her skull was crushed, and chips of bone were imbedded in her exposed brain. Her head was mottled with dried blood.

She had been dead for several days.

In the kitchen, the officers found a pair of small rugs. Underneath them, there were bloodstains—just as Bobbie Dodd had said there would be.

This was where the murder had been committed.

In the front room, the detectives found an iron pipe. There was a wastebasket filled with bloody tissue, which had evidently been used to clean the pipe and wipe it for prints.

The child was telling the truth. The kidnaper, it seemed, was also a murderer.

Who was this Gerald Bodde, the officers wondered? And what had impelled him to commit this gruesome crime? The answer was imbedded in a history that had begun more than a quarter-century earlier.

* * *

Gerald Lee Bodde was born on April 5, 1947, in Rock Rapids, Iowa. He was the byproduct of a broken home. His first act of outward rejection of society came at an early age, when he set fire to a neighbor's garage. His mother and stepfather decided, shortly after that, to move to another neighborhood.

They relocated in Houston, Texas. But they found that

young Gerald's conduct did not improve significantly. As soon as he started school, he began to have obvious difficulties getting along with other pupils. He also had difficulty with school work, and even special education classes failed to reach him.

Gerald Bodde quit school at the end of the seventh grade because, as he would later explain to a court-appointed psychiatrist who examined him, "I did crazy things. I felt like I had a little devil in my head." He frequently carried such things as snakes and spiders to school with him. He had a history of cruelty to animals, and he simply could not establish any relationships with other students.

At age fourteen, Gerald Bodde was committed to the Austin State Hospital, where he remained for nearly six months. His problem was diagnosed as an "adjustment reaction" of adolescence, and pyschological testing also indicated a "prepsychotic personality configuration." It was a warning of his conduct in the future.

Gerald Bodde was not a bright boy, but he was not abnormally dull, either. Intelligence testing later showed that he had an I.Q. of 85, which was within the normal range for the adult population—the lower end of the range, to be sure, but normal nevertheless.

It was as a youth that Gerald first began to have trouble with the police. His first conviction as an adult came when he was seventeen. He was convicted twice for theft, once for a firearms violation and once for the uncommon crime of bigamy.

But Gerald Lee Bodde's history was not as forbidding as that of many accused murderers. He had no known history of drug abuse, for example, and he apparently had no serious problems with alcohol. And although his home was a broken one, he was raised during most of his childhood by his mother and stepfather—a stepfather, named Bodde, who gave him his name.

The young man was attractive enough to women to be married five times (two of the marriages were at the same time, and that was the reason for the bigamy conviction). And he was able to secure some interesting employment on occasion. He earned part of his income singing in nightclubs, as the featured performer in a group called "Jerry and the Four Speeds."

But for the most part, he had difficulty succeeding at anything. As one of his lawyers would later say, "The only accomplishment we were ever able to find out that he made was that he memorized all of Elvis Presley's records." That had apparently been when he was with the Four Speeds.

The young man's wanderings eventually led him into the life of Jean Dodd, a divorcee and mother of three children. They met while she was working as a gas station attendant in an attempt to provide a living for her family. Gerald Bodde was down on his luck, and he was looking for anybody that would be a friend. Jean Dodd was looking for any man who could take on some of the crushing burden of supporting three children.

Soon they had set up housekeeping in a little apartment on Houston's north side. But almost as soon as they had moved in together, the relationship was near its end. Jean Dodd began to recognize Gerald Bodde's self-centeredness and immaturity. The man, she learned quickly, shared absolutely nothing. As Jean Dodd would later recall from the witness chair in open court, "Gerald would lock all his personal belongings in the closet. He got violently mad if one of the children touched his property, and he even locked up his cokes and candy bars."

Gerald Bodde probably never realized the real reason Jean Dodd walked out on him. It is likely that he saw it as one more failure in a life to which failure was the norm rather than the exception. But this failure was one too many, and it broke a thread that had been holding his life together.

During the first few days of the separation, Gerald responded to an advertisement in the newspaper and rented a room from an elderly lady, a widow living in a white frame house. His landlady's name was Bernice Hartsfield. From all outward appearances, it seemed that she too lived on the edge of poverty, since the house was an old one and the furnishings were worn.

But Bernice Hartsfield was not poor at all.

It was on the morning of January 3, 1975 that Gerald Bodde discovered how wealthy Bernice Hartsfield actually was. He stepped out of his room, walked through the breakfast area and went into the kitchen. His landlady was sitting with an elderly man in her breakfast room. She introduced the man to Bodde as her attorney.

She had more than ten thousand dollars worth of bonds spread out on the table.

She was preparing to re-write her will, Bernice Hartsfield explained. The gentleman with her was her attorney. He was helping her to record the bond certificate numbers.

Bernice Hartsfield was 81 years old, but still healthy and active. She was a widow, and had spent most of her adult life as a mathematics teacher in the Houston public schools. Her husband had been a teacher and an athletic coach. The salaries for their positions had been modest, but the combined incomes of husband and wife had been enough to allow them to save considerable amounts each year. Bernice Hartsfield had never given up her habits of thrift and modest living, and by 1975, she had accumulated an estate of over three quarters of a million dollars, simply by saving and investing wisely throughout her eighty-one years.

She banked at Houston's First City National Bank, a rock-solid financial institution and one of the area's largest. But she did not park her car at the bank when she visited. That was too expensive. Instead, the frugal schoolteacher left the car at the edge of town, on Houston's Polk Street, and rode the bus to the bank. That was the kind of thinking that had made Bernice Hartsfield rich in the first place. It was also the kind of thinking that made her take in a boarder for rent.

Her life came to an end on January 3, 1975, the day Gerald Bodde saw the bonds.

Before murdering his landlady, Gerald Bodde kidnaped little Bobbie Dodd from her home. He then returned to Mrs. Hartsfield's house for the last time, and he beat her to death with a steel pipe. He took her bonds, and the diamond rings from her fingers, and her silverware—and he drove, in her car, to San Antonio. It was from there that he made his ransom demand to Jean Dodd by long distance telephone.

The entire criminal episode was stupid. No one could have hoped to get away with it. But there was something even more stupid about it than that, because the bonds were non-negotiable. The certificates for which he had killed Bernice Hartsfield were of no value to anyone but her. As one of his attorneys would later say, everything Bodde took was "nonsaleable, traceable or valueless—pure junk. If you got $200 for what he took, you'd be doing good."

And Gerald Lee Bodde was stupid enough to leave an

unmistakable trail of physical evidence behind him, stretching from Houston to San Antonio—evidence that would eventually be used to convict him of capital murder.

THE GERALD BODDE MURDER CASE—the kidnapped child on the witness stand. Even under gentle questioning from Assistant District Attorney Doug Shaver, she was too frightened to testify. She glanced at the defendant out of the corner of her eye and started to cry. The prosecutors had to make their case without her testimony. The blackboard contains a diagram of the victim's house; the closet, and the body inside it, are at far right. (Photograph courtesy Houston Post).

THE GERALD BODDE MURDER CASE—booking photograph of the defendant. He kidnapped Bobbie Dodd, and he took her with him when he entered Mrs. Bernice Hartsfield's house and killed her with a pipe. He then took the dead woman's rings and bond certificates. Defense lawyers argued, at trial, that she could have "loaned" the property to him.

THE GERALD BODDE MURDER CASE—The victim (left), Mrs. Bernice Hartsfield, was 81 years old. The defendant beat her with a pipe, wrapped the body in a blanket tied with electric cords, and left it in a closet (top). He took her car, which was parked outside her house (bottom right) and drove to San Antonio with his kidnap victim, Bobbie Dodd, and Mrs. Hartsfield's rings, silverware and bonds. The elderly woman lived simply and modestly, but accumulated an estate that was inventoried at $789,000; Gerald Bodde killed her after she took him into her home as a boarder.

CHAPTER THIRTEEN
THE TRIAL OF GERALD LEE BODDE

A little girl, who was now six years old, sat on the witness chair in the 178th District Courtroom.

It was January, 1976.

A little over a year had passed since the murder of Bernice Hartsfield, and the trial of Gerald Bodde was finally under way. There had been six weeks of pretrial motions, during which Gerald Bodde's lawyers—there were three of them: Marvin Teague, Donald Rogers and Frank Shepherd—had tried to eliminate as much of the evidence against their client as they could. There had been a month of jury selection. Now, the trial itself was in its second week.

This was the crucial moment. The prosecution's only eyewitness, little Bobbie Dodd, was about to testify.

But before the child uttered a word, Marvin Teague stood and asked the judge to excuse the jury. Teague had been one of the Halloween Candy Case lawyers, and he was known for his technical expertise. He now showed the reason for his reputation. With a witness this young, he explained, there was always a question whether she understood the oath she was required to take. And she might be too young to separate fact from fantasy, or to relate her testimony coherently.

The judge should listen, first, to see whether she was qualified, Teague argued.

As it happened, this suggestion was the best defensive strategy of the entire trial. The events that followed it seemed to shake the prosecution's case to its foundations. Judge Walton, a cautious judge, agreed with Teague that the child should be examined first with the jury absent. In fact, he had already removed the jury in anticipation of this request by the defense.

The hearing began as Assistant District Attorney Doug Shaver began to question the child in an attempt to demonstrate to Judge Walton that she was qualified to testify. Shaver's questions were gentle and slow, because the little girl's nervousness was obvious.

"What's your name?" Shaver asked first, in this unusual hearing before the judge.

"Roberta," said the witness hesitantly.

So far so good, Shaver thought. "What's the rest of your name?" he asked.

"Roberta Dodd."

"Do you know what it means to tell the truth?" Shaver said next.

And with that question, the prosecutor suddenly reached an absolute impasse. There was an embarrassing, awkward silence. The witness sat in her chair, twisted her tiny hands, covered her eyes—and looked at Gerald Lee Bodde.

Shaver tried again. "Do you know what the difference is between the truth and a lie?"

There was no answer. The witness seemed to be frozen with fear. Shaver repeated the question again.

Finally, Roberta Dodd said, "The devil will get you if you don't tell the truth."

Shaver breathed a sigh of relief. That was part of what was needed to qualify the witness; it showed that she knew the difference between truth and falsehood, and she could therefore take the oath. But the hardest part was yet to come. Could Shaver get the little girl to talk enough so that Judge Walton could see that she was a competent witness?

Roberta Dodd sat with her lips pressed tightly together and her hands covering her eyes.

"What school do you go to?" Shaver asked. "What grade are you in? What room do you go to when you go to school?"

There was no answer.

At the defense table, Gerald Bodde looked on in impassive silence. Teague, Rogers and Shepherd all watched the little girl intently. At the prosecution table, three lawyers for the State—George Jacobs, Doug Shaver and David Crump—all stared at the witness. And Judge Walton, leaning to his left, looked down at the little girl—who, by now, was toying with her hands.

Roberta Dodd was deathly afraid of the defendant. She began to cry.

Shaver had anticipated that he might have difficulties of this sort. He had carefully let the child get to know him before the trial, and he had brought her into the courtroom so that it would be familiar to her. But the problem was far worse than he had hoped. It seemed that the little girl would not be able to tell her story—the story that she had related so completely and so accurately to Officer Mary Tobar on the day of her rescue. It seemed she would not be able to talk at all with the defendant present. And the defendant had a right, guaranteed by the United States Constitution, to sit in the courtroom and confront her. He could not be removed.

"Do you remember last Saturday, when we took you out and got you a Dilly Bar?" Shaver asked now. "Do you remember when we brought you up here to the courtroom, and let you sit in the chair?" The witness did not answer.

Twenty minutes passed. Shaver repeated, over and over, his gentle questions. For the entire time, awkwardly, the child cried.

"Just nod your head or shake your head," Shaver suggested at one point. But the child continued to cry, and occasionally she glanced furtively at the defendant.

It was excruciating to watch. And it was cruel to keep the child on the witness chair. But what choice was there? Should Gerald Lee Bodde be released? Shaver kept trying, for what seemed an eternity.

"We'll take a recess," said Judge Walton finally.

When the recess was over, Shaver brought the witness back. Three more times he tried to get her to speak, and three more times he was met with silence and weeping. Judge Walton had a reputation for patience, and he was true to that reputation. Each time, he took a recess and waited.

"Are you going to take another run at her?" Teague asked, at the end of the last recess. "Yes," Shaver answered grimly.

The child was seated in the witness chair once more. Judge Walton leaned down and said gently, "Bobbie, are you ready to answer their questions now? Nobody's going to mess with you or bother you."

The child rubbed her eyes, cried and fidgeted.

The judge looked at the prosecutors. He had made a decision. "I'm going to have to excuse the witness, Mr. Shaver," he said.

The child was led from the courtroom for the last time. The State's case seemed to collapse with her.

During the recess that followed, Bailiff Angelo Passante took Gerald Lee Bodde to the lockup behind the courtroom. The defendant was pleased at what had happened. "Aw," he said, "I've got this case beat."

He turned to Passante, and he added: "I'll be drinking coffee with you on your front porch by tomorrow afternoon."

* * *

The prosecutors pondered what to do next.

Was the loss of their only eyewitness going to mean that Gerald Bodde would go free?

That was certainly possible, they knew. But the case was, as yet, far from lost. Actually, there was still a formidable collection of evidence that was admissible before the jury. Jean Dodd had already testified about Gerald Bodde's damning confession: "I've just killed an old lady." The pipe and bloody tissue had been found in Bodde's rented room. The defendant had stolen the victim's car and had been arrested with the keys to it, which were on a ring that included all the dead woman's other keys. In the San Antonio boarding house where Bodde had stayed, Bernice Hartsfield's bonds had been recovered. So had her diamond rings, taken from her fingers. Marvin Teague was maintaining that the recovery of these items constituted an illegal search and seizure from his client, but it seemed likely that they would be admissible in evidence.

Then there were the items in the car—the silverware and other property belonging to Bernice Hartsfield.

There had even been a witness who had seen Gerald Bodde, together with Bobbie Dodd, driving the car from the house at the time of the murder. When the witness had asked him about it, Bodde had lied and claimed that the car was his.

And the killing itself had been accomplished in a locked house that showed no sign of forced entry. That was because Bodde had access to it.

In their research, Jacobs and Crump found several cases

in which convictions had been obtained with similar kinds of evidence. *The State of Texas versus Jones; the State of Texas versus Pulido*—these were cases in which circumstantial evidence alone had been held to be enough for a conviction. Lawyers know a famous saying about it: "Sometimes circumstantial evidence can be persuasive, such as when one finds a trout in the milk." The finding of a trout in the milk, in any reasonable person's mind, would support an inference that the milk had been improperly prepared.

The case against Gerald Bodde seemed equally convincing, even without Bobbie Dodd's testimony.

But even as they thought that to themselves, the prosecutors knew that their own evaluation of the case might be misleading. It was not they who would decide. It was the twelve people in the jury box. And jurors, by and large, do not find it natural to accept circumstantial evidence. The loss of the little girl as a witness might, for the jury, create an intolerable gap in the prosecution's case.

The prosecutors decided that it would be best if they could have the child's story told to the jury, even indirectly—through some other witness, perhaps.

* * *

The three prosecutors had divided their responsibilities during the trial.

Jacobs was the lead counsel, and he was in charge of the overall case. Doug Shaver was to question some of the key witnesses, such as Bobbie Dodd, and share the jury argument with Jacobs at the end. David Crump was to deal with technical legal problems in presenting the case.

In this trial, that was a job that kept him busy. And now, even more than before, technical points were going to matter. Crump and Jacobs began to consider whether there was any legal means to bridge the gap left by the loss of Bobbie Dodd's testimony.

"The Gerald Bodde case was a frustrating experience," says Crump. "With lawyers like Teague, and Rogers, and Shepherd defending him, we knew we were going to have to dot our i's and cross our t's on every technical point. The defense lawyers would make us. We knew we were going to have to fight to get every piece of evidence before the jury.

"It was going to be hard enough anyway, but when we saw what happened to our main witness, the little girl, it really took the wind out of our sails."

Crump was a former Assistant District Attorney, but now he was a professor and he taught in law school. He was assisting Shaver and Jacobs in the Gerald Bodde case as a special prosecutor, by appointment of the Houston District Attorney's Office. One of his specialities was the law of evidence—the complicated, confusing rules that determine what a jury can and cannot hear in the courtroom.

"Courtroom procedure doesn't always make sense," says Crump. "And if you want to understand how a trial works, you have to keep that fact in mind. A lot of the rules aren't there because of any sensible reason; they're there because they developed centuries ago, and they've been handed down from judge to judge until the present day."

A lawyer has to know all of these rules—and know how to use them. There are rules against hearsay, rules about expert witnesses, rules about confessions, and rules about almost every phase of testimony in a case. And there are exceptions, too, to every one of the rules. There are even, in some instances, exceptions to the exceptions.

"It's sort of like the Internal Revenue Code," Crump says.

"A great deal of the time," he adds, "the rules have the result of *hiding* the truth, rather than bringing it out." But although a lawyer might not like the rules, there is no question he has to learn how to deal with them if he is going to be a trial lawyer, because they can cause a case to be won or lost.

Now, Crump and Jacobs were confronted with a very practical problem. Since the main prosecution witness could not testify, was there any other way to get her story to the jury?

"The first thing we thought of," says Crump, "was getting Officer Tobar to repeat to the jury what the little girl had said to her when they brought her back from San Antonio. The problem was, repeating something someone else has said is hearsay. And hearsay can't usually be used in a trial. That's one of the oldest rules in the books.

"But there are exceptions to that rule against hearsay. A spontaneous statement by a victim of a crime, made close in time to the crime itself, is sometimes admissible in evidence.

And sometimes that kind of hearsay *can* be used. It comes within an exception to the usual rule against hearsay."

The prosecutors thought it through.

Could Officer Tobar relate, from the witness stand, what the little girl had told her a year ago? Might that be a way in which her story could be conveyed to the jury?

Crump and Jacobs were skeptical about the idea. But it might be possible. And if so, that would solve the problem.

The two lawyers went to the books. They found several cases decided by the Texas courts dealing with the issue, and some of the decisions looked promising. For example, there was a case, in 1964, in which a man named Hudgeons was accused of a sex crime with a little girl. The case was called *The State of Texas versus Hudgeons*. The interesting thing to Crump and Jacobs about the case was that the little girl had run home and told her mother about the crime, and then, when the case reached court, the mother was allowed to testify what the child had told her. Hudgeons was ultimately convicted, and he appealed. But the higher courts said the Mother's testimony was valid. The Texas Court of Criminal Appeals, in particular, said that the little girl's statement to her mother, even though it was hearsay, could properly be told to the jury—because it was spontaneous and close in time to the crime.

Crump and Jacobs nodded their heads to each other. Perhaps this precedent could be used to persuade Judge Walton to do the same thing in the trial of Gerald Bodde.

There were other cases. For example, there was a 1973 case in which a man named Beam was charged with robbery. This case was called *The State of Texas versus Beam*. What interested Jacobs and Crump about it was that the robbery victim had told a police officer what had happened, at the crime scene; and at the trial, the officer was allowed to repeat to the jury what the victim had said. The statement had been spontaneous and close in time to the crime.

A lawyer's reasoning process works by analogy. And the prosecutors felt that these cases were analogous to the trial of Gerald Bodde, in many respects. There were some dissimilarities, to be sure, but Crump and Jacobs also saw a good many points in common. And so maybe Judge Walton could, indeed, be persuaded to let officer Tobar testify concerning what little Bobbie Dodd had told her about the murder of Bernice Hartsfield. It would be a difficult legal argument to make, the prosecutors knew. But it might work. And now that the judge had ruled, finally, that the child herself would not be allowed to testify, what else could be done?

Crump and Jacobs collected the cases they had read, and they prepared a brief for Judge Walton.

* * *

Several hours later, the judge sat in the courtroom. He was studying the cases and evaluating the prosecutors' argument.

Finally, he was ready to rule.

"The court commends counsel for the state on the work they have done," the judge said. "But I do not consider these decisions applicable to the case."

That was the end of the matter. The little girl's story would not be heard by the jury, directly or indirectly. It was a judgment call, and Judge Walton had made a reasonable decision; in his view, the statement had simply not been spontaneous enough, or close enough in time to the crime, to fit within the exception to the hearsay rule. It was not analogous to the other cases.

The prosecutors pondered their case again. And they prepared to proceed with the evidence that was left.

The case was still not lost. The circumstantial evidence was compelling. And actually, there was a great deal more than circumstantial evidence. There was a clear confession of guilt, out of the defendant's own mouth. The statement that he had made to Jean Dodd about killing an old lady, together with all the physical evidence and the other testimony in the case, ought to be enough to convince the twelve citizens who were sitting in judgment of Gerald Bodde —even without the little girl's eyewitness testimony.

* * *

But as it happened, the prosecutors' difficulties were only just beginning.

Suddenly, there was a new development in the case that made Jacobs gag with frustration.

He had just returned from his office, where he had been in touch with HPD. "Do you know what those guys in the property room have done now?" he asked Shaver and Crump incredulously. "They've lost the tapes of the kidnaping demand."

The Houston Police Department's property room was a mammoth cavern where evidence was retained for safekeeping. Hundreds of weapons, dozens of items of bloody clothing, thousands of pieces of stolen property—all were kept under lock and key, with a sign-out system that was supposed to account for every item that was taken out.

But somehow, things were constantly getting lost in the property room.

The tapes, it seemed, had simply been misplaced. Trying to find them would be literally like looking for a needle in a haystack. The property room had already been turned upside down, and the tapes were not to be found.

In a way, it was understandable that losses would occasionally occur, because there were tens of thousands of separate items there. And with criminal court dockets being what they were, property was frequently checked out and returned over and over again. But still, Jacobs was thinking, in this case, a capital murder case, with a tape of a kidnaping ransom demand that was involved with the murder—it just seemed that that kind of evidence should not have been lost.

The defense, without a doubt, would lambast the prosecutors for this latest development. It was even conceivable that it might result in a dismissal of the case. In any event, Marvin Teague's job would be to try to persuade the judge that a dismissal was necessary.

Teague rose from his chair in the courtroom. He had considered the possibility, he told the judge, that the tapes might exonerate his client. They might show that Jean Dodd was lying. They might show that Gerald Bodde had not said anything about killing an old lady, after all.

Besides, Teague went on, "The jurors could listen to the tapes and decide whether it was really this defendant." But now, without the tapes, Jean Dodd "would have carte blanche to say whatever she wanted about what was in the conversations, and all we could do would be to say: 'Did that really happen?'"

The only fair thing to do, Teague said, was to suppress the testimony of Jean Dodd.

Fortunately for Jacobs, Judge Walton refused to do that. But he addressed the prosecutor sternly. "If it is found that this defendant's rights are prejudiced in any way, the result will be that any conviction will be set aside. This court will not hesitate to do so."

And there was one other danger that Jacobs had to consider in connection with the missing tapes. He had to consider the effect that this new development would have on the jury.

Even in the best of circumstances, an occurrence such as this would raise a red flag in any juror's mind about the prosecution's entire case. But in January, 1976, when the Watergate tapes were on everyone's mind, and the eighteen-minute gap was a recent memory, losing a tape was certainly not the thing for a prosecutor to do. It made the state's case look about as credible as Richard Nixon's defense had been.

If the loss of Bobbie Dodd had not already ruined the prosecution of Gerald Bodde, it seemed entirely likely that this newest development would be the end of it.

But even that was not the final difficulty for the prosecutors.

The HPD property room was also unable to find some of Bernice Hartsfield's stolen property. Her silverware, which had been found in Gerald Bodde's possession at the time of his arrest, was missing. And HPD had even lost a bronze eagle statuette, stolen by Bodde, that had the dead woman's name on it. These damning items of evidence, which linked the defendant to the victim, were going to be unavailable to the prosecution.

"My God," said Crump to Shaver. "Those guys can't keep track of anything over there."

And when the prosecutors learned *how* the silverware had been lost, the explanation left them even more dumfounded than the disappearance itself. It had happened when Gerald Bodde's father had come to the police station to pick up his son's personal effects. The man had had no intention to remove evidence, as such; he had simply made a routine request for the return of property belonging to a relative who was being held in police custody. But the officer in charge of the property room had given him everything he could locate that had been found in Gerald Bodde's possession. Without realizing it, the officer had thus surrendered several items of property that had happened to be there because Gerald Bodde had stolen them from Bernice Hartsfield. Those items had included the silverware.

Each of the prosecutors asked himself the same question. "How could this sort of thing be happening to us?"

Actually, it was unfair to blame it all on the police. There had been many difficult things that the Houston Police Department had done extraordinarily well. Houston police officers had disarmed and arrested a kidnap-murderer, without a single shot having been fired. They had treated him professionally while he was in their custody, so that there was no substantial question of any violation of his rights. They had recovered the victim, unharmed, within days of her capture. And they had solved a murder case almost as soon as they had learned of its existence.

HPD had done an excellent job of the things most citizens would think were important. It only remained to be seen what the twelve citizens who were sitting in the jury box would think of HPD's techniques for handling evidence.

Jacobs, Shaver and Crump—when they got over their initial shock—knew that they could still present a strong case. They ultimately presented 33 witnesses in all. There was a web of physical evidence from which there was no escape for the defense: a fingerprint analyst, a blood-typing chemist, and the stolen property. There was a witness whom the defendant had told "it was easy" to kill an old lady. There was going to be more than enough evidence to secure the conviction, even after the loss of Bobbie Dodd's testimony, even after the tapes, even after the silverware and the statuette. There would be more than enough, that is, unless the jurors had been so shaken in their confidence in the prosecutors' case that they would acquit anyone. And that was certainly possible.

The last piece of evidence that turned up missing was a set of photographs of the autopsy. "They can't locate them over at the medical examiner's office," Jacobs said. That meant that the prosecutors would be unable to show the jury the wounds that Gerald Bodde had inflicted upon Bernice Hartsfield.

By this time, the prosecutors were stoic. Crump sat at the

table and thought about it. Truth is stranger than fiction, the saying goes. And, as they also say, when it rains it pours. I only hope the clerk's office doesn't lose the indictment before the trial is over, Crump thought. But all he could say to Jacobs was, "That's incredible."

* * *

The defendant's lawyers did not present any evidence.

Marvin Teague rested his case immediately after Jacobs rested for the prosecution. That was the best defensive strategy, actually. It would allow the defense lawyers to argue, effectively, that the burden of proof was on the State and that a reasonable doubt remained in the case.

For a few minutes, there was a recess.

The lawyers—prosecutors and defenders alike—sat together in the judge's office, waiting for him to prepare the charge. It was a time for relaxation, like the lull that is in the eye of a storm. It was even a moment for companionship between two sets of tired adversaries.

"Can the jury be sent back to the hotel for the time being?" someone asked.

"Yes," responded defense lawyer Donald Rogers. He smiled, and added: "We want them in the best mood possible." A comfortable, contented jury might be more lenient toward the defendant.

"Are those good hotel rooms?" another defense lawyer asked.

"Yeah," said Doug Shaver. "The ones we saw were very good ones. Individual, private ones."

"We were over there reading the paper with Mrs. Black," said George Jacobs. He was joking with Rogers; Mrs. Black was a juror, and the jury had been sequestered in a hotel because of sensational publicity during the trial. Jacobs added, "We also read a few of the stories to Mrs. Tewsky." Mrs. Tewsky, as it happened, had been a subject of some interest to the six male lawyers in the case, because she was rather attractive.

Shaver, with his best effort at a straight face, said: "The jurors thought those flowers we sent them from the prosecution team were a nice touch."

But Marvin Teague was not one to be outdone, even at

gallows humor. "Did they like the candy old Bodde sent over?" he asked.

Everyone laughed in spite of himself. None of it was uproariously funny, exactly, but everyone in the room was emotionally drained and physically exhausted. Any kind of comic relief was welcome.

The conversation was typical of the situation in which these two teams of advocates found themselves, for the mark of a good trial lawyer is comradeship outside the courtroom and partisan zeal inside it. To each of the prosecutors, the defense lawyers were professionals. To each of the defense lawyers, the prosecutors were also professionals. They could all enjoy each other's companionship in a moment of relaxation. Then each could go to his respective table in the courtroom and do his best to destroy the opposing side's case.

There was a pause in the conversation, and then one of the defense lawyers said to Jacobs: "Gerald's not as friendly to you, George, as he was at first. I leaned over and told him, 'That man—the prosecutor—wants to kill you.'

"It's taken a long time, but I think he's finally snapped to it that that's what this whole trial is about."

"Give me another legal pad," said the Judge. He had the charge almost prepared.

A few moments later, the lawyers were standing before the jury to deliver their final arguments. The bantering was over. It was the adversary system, in full swing.

* * *

"I think they've proved that a kidnaping occurred," said Donald Rogers to the jury.

"But that doesn't prove a murder."

Rogers told the jurors that there had not even been proof that the property or the car was stolen from Bernice Hartsfield. For all anyone knew, he argued, she could have consented to the defendant's taking it. "It hasn't been disproved," Rogers added, "that Bernice Hartsfield could have loaned the property to Gerald Bodde."

What Rogers was suggesting was that an elderly lady, frugal almost to the point of miserliness, had loaned her bond certificates to a kidnaper and then turned up dead by coincidence. On reflection, that was hardly likely. But it was

Rogers' job to look for doubts in the case, and that was what he was doing. No one could rule out the chance that the jury might accept it.

Rogers' strongest argument, which he repeated over and over, was that "it's a circumstantial case." It was circumstantial, of course, because the little girl could not testify. But the State still had the burden of proof. That was the important thing.

"I ask you," Rogers went on, "has the state really proved that Gerald Bodde killed Bernice Hartsfield? And if he did, did they prove he had the specific intent to kill? And third, if he did, did they prove he did it in the course of a robbery?"

Again, Rogers reminded the jurors: "It's a circumstantial case."

The defense lawyers had agreed to divide their argument time among them. And so Rogers was followed by Frank Shepherd, who also argued for an acquittal. "What appalls me," Shepherd said, "is that they ask you to find this defendant guilty not only of murder, but of robbery-murder." Robbery-murder, of course, carried the death penalty, while ordinary murder did not. "It scares me," Shepherd went on, his voice rising. "It scares the hell out of me. On such flimsy evidence, they want you not only to find him guilty, they want you to KILL him."

Shepherd was shouting his words by now.

"The prosecutors may talk to you about cleaning up the community," he said passionately. "But you don't do any good at all talking about convicting a man"—here Shepherd reached his peroration, and also the peak of his volume—"a man who ISN'T GUILTY."

When the defense lawyers were finished, it was the prosecutors' turn.

Assistant District Attorney Doug Shaver had a different view of the case than the defenders. The defense argument, he told the jurors, reminded him of "when I was a little boy, and my daddy would take me fishing. He'd take out a lure and throw it.

"And if it didn't work, he'd throw out another lure. And if that didn't work, he'd throw out another lure. And he'd keep on like that, trying one after the other, just hoping that some fish'd bite at one of those pretty, bright, attractive-colored lures."

The point was obvious. "Don't you see," said Shaver, "That's what the defense is doing here. They want you to bite at anything to get him off the capital murder charge. They even tell you what I think is the most ridiculous statement I've ever heard: that she 'might have loaned it all to him,' including her car, her rings off her fingers, and her non-negotiable bonds."

George Jacobs ended the arguments.

"They've talked to you about circumstantial evidence," Jacobs said. "Well, circumstantial evidence can be good evidence. It's physical. It's there.

"But as you know," he went on, "we have more than circumstantial evidence here. We have a direct statement out of the defendant's own mouth. 'I've just killed an old lady. And I'll kill Bobbie too.'"

Jacobs started to go over the evidence, chronologically. The lawyer and Mrs. Hartsfield, looking at the bonds. The kidnaping, that same day. Bodde driving the car away, with the little girl, at the time of the murder.

The ransom demands, the attempted pickup, and the admission of the killing to Jean Dodd. And how had the police learned of the killing? "At this point, they still didn't know about the murder. It wasn't until they picked up the little girl, and questioned her, that the police went to Mrs. Hartsfield's house."

And how had that happened, Jacobs asked the jury? Then he answered his own question. They had learned of it because the little girl had been with Gerald Bodde—with the murderer, when he killed Bernice Hartsfield.

Jacobs lined up all the stolen property in the jury's view. The two diamond rings, taken from the dead woman's fingers. The keys, taken out of her pocket. The bonds, a stack of certificates nearly an inch tall, taken from her safe. The pictures of her car. The radio, the clothing—

"He took this pipe and killed her," Jacobs said, lifting the murder weapon for the jurors to see. "You can speculate, you can say, 'Maybe some guy crawled in through the keyhole and killed her, then got out without breaking the locks.' But that's not what happened, and you know it.

"We ask you to bring in a guilty verdict, because it's right. It's what the evidence shows."

It was a few hours later, shortly after five o'clock, that the jury returned with its verdict. The prosecution's evidence had been enough. Gerald Lee Bodde, the verdict said, was guilty—guilty of capital murder.

* * *

The penalty hearing lasted three days.

Most of that time was devoted to the hearing of objections by the defense. The evidence itself was short. It consisted of four character witnesses, who testified about Gerald Bodde's propensity toward violence, and of evidence about the defendant's prior criminal record.

Finally, it was time for argument on the question of life or death.

"I've been brought up to believe that no one has the right to take life," said Frank Shepherd. "We've been taking life since the time of Christ. It doesn't work. If we want to deter crime, why do we do executions behind closed doors in Huntsville? Why not do it all at the Astrodome, so everybody can see it?

"The prosecutors," Shepherd went on, "say, 'Wipe him out. Eradicate him.' Then we'll have two murders instead of one.

"And you,"—Shepherd looked at the jurors—"you will have participated." If he could make the jury feel guilty about the death penalty, the verdict would be one of life imprisonment.

It was a powerful argument. And Rogers and Teague both drove it home to the jury. "If there's a mistake, you can't change it—if you pull the switch," they told the jurors.

The defense lawyers also worked to humanize their client in the eyes of the jurors—to make them see him as a human being caught in a situation not his fault, and the crime as a tragic mistake. "The only possible conclusion," said Rogers, "is that he isn't very bright. This is a stupid crime." The argument was simplistic, but it might be effective. Everyone who owns a televison watches Kojak, where the crooks are all knowledgeable and clever; perhaps the jury would be persuaded to be more understanding of a crook who was not. That was the strategy.

Then it was time for the jury to hear from the other side.

Doug Shaver, for the prosecution, reminded the jury of

the crime. "Consider the evidence," he said. "She was hit with a pipe. Over and over again. Fragments went into her brain, fragments of her skull. And her face, all over, was black and blue."

There was plenty of other evidence of violent conduct by Gerald Bodde, Shaver went on. He quoted the defendant: "I can kill the little girl." That was what Gerald Bodde had said: "I'll kill the little girl and send her home in a pine box." At the time of his arrest, Bodde had had his hand on a pistol, Shaver reminded the jurors. It was loaded with five live rounds. The police had caught him before he had had a chance to use it.

George Jacobs, again, closed the argument for the prosecution.

"The defense lawyers," he explained to the jury, "want to put the fault on you." He was referring to Frank Shepherd's argument—that a death sentence would be another murder, in which the jurors would be participants. "They want to make it like it's your responsibility he's here in court," Jacobs went on. "But it's not your fault. It's not mine, or Mr. Shaver's. Gerald Bodde doesn't need to look any farther than himself."

It wasn't possible, he added, to think of two more innocent victims. "An old lady. A little girl." And as for Gerald Lee Bodde, Jacobs said, "there will always be a probability that he'll do it again."

The jury retired in late afternoon. That evening, they were back. They had answered both of the penalty questions "Yes."

That meant that they had sentenced Gerald Lee Bodde to death.

* * *

Why did the Gerald Bodde case end as it did?
Why did the defendant receive the death penalty?
It was certainly one of the strangest cases that any of the six participating lawyers had ever seen. There was the little girl who couldn't testify. There was the disappearing evidence. There were the intricate, technical points that decided what parts of the evidence the jury could or could not hear. Gerald Bodde's trial was an exaggerated version of the evidence problems in every criminal trial before a jury, in

which the unexpected is the norm. The jurors hear random bits and pieces of truth through a filter of complicated rules. The rules are supposed to ensure reliability of the evidence, but more often they result only in blindfolding the jury.

The key to the Bodde case was that the evidence was strong enough to filter through to the jury in spite of all the incidents that diluted it.

Actually, a combination of factors led to the ultimate verdict. For one thing, the jury was capable of responding to the evidence. For another, the murder itself was conscienceless and brutal. And the victims were both, as Jacobs pointed out, chosen by the defendant because they were helpless. But it was the quirks in the evidence—the accidents that hampered the prosecutors' case, and the way that technical rules affected the testimony—that set Gerald Bodde's trial apart.

Jacobs, Crump and Shaver will undoubtedly each remember, forever, one strange incident that was produced by the complicated, technical rules of evidence.

Crump and Jacobs were never able to persuade Judge Walton to let the child's story be told to the jury. The judge had ruled against that. In fact, the jury never even saw Bobbie Dodd. But Crump and Jacobs did manage to persuade the judge that the jury should not be left completely ignorant of what had happened. The prosecution, they argued, had the right to tell the jurors exactly *why* Bobbie Dodd could not testify. They showed the judge decisions by Texas courts that said so.

Judge Walton, when he was persuaded it was the law, agreed.

And so one of the last witnesses the jury had heard, ironically, had been Assistant District Attorney Doug Shaver, who had explained the little girl's absence from the list of witnesses.

"Do you know Roberta Dodd?" Jacobs had asked his colleague, when Shaver had seated himself in the witness chair.

"Yes," Shaver had replied, with the jury listening. "I last saw her here, in this courtroom. The jury was not present. I myself, and you, Mr. Jacobs, brought her into the courtroom."

The jurors had not known what was going on outside their presence. Until now, they had not been told why the child was not called as a witness before them. They had known only that they had been kept from the courtroom for several hours. They had learned the reason for the first time during this testimony from Shaver.

"Was she able to answer any questions?" Jacobs had asked.

"No," Shaver had said. "She covered her eyes."

That was all the jury ever knew. They had seen nothing of the little girl herself. They had not watched while she sat, in frozen fear, and glanced furtively at the defendant. And they never heard Bobbie Dodd's story.

When the final verdict came in, a group of elderly men and women sat in the audience benches in the back of the courtroom. For weeks, throughout the trial, they had been sitting there. They were the friends and relatives of Bernice Hartsfield. Each day, they brought their medicines to the courtroom and took them during the proceedings. Each day, in stoic silence, they watched the trial through their thick eyeglasses.

The United States prides itself on the equality of its justice. But it will be the last country in the world, it seems, to provide equal dignity to its elderly. Faced with poverty and loneliness, old people in America are victims of serious crime at an alarming rate. Many of them become prisoners in their own homes because of the fear of crime. That was part of the tragedy of Bernice Hartsfield's death; the schoolteacher had refused to accept the insularity and helplessness that goes with advancing age. She had rented a room to a young man down on his luck. Now her friends and relatives were sitting through a trial that had lasted three months and that resembled, at times, a game of chess more than an inquiry into the truth of her murder.

They knew the ordeal that Bobbie Dodd had suffered. They had watched the arguments and the technical objections. Each day, they looked at the man with the greasy hair, combed to a point at the front of his head, who had bludgeoned to death their sister, their friend. The man whose cowardice had led him to exploit the two most helpless victims he could find. The man who had killed Bernice Hartsfield for no reason at all.

The jurors had not been permitted to hear everything. But they had heard enough.

And they knew it too.

* * *

The trial of Gerald Bodde was extraordinary. But it was to be expected that it would be extraordinary; capital murder cases are nearly always extraordinary.

The trial of Kenneth Brock, for instance, had involved an unusual crime: a murder committed before the very eyes of six police officers. Certainly the Halloween Candy Murder case had been unusual as well. And the John Stiles Griffin case had been unusual not just in the nature of the killing, but in the personality and background of the murderer. It was not surprising, therefore, that Gerald Bodde's case was extraordinary too. Among capital cases, the extraordinary is the norm.

And at the time Gerald Bodde was tried, an even more amazing case—one of the most extraordinary capital cases the city had ever seen—was also awaiting resolution in Houston.

It was the case of a bizarre group of men who called themselves "The Brady Bunch." The members of the Brady Bunch participated in at least six brutal, execution-style killings—and confessed to them on television. Had it been told in an earlier, more peaceful time in this country's history, the story of the Brady Bunch would scarcely have been believed.*

---

*The following names in this chapter were changed, without alteration of the incidents in which the persons were involved: Mrs. Black, Mrs. Tewsky.

CHAPTER FOURTEEN
THE BRADY BUNCH, PART I: SUPPRESSION OF THE EVIDENCE

Jack Cato, of the Houston News Service, was the best known police reporter in the city.

He paced back and forth in the office and waited.

Larry Connors of Channel 13 was there too. So were Bob Wolfe of Channel 11 and Rick Hartley of Channel 2. All of them scratched their heads and wondered.

It was going to be a most unusual press conference.

The reporters were here at the Houston Police Homicide Division office for a simple reason—they had been summoned. But it wasn't the police who had asked for them. It was a group of prisoners.

Four prisoners, who wanted to talk to the press—that was what the reporters had heard.

"What's this all about?" one of them asked.

"I don't really know," said another. But he began to explain the rumors he had heard. There was a group of Mexican-American men who had confessed to a string of robberies and murders. It was said that the men were pretty brazen about it. The odd thing was, the members of the gang had asked to talk to the press. It was they who had called this press conference.

While the reporters were discussing this strange development, the police officers in the homicide division stood by and waited. The situation was strange to them too.

For the police department and the district attorney's office, it had been hard to know just what to do when these four prisoners had said they wanted to talk to the press. It was a damned-if-you-do, damned-if-you-don't situation. The publicity might endanger a prosecution. But on the other hand, the American Bar Association's guidelines say that it is proper to let a prisoner be interviewed when he has consented. And this was a situation in which the four men had not just consented, but *demanded* to see the press. You ought not to stop someone who wants to talk to reporters from talking to them.

All across the country, the police officers knew, there had been lawsuits by prisoners denied access to the outside world. The courts had often prodded wardens to allow contact with prisoners. And it usually looked, to the public, like a cover-up if the press was excluded, anyway.

That was why the decision had been made to allow the press conference. That was why the four prisoners were on their way to the homicide office now.

One of the reporters said, "I hear they call themselves 'The Brady Bunch.'"

"The Brady Bunch?" said someone else. "Why the 'Brady Bunch'?"

The explanation for the name was really quite appropriate, it seemed. There was a television show called "The Brady Bunch." The name of this group was a take-off on that. It was rumored that the four men had committed their first robbery-murder on Houston's Brady Street. It had been reported in all the papers as the "Brady Street Murder." From that, it was said, the four men had started calling themselves the Brady Bunch. The name stuck.

The Brady Bunch. A group of Chicanos who had given themselves that name, and who wanted to get on television to talk about their crimes. It sounded like news; it might make some footage for six o'clock.

The reporters set up their lights and cameras at one end of the room. And they waited.

* * *

Bernardino Sierra was a thin man with a tooth missing in front. He had greasy hair combed in ducktails and a huge, spidery tattoo on the front of his neck.

He was the chief spokesman for the Brady Bunch.

A few seconds ago, the door to the office had opened. The reporters had seen four men, in prison whites, walking languidly into the room while a small army of officers kept them under guard. The four men had been brought across the room. They had given their names: Sierra, Vargas, Ruiz and Fuentes—the Brady Bunch, Now, as they stood blinking at the television cameras, Bernardino Sierra stepped into the limelight. The questioning began almost immediately, with Jack Cato.

> Cato: "The Officers and the District Attorney's Office say that you were involved in a ring that was killing people. Is that right?"
> Sierra: "Well, that's what I—you could—yeah, that's right."
> Cato: "Can you tell us about it?"
> Sierra: (Unintelligible)
> Connors: "Tell us the best way you can, Mr. Sierra."
> Sierra: "Let Richard tell you about it."

Richard Vargas stood beside Bernardino Sierra. His appearance was different from Sierra's, but he was no less threatening. Richard Vargas was a short, stocky man, with a strong build. He had a burr haircut and smoldering eyes.

Now, the newsmen turned to him.

> Cato: "What started it? Why did it start, you robbing places?"
> Vargas: "No reason at all."
> Connors: "What started the killings? Do you know how many you killed?"
> Vargas: "Well, one on Almeda—two on Almeda, and one on Brady."
> Connors: "Why?"
> Vargas: "For no reason."
> Cato: "Do you feel bad about it since there was no reason?"
> Vargas: "It don't bother me."

The newsmen were incredulous. They had never seen or heard anything quite like this. Here were these four men, nonchalantly saying, with soft, calm voices, that they didn't care about killing. They were having obvious trouble remembering just how many people they had killed. It was going to make better footage than the reporters had anticipated.

The questioning went back to Sierra. The reporters were interviewing these four murderers as though they were visiting dignitaries.

Cato: "You shot somebody over on Middle Street, didn't you, a man that you didn't know?"
Sierra: "I didn't shoot him."
Cato: "Who did?"
Sierra: "I ran over him."
Cato: (surprised) "You ran over him?"
Sierra: (nonchalantly) "Umhum."
Cato: "Why? Why did you pick this man out?"
Sierra: "He was messing with my woman."
Cato: "And what did you do?"
Sierra: "Robbed him."
Cato: "And then what?"
Sierra: "Ran over him."
Cato: "How did you feel about it after you did all this?"
Sierra: "All right."

While Sierra talked, matter-of-factly, about the Middle Street Murder, Houston Detective James A. Pierce was watching. And he thought about the Middle Street case too.

The mangled body of a Chicano man had been found in an empty field on Middle Street. It had taken the police department months to identify the body. It had been crushed and deformed to such a point that it was nearly unrecognizable. It had finally been identified through fingerprints.

The autopsy report on the Middle Street Murder had shown a killing of unusual ferocity. The report had listed eight different factors in the cause of death, ranging from "1. fractured skull" to "8. multiple lacerations and abrasions of head, trunk and extremities." In lay terms, the autopsy had come down to this: The victim had been stabbed repeatedly in the head and other places with a large blade. Then he had been dragged by a car. Then he had been run over several times.

In other words, it had been exactly as Sierra was now saying.

When the police had finally identified the victim of the Middle Street Murder, they had been surprised at who he was. It would have seemed, given the nature of the homicide, that he would be an uncommon person—a person with enemies, or at least a person with a police record. But this victim was just an average citizen. He had worked at a bookstore. Yet he had been stabbed, dragged and run over with a car, and now that the Brady Bunch were describing how they had killed him, it sounded as though they were describing how the milkman delivered the milk.

Actually, most of the Brady Bunch cases were execution-style killings. Sierra and Vargas were talking about them freely now, with evident pride, in their soft, polite voices. Somehow, the politeness made the cases all the more frightening.

The press conference was now in high gear. Sierra and Vargas had overcome some of their initial shyness. They were talking naturally and pleasantly, correcting the reporters whenever they had their information wrong. The reporters were loosened up, too. They had started this interview not knowing exactly what they had; and now that they knew, they wanted to find out as much as they could.

> Cato: "How about that store owner over on Harrisburg you shot down?"
> Sierra: (correcting him) "Navigation Street, you mean?"
> Cato: "Navigation, yeah."
> Sierra: "Umhum."
> Cato: "Did you feel bad about that one afterwards?"
> Sierra: "No, I don't feel bad.... They can only burn me once, anyway."
> Cato: "Why did you call this conference? You don't have to put up with all these questions. Why did you call it?"

And then Jack Cato answered his own question: "You wanted to be in the newspapers and on TV, didn't you?" He said. "Do you feel it will help you, talking to the people out there about what you all did? Do you feel good about it?"

"I don't feel bad about it," Sierra said. "I wanted to say something."

The press conference went on.

The newsmen tried hard to pin down the killings—how many there had been, and where they had been. No one could be sure. At times, it seemed the Brady Bunch members themselves could hardly be sure. But there were at least five that were certain. The original one, on Brady Street. That was one.

Number two was on Navigation. Number three was on Almeda Road. Number four was on Middle Street. That was the one where Sierra said he didn't shoot the victim, he "ran over" him.

Number five was in Fort Bend County, Texas, just outside the city limits of Houston. And that, it appeared, was all of them.

Once the murders were sorted out, the next question was—Why? Why had they done it?

Of all the Brady Bunch members, Richard Vargas was the most eloquent in explaining the motive—or lack of it—for the killings. Did he ever feel bad about killing anyone? "No, sir." Did he ever even think about it? "No, sir." If he were out on the streets now, would he do it all again? "I guess so." Why would he do it again? "I guess just for kicks."

Did he enjoy it, the reporters wanted to know? "Yes," Richard Vargas told them, "it was all right." And what had he thought about, when he saw the victims dying, bleeding to death from gunshot wounds and knife wounds? "Well, they was gonna die, that's all," said Vargas pleasantly.

But perhaps the most unusual exchange happened just before the news reporters packed their gear to head back to their stations.

"I got something else to say, man," said Richard Vargas.

"You got something else to say?" Cato answered, turning toward him. "Go ahead, Richard, just tell us."

"Well," Vargas said, "How come they don't want us to tell you about the Murder in the County Jail?"

To the reporters, this was a complete surprise. Besides the five murders they had heard about, there was a sixth one—a Murder in the County Jail.

Vargas began to explain. It seemed the police had not known it was a murder. They had thought the victim died of a heart attack. Vargas had finally told them about it, but they didn't want to make it public because it was—well, it was embarrassing to the police. They hadn't solved the crime or even known about it.

Vargas, now, was going to enjoy embarrassing them.

He explained how he and Sierra had done it. Using a plastic bag, they had suffocated a fellow inmate in order to rob him. It had happened because when the Brady Bunch had first been arrested, the police had not known how violent they were, and they had put them in a community jail tank. Sierra had held the man down by sitting on his chest. Vargas had held the bag over his face.

"Well, the man came in," Vargas said, "and, uh, he was

wearing a diamond ring. He started shaking. I started talking to him, you know, and he told me that his wife sent him in here for drunk.

"And later that night we killed him and took his ring."

That was all there was to it. The Murder in the County Jail.

The reporters dismantled their equipment and packed it up. Then they rushed back to their stations to get the Brady Bunch—plus, of course, the Brady Street Murder, the Navigation Street Murder, the Almeda Road Murder, the Middle Street Murder, the Fort Bend County Murder, and last, but not least, the Murder in the County Jail—on the news at six o'clock.

* * *

The press conference had been held on August 27, 1974.

Now, four months later, Assistant District Attorney Stu Stewart flicked off the tape recorder as he finished listening to it one more time.

It was unbelievable, he thought.

And the most unbelievable thing about it was that the press conference would not be admissible before the jury at all, during any of the trials of the Brady Bunch members. The jury could never even be told about it.

Once again, Stewart read the provision of the law that said so. It was article 38.22 of the Texas Code of Criminal Procedure, and there was no way around it. The tapes and videotapes of the press conference could not be used as evidence, because article 38.22 said that if a prisoner was in custody, only a signed, *written* statement was admissible in evidence. An oral confession—even if it was recorded—couldn't be used at all.

Charles Dickens once wrote that "the law is an ass." Here, the law said that a written statement would be admissible, but it allowed the Brady Bunch members to call a press conference before television cameras and tell the whole world how much they enjoyed killing—then keep it hidden from the jury that would decide the case.

Charles Dickens was right.

At least, Stewart reflected, there was a set of admissible confessions. The Houston Police Department, aware of the provisions of article 38.22, had gotten written statements at the same time as the press conference. The statements recited all the warnings required by the Supreme Court's decision in *Miranda v. Arizona*. They were all signed. And these written confessions were completely voluntary; everyone connected with the events, including the television newsmen, could testify to the circumstances.

It was unfortunate, Stewart thought, that there was no way to show the jury the chilling, frightening quality of these murderers that the press conference showed so graphically. The written confessions contained a description of the crimes on paper. They would not give the jury the insights that the press conference did into the kinds of men these Brady Bunch members were.

Still, Stu Stewart was never one to quarrel with the law. Or to try to circumvent it.

Even his opponents held Stu Stewart in high regard. In fact, one might say, especially his opponents—they respected him. "He's stronger than a Mexican plate lunch," said one lawyer who fought against him in court. "But he doesn't pull any bullshit tricks on you, either. Nothing cheap, no cheap shots.

"He beats you fair and square, or not at all. He's just a good guy."

Stewart was a big man. He radiated strength and solidity. Born in Texas, he had gone to college in Tulsa, Oklahoma, where he combined a starting position on the football team with a high grade average. He came to the District Attorney's office after graduating at South Texas Law School in Houston, and he had been a prosecutor for over seven years when he was assigned to handle the Brady Bunch cases.

Now, as he prepared these extraordinary cases for trial, he knew what the defense would do. The defense lawyers would not be satisfied with exclusion of the press conference. They would try to get the written confessions thrown out of court too. They would say the confessions were coerced and involuntary, and they would claim that their client's rights under the fifth, sixth and fourteenth amendments had been violated.

Stewart turned on the tape recorder again. He heard the voice of the news reporter, Jack Cato, asking the Brady

Bunch members something that would be of the utmost importance in the pre-trial hearing concerning the confessions.

> Cato: "You've been treated all right? You haven't been hit or mistreated?"
> Voices: (all defendants) "No."
> Cato: "Do all of you agree on that? You haven't been mistreated?"
> Voices: (Unintelligible)
> Cato: "Nobody's laid a hand on you, have they?"
> Voices: (several responses, of defendants) "No."
> Cato: "On you?"
> Voices: "No."
> Cato: "Let's see, all four of you agree. Nobody's—. Okay."

That, Stewart thought, made it pretty clear. The defense lawyers might challenge the confessions. In fact, they were certain to. But in the pre-trial hearings before the judge, the tape recording *would* be admissible. And it showed how spectacularly evident the voluntariness of the confessions really was.

Stewart shut the tape recorder off and began to prepare his case.

* * *

Defense Attorney Stuart Kinard was studying the press conference too. He had a different view of it than the prosecutor.

Stuart Kinard was Vice President of the Texas Criminal Defense Lawyer's Association. He taught an evening course in criminal defense trial practice at a local law school. He was smart, and tough, and a seasoned criminal lawyer.

His appointment to represent Bernardino Sierra had come back in August of 1974.

The case against Sierra, he knew, contained all the elements of a death sentence case. A written confession to five murders. A trail of robberies with eyewitnesses who could identify Kinard's client. Sierra had even been arrested while he was committing a robbery, and the gun he was using was the weapon he had used to commit one of the five murders.

Kinard wanted to save his life. But even that would take a

miracle.

"There's no question about it," he thought to himself, "I've got to try to get the written confessions thrown out. Not just the videotape of the press conference—because article 38.22 does seem to exclude that, in any event—but the written confession, too."

Kinard went over the transcript of the press conference with a fine-tooth comb. It would not be admissible before the jury, but it would be seen by the judge during the pre-trial hearings.

It was the key to the case.

And Kinard found several things that seemed promising to the defense.

During the press conference, Sierra had been asked whether he had been promised anything by the officers to get him to confess. Sierra had said, "Yeah, I been promised that my mother was gonna get cut loose."

In fact, Sierra's mother had been arrested along with the Brady Bunch members. She had been in possession of a cache of stolen property. The police had released her immediately after the last of the confessions, because all the Brady Bunch members said that she didn't know the property was stolen.

Kinard read on in the transcript.

It seemed that Sierra had been fairly persistent in naming his mother's arrest as one of the reasons he had confessed. When Jack Cato had asked, "Why did you call this conference?" Sierra had answered, "Well, uh, my mother, you know, like I say, she was gonna be charged with something she didn't do, so, uh, I didn't want her to be in jail no longer."

That would be his theme, Kinard decided.

Sierra wasn't beaten. No one laid a hand on him. He wasn't mistreated in any way. Kinard's defense would be that he was forced to confess in order to free his mother from prison. It was not physical coercion, but it was coercion nonetheless.

It would be a hard argument to make. The police were not outside the bounds of propriety if they arrested Sierra's mother with probable cause, and it seemed they had that, since they found her in possession of the property. And they were not outside the bounds of propriety if they released her when they got information which they believed, which showed them that she hadn't known the property was stolen.

But if Kinard could show that the police had arrested Sierra's mother for the purpose of using her as a hostage, and threatening to hold her without evidence until the Brady Bunch members confessed—if he could do that, the confessions might be considered involuntary. And that would mean they would be thrown out.

The press conference itself, and the ghoulish delight that the Brady Bunch members took in bragging about their exploits, was the prosecution's answer to the defense theory. To counter the press conference, it would be Kinard's job to put on evidence of coercion so powerful that it resulted not only in the written confessions, but in the press conference too.

It seemed far-fetched at first. But it might work.

The lawyers who represented Richard Vargas agreed to let Kinard take the lead in the pre-trial hearings. Vargas didn't have a mother in jail, and he had almost nothing that could be used to dispute the confessions—outside of whatever might splash over from Kinard's attack on them on Sierra's behalf. Fuentes and Ruiz's lawyers, too, were content to let Kinard take the lead.

This defense became known as the "Sierra's Madre" Theory, and it went like this: all of the written confessions, and the press conference with its appearance of voluntariness, were in fact the result of pressure that was applied to *all* the Brady Bunch members, through the fear that Sierra's mother might have to take a bum rap. The four men's voluntary appearance at the press conference was a put-on. It wasn't really voluntary. The Brady Bunch members had turned in an Academy Award performance in front of the television cameras, and they had done it because the police had forced them, psychologically, to do it. Kinard was enough of a wag to refer to his theory as "The Pressure of Sierra's Madre."

* * *

"I think it's incomprehensible," Judge Jefferson said, "that that sort of thing could happen in this country."

Judge Jefferson wasn't talking about the crimes the Brady Bunch had committed. He was talking about the press conference.

As he saw it, the broadcasting of the confessions was an attempt to taint the trial with publicity. Stu Stewart protested; the "Bunch" members had demanded to see reporters, and that was why they had been allowed to see them.

Judge Jefferson didn't see it that way.

The frame of mind that Andrew Jefferson brought to the case was going to matter a great deal. He was the judge of the 208th Criminal District Court of Harris County. And as it happened, the Brady Bunch cases had all been consolidated and assigned to the 208th for pretrial hearings.

Judge Jefferson was an impressive man. He liked to use street slang whenever the King's English was insufficiently expressive, but he had come a long way since his beginnings. As a black man he had graduated from the most prestigious law school in the State—the University of Texas—at a time when black law students were all but unheard of. From there he had become an Assistant United States Attorney. There, his obvious capabilities and his background appealed to many potential employers—both in and out of government. It was not long before he was employed in the office of the general counsel of what is now called the Exxon Corporation, and that made him one of the chief legal officers of one of the largest companies in the world.

He had been appointed to his present position about a year before the Brady Bunch cases came to him.

Judge Jefferson's diction and his command of the English language were part of what made him a commanding figure in the political arena. It was said that he was as good a speechmaker as Congresswoman Barbara Jordan, who was a friend of his, in fact.

There was one other noteworthy thing about Judge Jefferson—something that was of particular importance to Kinard and the other Brady Bunch defense lawyers.

The judge had a dislike for some of the policies of the District Attorney's Office that seemed to have blossomed into a personal animosity toward the District Attorney himself. The District Attorney, in turn, had publicly criticized some of the judge's decisions. Judge Jefferson apparently did not believe that the District Attorney ought to do that.

Relations between the two men had become so strained that Judge Jefferson, on one occasion, interrupted a public hearing, for which he had summoned the District Attorney to his court, to ask him, on the record: "What is your attitude toward criticism of judicial decisions, Mr. Vance?"

The District Attorney had replied, in so many words, that no public official holding an elective office was immune from criticism. That was legally correct, of course, and the first amendment to the Constitution said so; but it did little to ease the tension between these two powerful men.

It was early January, 1975, when the hearings on the Brady Bunch confessions got under way in Judge Jefferson's court.

"Any opening remarks, Mr. Stewart?" Judge Jefferson asked.

The prosecutor stood up. "We recognize, your honor, that the burden is on us to show that the confessions were voluntary," Stu Stewart began. "We intend to more than shoulder that burden."

He would produce the tapes of the news conference, Stewart went on. He would produce as witnesses the newsmen who were present at the conference, to show how it was conducted and to testify about the demeanor of the Brady Bunch members. He would produce all the police officers who had been present and a number of lay witnesses.

And so the hearing began.

Officer James A. Pierce, who had been present when Sierra signed his written confession, was one of the first to testify.

"Did you ever make any promise, or offer any inducement to them?" Stu Stewart asked.

"No," was Pierce's answer.

As to Kinard's charge that he had used Sierra's mother to get Sierra to confess, Pierce said, "He heard his mother was in jail. He asked to see us, not the other way around. He wanted to tell me his mother had nothing to do with it.

"We told them we couldn't make any promises."

When the Brady Bunch members had asked to go on television, said Pierce, "I called the District Attorney's Office." The decision to allow the newsmen and the prisoners to get together was made personally by the District Attorney, on the ground that if inmates wanted to talk to the press, and you didn't let them, it would create more problems, and violate their rights to a greater extent, than if you kept them incommunicado.

Stuart Kinard's questioning was acute. He wanted to know why Sierra's mother was marked "hold for investigation" on homicide division records instead of burglary and theft records.

"We had information there were other killings besides the ones we knew about," Pierce answered. At the time, there were only two cases—the Navigation Street Murder and the Almeda Road Murder—that the police had solved. "The families of these men had property including guns used," Pierce said. "We didn't know the extent of this thing."

The explanation was plausible. The judge might accept it. But Kinard had some other points to make.

Wasn't it a fact, he asked, that all of the Brady Bunch lawyers had been appointed before the press conference? And none of them were notified that the press conference was going to take place?

And wasn't there a time when not only Sierra's mother, but Joe Ruiz's mother and father were under arrest and in custody?

There was, indeed, Pierce replied. But Ruiz's parents, too, had been found in possession of stolen property, and they had been arrested for that offense. It was an arrest on probable cause, and it was not used in any way to elicit the confessions. As far as the lawyers were concerned, the Brady Bunch members had full access to them, had met with them, and had been advised of all their rights. They hadn't wanted to consult their lawyers. They had wanted to get on television and brag about their crimes.

After Pierce, Stewart called a news photographer, Nancy Redding, to the stand. She identified photographs she had taken at the time Sierra and Vargas had made and signed their confessions. The photographs showed them smiling in amusement. One of the pictures showed Richard Vargas, seated at a desk, looking at something. His face had a look of bemused interest in it. The witness explained that Vargas was looking at a photograph of one of his victims, which he had asked the police to see.

But the star witness in the case was a tape recorder.

The chilling, calm voices of the Brady Bunch members wafted through the courtroom. Judge Jefferson listened intently. He heard Sierra talking about the Middle Street

Murder, telling reporters he hadn't shot the man but had "run over" him. He heard Vargas tell how much he enjoyed the killings and how he "guessed" he would do it again. And he heard the astounding revelation of the Murder in the County Jail, which the police, far from forcing the Brady Bunch to confess, had wanted to keep confidential.

Judge Jefferson heard the entire press conference.

Finally, Stu Stewart rested his case. He had put on nearly two dozen witnesses; it had taken seventeen days. The evidence that the confessions were voluntary, he thought, was overwhelming.

* * *

During most of the hearing, the four members of the Brady Bunch—Sierra, Vargas, Ruiz and Fuentes—sat in the empty jury box.

That seemed the most appropriate place to put them. The hearing had started with them at counsel table with their lawyers, but that had not worked out at all. They had spent a great deal of the time talking among themselves and laughing.

There had been one point in the hearings when Judge Jefferson had said something about holding Stu Stewart in contempt and putting him in jail. That had been the high point of the trial for the Brady Bunch, who had been unable to restrain their glee. They were laughing at a system in which the judge presumed them innocent after they had confessed to six sadistic murders on television, but threatened to put their prosecutor in jail.

Now, it was time for the Brady Bunch themselves to testify.

One by one, each of them claimed that he had confessed because of the fear that his own mother would be arrested by the Houston police.

"But your mother wasn't in jail," Stewart said to Richard Vargas. "How did they make you confess?"

"They told me they'd go arrest her," Vargas answered.

To Fuentes, Stewart said, incredulously, "Your mother was in Matamoros, Mexico. How did they make *you* confess?"

"They told me they'd find her," Fuentes replied.

It was too much for Judge Jefferson to believe, the

prosecutor decided. The Sierra's Madre Theory just required too much imagination for anyone to swallow it. It required one to believe that the arrest of Sierra's mother, on probable cause, had led to a series of events that culminated in the press conference, at which the four men, in spite of their low intelligence, fooled everyone into thinking they were acting voluntarily when in fact they were not.

* * *

It was only a short time later that Judge Jefferson made his decision public.

". . . .the court finds that the state has failed to meet its burden to prove by a preponderance of the evidence that the said confessions were voluntary," the judge's order read. And with those words, he threw out the written confessions of Sierra and Ruiz.

Two days later, he entered another order, throwing out the confessions of Vargas and Fuentes.

The four men had confessed on television, put it in writing and signed it, and said they were never mistreated by the police—and yet there it was. None of it could be used in court against them. Judge Jefferson had accepted the Sierra's Madre Theory. And there was nothing that Stu Stewart could do about it.

Within a matter of months, before any of the Brady Bunch cases was settled by trial, Judge Andrew Jefferson resigned to enter private practice.

And he went into partnership with two of the lawyers who had represented Brady Bunch members in the hearings before him.

There was no impropriety in this, of course. The judge had a right to resign, and he had a right to form a partnership with whomever he chose. But there were some people who thought that the arrangement had a strange appearance to it. One prosecutor, in fact, summed it up with the street slang Judge Jefferson himself occasionally liked to use: "It sure showed where his head was at during the hearings on the confessions."

For Stuart Kinard, the confession hearings were an amazing success. It had looked like an impossible argument for the defense. Now, his "impossible" task of defending

Bernardino Sierra had moved a little closer to accomplishment. Of course, the prosecution could still proceed to try the Brady Bunch members, using the evidence they had left—eyewitnesses, circumstantial evidence, and the like—but the confessions, the most damning evidence, were out of the picture.

Stu Stewart, the prosecutor, had a different perspective.

"That was the strangest hearing I've ever seen," he said, when it was over. And he added: "Or that I ever hope to be a part of."

But every trial lawyer is used to adverse decisions, including ones that are incomprehensible to him. And so Stu Stewart, now, got ready to try his case against the members of the Brady Bunch. The first of the cases to reach a jury was the one against Richard Vargas. And as it happened, the suppression of the confessions was only the beginning of the courtroom battle over Richard Vargas' life.

THE BRADY BUNCH—This bizarre group took its name from the fact that one of its first robbery-murders was this brutal killing at an address on Houston's Brady Street.

THE BRADY BUNCH—the members of the group demanded to meet with news reporters. From left to right, Richard Vargas, Joe Ruiz, Bernardino Sierra and Angel Fuentes meet the press (Photograph courtesy *Houston Post*).

THE BRADY BUNCH—Bernardino Sierra, shortly after the giving of his confession concerning the Fort Bend County Murder. This was two days after the press conference. Detective Chuck Lofland has just said something funny, causing Detective Terry Pierce (standing) and Sierra to laugh. (Photograph courtesy Nancy Redding).

THE BRADY BUNCH—when he confessed to Fort Bend County authorities, Richard Vargas wanted to see police photographs of his victim. Here he studies those pictures, with a newspaper containing front page coverage of the press conference in front of him. (Photograph courtesy Nancy Redding).

THE BRADY BUNCH—homicide scene photograph of the Middle Street Murder. The victim, an ordinary citizen who worked at a bookstore, was stabbed in the head, chest and extermities with a large blade, then run over and dragged with a car.

THE BRADY BUNCH—homicide scene photograph of the Almeda Road Murder. The victim, who had completed the requirements for a college degree in pharmacy and was awarded his diploma posthumously, worked as night manager of a grocery store to put himself through. He was forced to lie here, behind the cash register, and shot in the back of the head.

THE BRADY BUNCH—homicide scene photograph of the Navigation Street Murder. Sierra, accompanied by Vargas and Ruiz, entered the Crescent Food Market on Navigation Street and committed a robbery. Sierra then shot an employe in the chest, wounding him critically, and shot and killed a customer named "Papa Joe" Picinich, who was approaching his sixtieth birthday.

THE BRADY BUNCH—one of the robbery victims in the Navigation Street Murder re-enacts the crime by showing the position in which he was forced to lie.

> with to kill him or I would have killed him then, I was just
> Richard left in Ernest's car and went to a U-Tote-Em on Almeda. He an
> RICHARD went in there and robbed the place, everyone else stayed in the
> car. Richard shot that man that was there with a .22 pistol. Then we
> left. Sometime in June, me, Joe and Richard took Hoya's car and went
> to the Cresent Food Market on Navigation and robbed the place. We all
> was inside and I shot two men during the robbery. One died and one
> lived. After that we kept on robbing and then about 8 hours later we
> went to Early Robert's and that's where I was busted at, pulling a
> robbery at Larly Robert's. Robbery Division confiscated my .32 that I
> had used at the Cresent robbery and about $350 that I had on me. After
> we were busted we were put into the County Jail. THERE was an old white
> man there, he was about 50, heavy and he was in the same tank with us.
> They put him in the same cell with us, 6 cell, and me, Richard, Angel
> and Ernest Hoya. This man, he was telling us about this ring he had
> on that cost $1,500 and we decided to rob him so Richard held a plastic
> bag over his face, the rest of us were holding him down. Richard held
> the bag over his face until he died. Then I took the ring off him

THE BRADY BUNCH—part of a transcription of Bernardino Sierra's confession, which was signed and verified after it was transcribed. This excerpt tells about the Almeda Road Murder, the Navigation Street Murder, and the Murder in the County Jail. Shortly after giving this confession, Sierra joined Vargas, Ruiz and Fuentes at a press conference held at his request.

THE BRADY BUNCH—the wounds of one of the victims of the stabbing inside the county jail. Sierra smuggled in a pair of scissors and attempted to kill two other inmates with them. This episode followed Sierra's escape from jail (he was apprehended without violence) and the incident in which Sierra and Vargas successfully killed an inmate to steal his ring.

CHAPTER FIFTEEN
THE BRADY BUNCH, PART II: THE TRIAL OF RICHARD VARGAS

"I been nervous a long time," the prisoner said. He stared down at the floor.

The psychologist looked at him. "Have you gotten any medicine for it?" he asked. "Or any treatment?"

"No," said the prisoner indifferently.

The man was trying to be as unresponsive to the questions as possible, the psychologist noticed. In fact, he was acting out a classic example of what psychologists call "passive-aggressive" behavior. Inside, he was smoldering with hostility. Outwardly, he expressed that hostility by ignoring the interviewer.

He told the psychologist his name was Richard Vargas. And he added that he was a member of the "Brady Bunch."

The psychologist tried again. For him, the purpose of the interview was fairly simple; he had some straightforward questions that had to be answered. Was Richard Vargas rational? Would he be able to communicate with his attorneys and assist them in his defense? The law said that before any individual could be tried for a crime, he had to be mentally competent.

It was the psychologist's job to find that out.

The prisoner was only minimally cooperative, and he expressed his aggression by grunting, staring or saying "I don't know." But that was a mode of behavior the psychologist knew only too well, and he knew of standard methods for dealing with it and getting the information he needed. And so in many respects, the process was routine.

But in another way, it was anything but routine.

The interview was taking place on the ninth floor of Houston's Jefferson Davis Hospital. That was where the maximum security wing of the hospital was located. And the subject of the evaluation, Richard Vargas, was charged with multiple counts of capital murder.

The first step in a psychological interview is to take a history. That was hard to do, given this subject's lack of cooperation, but it could be done with patience and repetition of questions. And so, slowly, the psychologist began to learn something about the unusual human being who sat before him.

Richard Vargas was born May 30, 1951, in Brownsville, Texas—deep in the fertile Rio Grande Valley, just across the border from Mexico. Reports on the number of his brothers and sisters varied, but it was clear there were a lot of them. His mother had said that there were seventeen children in all. Richard Vargas, when he was asked about it, said that he "wouldn't try" to figure out where he ranked in age among them.

The prisoner's work history was sporadic and unstable. He had been employed mainly as an unskilled laborer. That, in turn, was tied to his lack of success in school; for although Richard Vargas had made it through the elementary grades, he had progressed only into the first year of junior high school. In 1965, the psychologist learned, Richard Vargas had earned his first institutional commitment—to the State Reform School in Gatesville, Texas. That marked the end of his formal education.

That may also have been when drugs became a regular part of Richard Vargas' life. The psychologist learned that this prisoner had used LSD, amphetamines and barbiturates on a regular basis. But the drug Richard Vargas used most frequently, he said, was alcohol. Becoming intoxicated was an everyday occurrence for him.

As the history progressed, in spite of Richard Vargas' hostile resistance to the interview, the portrait of a killer emerged. Bit by bit, the doors to the information the psychologist needed began to open. The keys to the doors were sometimes under the surface—not just in the prisoner's answers themselves, but in his behavior too.

Now, the psychologist began to ask direct questions aimed

at finding out whether the prisoner perceived the situation he was in. Did the prisoner know what he was charged with? Yes, he did; they were murders and robberies. Did the prisoner understand that he could get the electric chair, the death penalty, for the crimes he was charged with? Yes, Richard Vargas said, he understood.

"I don't think about it," he added. "They can only burn me once."

By now, the man's basic mental condition was clear enough to the psychologist. Richard Vargas was sane. He was competent to stand trial. He had a rational understanding of the reality that surrounded him. Hostile, aggressive, even cynical—but rational.

Still, the interview wasn't enough by itself.

Because of the seriousness of the charges, the psychologist knew that further examination would be appropriate— just to make sure. And so he turned to the diagnostic techniques of modern psychology. By testing the prisoner with ink blots, drawings and carefully prepared questions, he hoped to get an inside view of Richard Vargas' brain.

* * *

The Bender Gestalt Test is used to determine the presence, or absence, of physical brain damage.

It was the first of a battery of tests that the psychologist administered to Richard Vargas.

The Bender Gestalt Test is deceptively simple. All it consists of is a sheet of paper with diagrams on it. At the top of the page is a circle and a diamond, with a row of twelve dots beneath them; the rest of the sheet is a complex pattern of dots and squiggles. The test subject is given this sheet, together with a blank sheet and a pencil, and he is asked to copy it.

A subject with brain damage produces a characteristically distorted pattern. That was what the tester had to look for.

The psychologist waited while Richard Vargas copied the Bender Gestalt pattern. Then he looked at the results.

The prisoner's drawings were sloppy and crooked, and there were blanks that were attributable to his laziness and lack of cooperation. But the spatial relationships of the dots and squiggles on the copied sheet was generally faithful to the original Bender Gestalt Test pattern. That was the important thing. It meant that there was no organic damage to Richard Vargas' brain.

And so the Bender Gestalt Test told the psychologist that Richard Vargas' brain was normal—at least physically.

Now, the next test.

The psychologist showed Richard Vargas a sprawling, discolored ink blot with a series of white spaces in the interior. It was the first "plate" in the famous Rorschach, or "ink-blot," test.

The first plate in the Rorschach test is sometimes called "the bat," because that is the most popular description of this symetrical smear. The psychologist got Richard Vargas to give a "free-association" description of the "animal" he saw in the blot. Then he asked about the details of the figure that Richard Vargas said he saw.

Then, one by one, the psychologist repeated the process for each of the other plates in the Rorschach series. There were ten in all.

The Rorschach test is probably the most widely used test in all of psychology. It is simple to administer and it is marvellously versatile. It is capable of detecting both psychoses and neuroses, as well as a wide variety of other personality imbalances.

If the subject gives wildly unconventional descriptions of the imaginary anatomy he sees in a particular blot, for instance, it may lead to a diagnosis of schizophrenia. If he responds with explanations that indicate fear or disgust, it may be an indication that the schizophrenia is of the paranoid type. The emotional content of the response, the number and type of details that the subject perceives, and the part of the blot that is described—all of these are windows into the personality of the subject, for a psychologist skilled in the art.

And so it was in Richard Vargas' case.

The psychologist found no evidence of delusions or hallucinations. There was no interference with the prisoner's rational thought processes. The prisoner was not suffering from any known psychosis or neurosis. And that, in itself, was significant.

The results of the ink blot test, in other words, were consistent with the psychologist's conclusions from the interview.

That left one more major area to be tested: It was necessary to know something about the prisoner's level of intelligence.

Using a technique called the "Ammons Q. T. Test," the psychologist soon had an evaluation. Richard Vargas' responses indicated an I.Q. of 75. But that score did not take account of the language barrier. Since Richard Vargas' primary language was Spanish, the true value would be slightly higher. The psychologist estimated Richard Vargas' true I.Q. to be between 80 and 90.

Again, the findings show no abnormality. Richard Vargas had a level of intelligence that was only slightly below the average of the adult population in the United States.

Now the psychologist's test results were complete.

They showed something that was really quite startling. The prisoner was normal, in most respects.

He was of normal intelligence. There was no brain damage. And he had no delusions or interference with his rational processes. The psychologist's report was simple: Richard Vargas was sane and competent to stand trial.

But that, of course, left the biggest question unanswered.

Why was this man a killer?

The textbooks call it "antisocial personality." This label, the textbooks say, "is reserved for individuals who are basically unsocialized and whose behavior pattern brings them repeatedly into conflict with society. . . . They are grossly selfish, callous, irresponsible, impulsive, and unable to feel guilt or learn from experience or punishment."

That description fit Richard Vargas perfectly.

But the label, "antisocial personality," is not a very useful label.

At different times during the history of psychiatry, people with what is now called "antisocial personality" have been called "psychopaths," "sociopaths," or other names. The psychiatric profession has changed the name of this particular personality disorder repeatedly, every few years. And the changes are really quite important, because they are an indication that the psychiatrists do not know very much about this condition. Every few years, they change their collective mind about what "antisocial personality" (or whatever it is called) really means.

It is also a fact that the psychiatric profession is utterly unable to agree on the causes, the nature and the treatment of an antisocial personality. Little, if any, treatment is possible.

In Richard Vargas' case, it was like saying that he was a criminal because he had a personality that was suited to his being a criminal. That was the best that experts on the human mind could do.

The psychologist finished dictating his report. He flicked the tape recorder off.

* * *

At the courthouse, Assistant District Attorneys Stu Stewart and David Crump studied the evidence against Richard Vargas.

The evidence included the reports of the psychiatrists and psychologists who had examined him.

Usually, the psychologist is viewed as a witness for the defense. He is an expert on the issues of insanity and mental incompetence. His normal function is to give evidence on whether the defendant can "tell right from wrong," has a "mental disease or defect," has "capacity to conform his conduct to the law," or whatever other language is used to express the test for insanity. The prosecution, too, sometimes uses psychologists, but it is almost always in answer to a claim of insanity or incompetence that has been raised by the defense.

But the trial of Richard Vargas was going to be different.

When it comes to the death penalty, a psychiatrist or psychologist can give information that is useful on matters unrelated to sanity or mental competence. A psychiatrist or psychologist can give evidence that relates to the basic issue of the appropriateness of capital punishment.

In a capital case in Texas, the jury has to answer a question about the defendant's tendency toward violence in the future. This is a subject on which the psychologist's expert knowledge can be revealing.

As they prepared for trial, Stewart and Crump decided to introduce psychological testimony in the trial of Richard Vargas. It had been done in a few cases before. It had never been done in Houston.

Prediction of future violence, they knew, was difficult even for experts in the field. It was particularly difficult in marginal cases. But with a clear case—a strong case, someone like Richard Vargas—the psychologist might be able to say something that the jury could hang its hat on.

It was decided that Stewart would handle the case during the first trial, the trial on Richard Vargas' guilt or innocence. He would prove the elements of the offense. He would put on the evidence that would secure a conviction for capital murder.

The second trial—the penalty hearing—would be handled by David Crump.

And in the penalty hearing, the prosecution would present a picture of the personality of the killer, a psychological portrait.

That meant that the prosecutors' preparation for the penalty hearing would be unusual. It would require knowledge about the techniques of psychiatry and psychology that were used to evaluate Richard Vargas. That would require, in turn, an understanding of the Bender Gestalt Test, the Rorschach Technique, and the Ammons intelligence test—the tools that the psychologist had used.

These were technical concepts. Their use was generally confined to practitioners in white coats who inhabited the realm of ideas about the human mind.

But in the trial of Richard Vargas, they were about to become weapons in a battle over life and death.

* * *

The trial of Richard Vargas was in its second week when Stu Stewart rested the case for the prosecution.

The evidence of the defendant's guilt was overwhelming.

Stu Stewart had presented a total of nearly two dozen witnesses. Three of them were eyewitnesses to the killing itself. Their testimony showed a murder that was strikingly devoid of any reason or justification.

The four members of the Brady Bunch had stopped at a grocery store during the evening of June 22, 1974. Bernardino Sierra and Richard Vargas had gone inside. They had made everyone in the store—patrons and manager alike—lie face down, on the floor.

Vargas had sat on the counter, the witnesses said. He leaned over it and pointed his gun downward, into the area behind the cash register. That was where the store manager was lying.

And in that position, Vargas had fired his .22 pistol twice.

"Did he ever change expression, the expression on his face?" Stewart had asked one of the witnesses.

"No," was the witness' answer.

There had been no need for the killing. The manager had not resisted; in fact he had not moved at all after lying down. The autopsy pictures showed the jury where the gunshot entry wounds were; they were squarely in the back of the manager's head.

The only plausible explanation was that Richard Vargas had killed the man for amusement.

Houston Police Officer R. A. Noskrent had been the first investigator on the scene. He described the victim. In life, Ashokkumar Patel had weighed only 120 pounds. He was a tiny man, just over five feet tall. As it happened, he was a citizen of India, from the state of Madras, going to school in the United States and working his way through by managing this grocery store.

Now, a year and a half later, Noskrent was visibly shaken by the effort of testifying about the murder.

He had arrived as Patel was dying. In court, he told the jury he had heard the victim chanting in his native tongue as the officer wrapped his exploded head in a towel and waited for an ambulance.

"What did he appear to be saying?" Stewart asked.

"It appeared to me he was praying," Officer Noskrent said slowly.

* * *

Victor Blaine is one of the best criminal lawyers in Harris County.

He is also one of the most straightforward and honest.

The two attributes do not always go together. In fact, it takes a real effort to combine them. The criminal law is a cesspool of injustice, and the frustrations of practicing it day in and day out can soften any man or woman to the easy temptations it presents. And that leads to dishonesty, to the opposing evils of selling out a client or suborning him to perjury.

Vic Blaine and his partner Bob Carroll were well known and respected at the courthouse. They represented their clients within the boundaries of the law. But they did it vigorously, and they always gave those to whom their duty was owing a skillful defense.

Now Blaine and Carroll were applying their talents to the defense of Richard Vargas.

Blaine—with his curly, salt-and-pepper hair and his accent that told of his youth in Mississippi—had an excellent record in capital cases. Since the capital murder statute had been enacted in Texas, he and Carroll had defended three cases—and saved their client from the death penalty each time.

In this case, though, Blaine and Carroll were going to have a difficult time of it. The evidence was strong, the crime was brutal, and the defendant—the defendant would be seen by a jury, after all the evidence was in, as a person who ought to be subject to the death penalty. It would take a vigorous defense to prevent that from happening.

Blaine and Carroll decided to make an issue of the witnesses' identification of the killer. The witnesses were mistaken—that was their defense. The two defense lawyers presented a witness who had seen the killing and who had not been called to the witness stand by the prosecutors. The witness said he was not sure whether it was Richard Vargas who had pulled the trigger in the grocery store that night. He was unable to identify the killer at all. He said it "could have been" Richard Vargas, or it "could have been" someone else; he just didn't know.

It was good defensive strategy, even though the testimony was not highly credible. The prosecution had the burden of proof, and that burden was to show the defendant guilty beyond a reasonable doubt. As a practical matter, jurors demand much higher proof in a death penalty case. Could this testimony create the doubt Blaine and Carroll needed to acquit Richard Vargas?

It was possible.

But as with every strategic decision, this one had some risks associated with it.

The robbery-murder of Ashokkumer Patel was not the only crime Richard Vargas had committed on June 22, 1974. He had committed a series of ten robberies, plus a murder and an attempted murder in addition to the crime he was now on trial for. Up to this point in the trial, Texas law had prevented the prosecutors from telling the jury about those other crimes.

But the rule against "extraneous offenses" in Texas has some important exceptions. And one of them says that if the defense challenges the identification of the suspect by the witnesses, the prosecution can put evidence before the jury concerning all other similar crimes committed by the defendant.

And so it was that Blaine and Carroll's calculated risk opened the lid to a Pandora's box for the defense. With witness after witness, Stewart traced the path the Brady Bunch—Vargas and Sierra together—had followed on that day in March. Stewart called an associate of the Brady Bunch who had turned State's evidence after Vargas and Sierra had threatened to kill him; there was no question of his being mistaken in his identification. The license number of the car was traced to a friend of Vargas'.

Stewart even showed that Vargas was wearing a disguise at the time of his arrest.

Blaine and Carroll had made a decision that had much to recommend it when they raised the issue of mistaken identity. It was just that it had backfired on them.

The jury returned a verdict saying that Richard Vargas was guilty as charged.

* * *

It was three days later, when the penalty hearing was well under way, that the State called its expert witness.

"What, if anything, did you observe about the way in which Richard Vargas regarded the future or its consequences?" David Crump asked.

"He doesn't care much for the future or its consequences," the psychologist answered, "especially as compared to what he wants at the immediate moment."

"Did he appear to have a high regard, or a low regard, for the fate of other human beings, including himself?"

"A low regard," the psychologist answered.

It had taken the jury a little over an hour to find Richard Vargas guilty of capital murder. But as is usually the case with a death penalty trial, that was only the beginning of the battle.

Blaine and Carroll had offered the testimony of Richard Vargas' mother. Pleading with the jury for his life, Mrs. Cruz Vargas had looked down at her feet and said, "my son is sick." And they had offered the testimony of a college administrator who had known the Vargas family for several years. "I'd take a chance on him," this witness said to the jury, earnestly. "I think his prospects are good."

Now, the jury was hearing the State's psychologist. This was the key witness. And his opinion of Richard Vargas was different.

The testimony was strong, and the jury was listening to it closely. The psychologist described Richard Vargas as impulsive, hedonistic, sensation-seeking. He described Vargas' passive-aggressive behavior during the interview. Such an individual would probably not cooperate to any greater degree with a psychiatrist who was trying to treat him, and there was no real "cure" for the antisocial personality anyway. The psychologist added that Richard Vargas was perfectly sane, and capable of conforming to the law if he chose to do so, but his attitude of contempt toward the law prevented him from it.

"The best indicator of future conduct is past conduct," the witness said near the end of the examination. There would be "a high probability," he added, that Richard Vargas would commit violent crimes in the future if he got the chance.

Both sides rested the case. The evidence was closed.

* * *

The courtroom filled with spectators.

The front row was occupied by lawyers. The rear was crowded with news reporters.

The prosecutors' argument to the jury was about to begin.

Crump and Stewart had agreed to split their argument time, with Crump opening and Stewart closing. In between would come the arguments of Blaine and Carroll for the defense.

Crump's argument was concerned with evaluating the facts of the case. But it was also concerned with another issue: the death penalty itself.

"Why is this a death penalty case?" he said to the jury.

"Well, in law school I learned several basic purposes of sentencing. I'd like to talk to you about them.

"For one thing, those purposes include *justice*. Justice to society. And justice to the victims. Justice to people like Mr. and Mrs. Ashokkumar Patel.

"Another purpose is *rehabilitation* of the offender to return to society—if that is feasible.

"Another purpose—the third purpose—is *protection*. Protection of society, victims, witnesses and everyone else from the offender.

"The fourth purpose is to have a penalty that will make other people stop and perhaps not commit crimes. In other words, *deterrence*."

Here the prosecutor paused, then said: "Let's look at those things.

"First, a society that loses its ability to do justice," he said, "soon loses everything."

"Every society has to have some way of securing justice in a murder case. Justice that is equal to the crime."

The jury was listening, Crump saw. He went on.

"In primitive societies, it's done by one's kinsmen and tribesmen. They go out and avenge their slain relative.

"Today, we don't do that. But it's clear that sometimes people in our society still take the law in their own hands. If we are to have a government of laws, we should keep the function of administering justice in the place where it belongs—with the jury. People will do that so long as, and only so long as, they are confident the jury will do its duty."

Crump talked about Ashokkumar Patel. The victim had been in his final year at Texas Southern University. He had been studying pharmacy. He had been awarded his pharmacy degree—posthomously. He had left a wife, who happened to have been pregnant at the time; he now had a son. A son whose father Richard Vargas had murdered.

Justice demanded the death penalty in this case.

The next thing to discuss was rehabilitation.

"Rehabilitation?" Crump went on. That's proper in many cases; maybe in most. But there comes a point where the chance for that is slim—remote—in this case impossible.

"This man's character is so hopeless, this man's crime is so deliberate, unnecessary, inexcusable, monstrous, that if we dream about rehabilitation, all we're doing is saying, 'Let's ship him off to somebody else and let them take care of him.'"

At this point, the prosecutor reminded the jurors of the testimony of the psychologist.

And then he moved on to another reason for capital punishment in this case.

"Basically," he said, "we need protection from this kind of homicidal, violent killer. That's the third consideration.

"We can't just foist him off on somebody else. Violent crime—from rapes through fist fights through robberies through maiming, mayhem and murder are a danger to people inside prisons. Prisoners in the prison system are entitled to be considered as people, too.

"Think about it. What's the major reason *you* wouldn't want to be locked in a prison today? I bet high on the list is the fact that there are people like Richard Vargas inside there too.

"You could never be sure of your plain old, physical, personal safety if you were locked up together with him."

This was the strongest point, Crump thought. Protection. People might debate whether capital punishment was just. They might debate the deterrent value of it. But this factor—protection—was an absolute. There was no other way to prevent this unbelievably dangerous man from killing again.

And so the prosecutor hammered the protection argument home.

"There's no way to build a prison that complies with our laws that will ensure safety for inmates, guards, wardens, case workers, librarians, doctors, teachers and everybody else that's in the environment. There's no way to keep this man from getting access to spoons, mattress covers, and any one of a thousand other things that can be used in violence. How will he shave? Eat? Sleep? Bathe? Or do any of a hundred other daily chores that will bring him in touch with free world persons?

"And I don't have to tell you that just because a man is in prison for a term, is no guarantee that he won't come into contact with people on the outside."

Richard Vargas, of course, was the man who had committed the Murder in the County Jail, plus at least five others in the free world. And bragged about it on television.

But the jury didn't know any of that, because it wasn't admissible in evidence. Crump just had to hope they had heard enough.

The prosecutor moved on to the subject of deterrence.

"Finally," he said, "there was a great judge who once wrote, 'the law must keep its promises.' People who break the law ought to know that definite consequences come from it.

"If you commit a robbery, you know, you've already committed an offense for which you can get life imprisonment. Why not kill everybody in a robbery?... In this state, that kind of murder carries the death penalty. Now, by itself, that won't stop crime. It won't stop every robbery-murder, by any means. But we can't just throw up our hands.

"If it will prevent any one robber from killing any one innocent person lying on the floor groveling and begging for his life, it's justified."

The remainder of the argument consisted of a summary of the evidence. Crump tried to show the jury that the answers to the two questions they would have to answer was "Yes." The killing was obviously deliberate. And all the evidence—from the crime itself to the psychologist's description of the killer's personality—made it clear that Richard Vargas was likely to commit future crimes of violence.

The argument lasted about thirty minutes. For a jury argument in a capital case, that was not very long. But Crump felt mentally drained when he finished and sat down.

Now it was Blaine and Carroll's turn.

* * *

Bob Carroll's argument emphasized that the burden of proof was on the State. "I don't think I'd want to have somebody spend two hours with you and decide you should get the death penalty," he said, referring to the psychologist.

"There is a man who is dead. But that doesn't answer the question. Each of you told us you'd require them to prove their case to you.

"Ask yourself: have they proved it to you? What they've given you is like tossing you a life preserver.

"I think he should get life imprisonment. If he goes to the penitentiary and goes to school, I think he'll get educated.

"Life's a heck of a good thing."

Victor Blaine took up that theme, too.

"Where the death penalty is still invoked, that is where the crime rate is highest," he said. "People are going to have a low regard for life if we take life.

"The only question is—if you don't burn him, would he do it again?

"The psychologist said he 'probably' would," Blaine said emphatically. "He can't prove it to you beyond a reasonable doubt."

The final argument—the last of the four—was Stu Stewart's.

"You have a fact situation that cries out for the death penalty," the prosecutor said, his voice shaking. "What else can you do in this case?"

"I asked all of you, could you give the death penalty in a proper case? Your answers were unequivocal that you could.

"Our system is based on evidence and responsibilities."

* * *

The jury was out until late afternoon.

The courtroom was still full when they returned.

Judge Peter Solito read the verdict. First, the deliberation question.

The jury's answer was "Yes."

The answer to the second question, the violence question, was also "Yes."

"The defendant will rise and face the jury," the judge said. And he assessed the sentence of Richard Vargas at death.

Stu Stewart was outside the courtroom. Victor Blaine walked with Richard Vargas back to his cell. And Bob Carroll shook David Crump's hand. He refused to listen to any condolences. "If you can't drop one, you've got no business trying it," he said.

* * *

It was several days later when Crump tried to reconstruct what had happened.

What were the reasons that Richard Vargas had been sentenced to death?

The answer lay in the evidence.

The jury in the Vargas trial was attentive, intelligent and strong-willed. They were able to follow the court's instructions in the case, and decide it as the law required. But of course, there was another side to that coin; the defense lawyers had had a hand in selecting the jury too. They knew that they had selected a jury that would find against the state if the prosecutors failed to carry the burden. The answer was that the evidence made the life-or-death difference.

The case showed, once again, how quirks of fate could govern the availability of the evidence. The confessions that were suppressed: that had started the process with the state being put at a disadvantage. But the eyewitnesses to the crime had been convincing and sure. They had made the case for the prosecution.

The raising of the identity issue by the defense may have been another factor. For Vic Blaine and Bob Carroll, that had been a tactical decision, and a reasonable one. But it had meant, under the rules of evidence, that the prosecution had been able to give the jury a glimpse at the rest of Richard Vargas—other robberies, another murder, another attempted murder.

The murder in the county jail—that had not been admissible. But the jury had heard enough that was.

Then there was the penalty-hearing evidence. The testimony of the psychologist—and his insights into the mind of a sociopathic killer—that added the last convincing touch to what was already a strong case.

Many factors go into the decision of a criminal case. The composition of the jury, the decisions of the judge, even the personalities of the lawyers—all these can influence the outcome of a trial.

But it was the evidence, and the evidence alone, that made the life-or-death difference in the trial of Richard Vargas.

* * *

Richard Vargas was the first of the Brady Bunch to be

tried before a jury.

After Vargas had been sentenced, Stewart began to concentrate on the cases against other Brady Bunch members.

Angel Fuentes was one of the Bunch. But he was a hanger-on, and his involvement in the violent activities of the Brady Bunch was peripheral. In Fuentes' case, Stu Stewart was satisfied to ask for a sentence of fifteen years. Joe Ruiz, the third man, was more deeply involved than Fuentes—but still not as culpable as Vargas or Sierra. Ruiz was convicted of capital murder and given a sentence of life imprisonment.

That left Bernardino Sierra. Sierra, the leader of the group; Sierra, the pathological killer. Sierra, whose case was to become a paradox, because he would never be convicted before a jury of any of the six murders he had committed.

CHAPTER SIXTEEN
THE BRADY BUNCH, PART III:
THE NAVIGATION STREET MURDER

The judge's bench in the 209th District Court is low. It bears little resemblance to the towering masses that dominate Houston's more traditional courtrooms.

A judge sitting at this bench sits only a few inches off the floor. He is almost at eye level, in fact, with a person standing in front of him.

On July 7, 1976, Judge Frank Price sat at the bench of the 209th and looked at the prisoner who faced him just a few feet away. The man was a slender Mexican-American with greasy hair. He had a tooth missing in front and a sprawling tattoo on his neck.

"You are Bernardino Sierra?" the judge asked, in the tone of voice of a man reciting a familiar ritual.

The prisoner looked briefly at the two lawyers at his side, the lawyers who had saved his life. Then he looked back at the judge.

"Yes," he said.

"Is that your true name?" the judge went on.

"Yes," said the prisoner.

"You're here in court with your attorneys, Mr. Stuart Kinard and Mr. Terry Gaiser," the judge said. "You're charged by indictment in cause number 214,983 with the offense of murder. How do you plead, guilty or not guilty?"

The judge spoke quietly and politely. There was none of the strident adversity that accompanies a contested jury trial. In fact, no jury was present. The courtroom was nearly deserted.

"Guilty," Bernardino Sierra said softly, in answer to the question.

The outcome of this proceeding had been agreed upon in advance. All that had to be done was the ceremony that the law required for every plea of guilty. It was a ceremony familiar to any criminal lawyer—the completion of a plea bargain. Bernardino Sierra was pleading guilty for a lesser sentence than he might otherwise get.

But this was no ordinary plea bargain.

It was the Plea Bargain of the Century.

Why was it happening? Why wasn't a case of this magnitude being decided by the adversary processes of trial? The answer to that question lay buried in a history that spanned Bernardino Sierra's life, his commission of the Navigation Street Murder, and a death penalty trial that failed to produce a verdict. It was a long history, and one that was both fascinating and repugnant.

* * *

It had seemed, at one time, that there was no one in Houston who was a better candidate for capital punishment than Bernardino Sierra.

The four capital murder indictments pending against Sierra were only the tip of the iceberg. He also had one other murder case—for non-capital murder—pending against him, as well as too many robbery indictments to count.

He had even killed inside the county jail. He had participated with Richard Vargas in the incident resulting in the suffocation of an inmate to steal his diamond ring. But Sierra had taken up where Richard Vargas left off. On another occasion, again inside the county jail, Sierra had gotten a pair of scissors smuggled to him—and he had tried to kill two more inmates, stabbing them over a dozen times.

He had escaped from the county jail at least once. And he had arranged with other members of the Brady Bunch to try to kill the witnesses against them.

Who was this man, who was pleading guilty to three murders?

Where had he come from, and why had he done what he had done?

Bernardino Sierra was 27 years old. He was born March

16, 1947, in the city of San Marcos—on the plains of central Texas, a beautiful, lush country with rolling hills and the best ranching land in the world. When he was a child, his father and mother separated. His mother, who raised thirteen children in addition to Bernardino, moved often from place to place.

Bernardino Sierra finished school through the seventh grade. He was put in a class for slow learners and failed the second grade. There was no question he had difficulty in school, but it was hard to see why—since psychological testing showed that he had an intelligence comparable to the average in the adult population, in the 95 to 105 range.

He was raised primarily by his stepfather—a man with a reputation for large alcohol intake and a bad temper. At an early age in his teens, young Sierra quit school to go to work in a restaurant. During his childhood and early youth, he was abused by his father, who was often angry and drunk at the same time.

It was not long before Bernardino Sierra patterned himself on his father's habits. He had tried drugs of different kinds, but his drug of choice was alcohol. "A case of beer," he once said, "goes down easy." When he was evaluated psychologically, he gave a history of arson and cruelty to animals as a child.

Young Bernardino married at the age of seventeen. He worked successfully for a time. He even had two children, and was able to support them and his wife. His criminal history began in 1970, at the age of 23, when he was convicted of burglary. He was released on probation, without imprisonment. But a year later, he committed another crime, and his probation was revoked.

He spent three years in the Texas Department of Corrections. He was released March 21, 1974.

He came to Houston, got a job as a forklift operator, and stayed out of trouble for only a few months before he was arrested and charged with a string of capital murders and robberies.

A psychiatrist who examined him found him "nonchalant, almost proud of his current situation, almost proud of the publicity he has received."

There was nothing wrong with Bernardino Sierra's mental abilities. He was perfectly sane, perfectly rational.

And yet the psychiatrist reported that he "seems to have no remorse, whatsoever, about the recent episode."

The psychiatrist's report concluded with a summary of his findings about Bernardino Sierra. It said, "Impression: Antisocial personality, manifested by violent acting-out, marked negativism, extremely poor impulse control, manipulativeness, passive-aggressiveness and destructiveness."

That was Bernardino Sierra.

And so a quarter-century of development lay behind the guilty plea that was taking place in the 209th. It was the development of a personality that could kill, sadistically, without conscience of remorse. That was part of the history behind the plea bargain.

But there was another history, a shorter one, that was equally important. It was the series of legal maneuvers that had led the prosecutor to recommend a life sentence, rather than death, for Bernardino Sierra. It was a history of difficulties for the prosecution—strange quirks in the law, strange quirks in the rules of evidence—that made it possible for Sierra to escape the ultimate penalty of death.

* * *

The history began before the trial date of Bernardino Sierra.

In his office, Stu Stewart sighed—and looked, once more, at his file.

Four indictments for capital murder. And every one of them, Stewart knew, would present problems for the prosecution. The suppression of the confessions by Judge Jefferson had been an omen. It had signalled how the rest of the case might go.

This case, Stewart knew, was going to be different from the case against Richard Vargas.

The trial of Richard Vargas had involved powerful, and positive, eyewitness testimony. There had been a number of people inside the store who had been able to see what happened, and one of them was close enough to see the killer's fingers tighten when he pulled the trigger. The cases against Bernardino Sierra, although there were a lot of them, did not involve any such powerful evidence.

To Stewart, it was frustrating. He knew that the

availability of evidence was controlled by chance; but still, it was frustrating.

As it happened, the strongest case against Sierra that the prosecution had was a capital murder committed in the course of a robbery of a small grocery store called the Crescent Food Market. Sierra had shot and killed a customer, execution style. He had also shot, and critically wounded, a store employee.

It was called the Navigation Street Murder, because the Crescent Food Market was located on Navigation Street.

There were plenty of other Brady Bunch cases, but each one of them had problems for the prosecution insofar as convicting Sierra was concerned. Four of the murders—the Brady Street Murder, the Middle Street Murder, the Fort Bend County Murder, and the Murder in the County Jail—had very little evidence other than the confessions to prove them. For all practical purposes, Judge Jefferson had thrown those cases out when he had ordered the confessions suppressed.

The fifth case, the Almeda Road Murder, was a strong case—but that was the one Richard Vargas had committed. It was the murder of Ashokkumar Patel. Sierra had participated in the robbery on Almeda Road, and so he might be guilty of the murder as a principal; but Stu Stewart concluded that it would be inappropriate to ask a jury to sentence him to death when he had not personally participated in the killing.

That left the Navigation Street Murder as the logical one for the prosecution to focus on.

The trouble with the Navigation Street Murder, though, was that no one had actually seen Sierra pull the trigger there. Everyone in the store had been lying face down. The witnesses had all been located where they could not see the murder itself. Several of them could identify Sierra, Vargas and Ruiz as the robbers, but the evidence that could put Sierra behind the murder weapon—the evidence that might get him the sentence Stewart felt he deserved—was all circumstantial.

There was a time, Assistant District Attorney Stu Stewart says now, "when I didn't know what to do.

"I got ballistics tests run on the gun Sierra was arrested with. It was the same type of gun used in the Navigation

Street Murder. But the bullet was too deformed from colliding with the victim's body. It went clear through it, from side to side. And an identification of the gun wasn't possible.

"All the eyewitnesses were on the floor and none of them saw anything.

"No one saw it but Sierra, Vargas and Ruiz. And I couldn't exactly put them on the witness stand."

At least, Stewart could show that Sierra was the only one carrying the kind of gun that had been used in the murder. That was some evidence. But he faced the prospect of going to trial with no proof of the murder itself that would stand up in a court of law.

Finally, Assistant District Attorney Stu Stewart went to the books for help. He re-read the Texas criminal code.

And he found a provision that seemed to fit the case perfectly.

It was a new law, just recently passed by the Texas legislature. It said, in essence, that if a person entered into a conspiracy with any other person, he would be guilty of any crimes that he "should have anticipated" his co-conspirators would commit.

As Stewart re-read these words, it dawned upon him: here was a way to prove his case. It was clear that Bernardino Sierra had entered into a conspiracy. He had formed a tacit agreement with the other members of the Brady Bunch—a conspiracy to commit robberies. And from the whole picture, it was clear that that murder was a result that "should have been anticipated" by all the members of the Brady Bunch.

Generally, to be a principal in someone else's crime, a person had to share the intent to commit it. That was what could not be shown in Sierra's case, with reference to the Navigation Street Murder. But this new provision said that in a conspiracy situation, the defendant could be guilty of a crime that "should have been anticipated," even if he had no intent to commit it at all.

And so, irony was piled upon irony. Sierra had, of course, admitted in his written confession that he had pulled the trigger in the Navigation Street Murder. He had even bragged about it in a press conference which he himself had called. The case had been assigned, then, to Judge Jefferson, and he had decided to suppress the confession; and that had left the prosecution unable to prove his act of murder directly.

Now, however, there *was* a way to prove Sierra guilty. Not as a murderer in his own right, which he was, but as a conspirator in the robbery which produced the murder he himself had committed.

"Sometimes the law makes sense," Stewart said. "Sometimes it doesn't. And sometimes it makes sense in spite of itself."

Of course, whenever the law "makes sense in spite of itself," it begins to look like nothing more than a game of words.

So it was in Bernardino Sierra's case.

Sierra had pulled the trigger, but the evidence to prove he had pulled the trigger had been thrown out, and therefore he could not be guilty of pulling the trigger. But he could be guilty of conspiring with the person who pulled the trigger, or in other words, with himself. The long and the short of it was that Sierra could be proved guilty as a principal in a murder which he himself had committed.

* * *

This conspiracy theory was Stu Stewart's key to the whole case.

The jury began to get a view of it, finally, when the trial of Bernardino Sierra was in its fourth week.

When the prosecution began to put in its conspiracy evidence, Stewart's first manuever was an unusual one. He offered into evidence a large map of the city of Houston. And he held in his hand a set of little red flags, each of them glued to a pin.

He explained to the judge what he intended to do. Each one of the red flags would represent the site of a murder or robbery committed by Bernardino Sierra, together with the Brady Bunch, on June 22, 1974.

That was the day of the Navigation Street Murder.

By showing that Sierra had repeatedly committed robberies together with his companions, Stewart knew, he could legally prove that a conspiracy to commit robbery existed. For the Navigation Street Murder had not been the only crime the Brady Bunch had committed that day. They had started in the morning, and they had pulled one "job" after another until the wee hours of the following morning.

Of course, Stuart Kinard—as Sierra's chief defense lawyer—did not accept the conspiracy theory. He argued strenuously to the judge that it did not apply in a capital murder case. And at the first mention of an offense other than the Navigation Street Murder, he stood up and objected that his client was not being given a fair trial.

"It would show an extraneous offense, your honor," he said.

Stewart, as prosecutor, had anticipated this objection. He was well aware that the Texas law usually excluded from the jury's consideration evidence about crimes other than the one for which the defendant was on trial. But he thought he had a right, under the law, to show the jury this particular crime spree, since it happened all in one day. It was a continuous event.

"It goes to show that Bernardino Sierra was involved in a conspiracy with Richard Vargas and Joe Ruiz," he argued to Judge Price. "That's the whole issue in the case."

Since the prosecution could not produce an eyewitness to the actual shooting, Stewart said, the conspiracy provision came into play.

"It also goes to show that murder was a result they all could have anticipated," Stewart said. "That's what the law requires us to show. And the fact that they committed all these robberies, plus shooting three people, goes to show that."

Judge Price pondered the issue for some time.

There was no precedent for what Stu Stewart was trying to do. There could not be, because the conspiracy provision had just been passed recently by the Texas legislature, and no one knew exactly what it meant. It was a pure judgment call. And Judge Price knew the penalty if he guessed wrong: the Court of Criminal Appeals of Texas might reverse the conviction and require a retrial of the case.

But the judge was persuaded by the prosecutor's argument.

"I'm going to let the evidence in," he said. "The objection is overruled."

Stu Stewart looked at his list of witnesses. If he was going to be allowed to present them all, it would be a very long trial.

Aided by Assistant District Attorney Vic Driscoll, he set

up his huge map on an easel and had it received into evidence. And he stuck the first red flag into it, near the center of the city of Houston.

* * *

"Is that where your store is located?" Stewart asked the man from the U-Tote-M Store.
"Yes," the robbery victim replied.
Upon getting this answer, the prosecutor walked between the jury box and the judge's bench, glancing at the witness. He reached toward the big city map and put another red flag near the center of the city. The witness nodded.
There had been a parade of witnesses to the activities of the Brady Bunch on June 22, and the map was already becoming congested with little red flags. The map was probably the most powerful piece of evidence Stewart had.
The first crime of the day had been the robbery of a "Stop-N-Go" store—a small grocery chain. Stewart had produced witnesses from the store who told how Vargas and Sierra had come into the store and robbed it.
That was the first flag on the map.
The second flag marked the location of a fast food store called Shipley's Do-Nut Stand. Again, Stewart had called the victim to the stand to identify Sierra and tell about the robbery.
The third flag was the robbery of a small pinball-and-pool establishment called the Fun Arcade, near the center of Houston. The fourth was the Navigation Street Murder itself.
The fifth flag marked the site of the Almeda Road Murder—the crime in which Richard Vargas, in Sierra's company, had flushed away the life of the little Indian immigrant, Ashokkumar Patel.
Still, the Brady Bunch had not been finished after that murder. And now, neither was Stu Stewart.
The sixth flag in the map was a "Seven-Eleven" grocery store. The seventh was another "Stop-N-Go." The eighth was a U-Tote-M store, another small grocery chain.
The ninth stop for the Brady Bunch—and the ninth flag for Stu Stewart—was a second location of Shipley's Do-Nut Stand. Apparently, the Bunch did not mind hitting the same

store chain twice, as long as it was at different locations.

And then Bernardino Sierra had made the last stop alone.

He had gone into a restaurant, called the Early Roberts Cafe, and he had stuck a gun under the manager's face. As it happened, Houston Police Officer George Rojas was in the cafe having breakfast in the wee hours of the morning. He hadn't quite believed what he was seeing.

Rojas had stepped up from his chair, stuck his own gun in the robber's back, and told him to "Freeze."

And so now, as Stewart stood in the courtroom and pushed the tenth and last pin in the map, he marked the location of the Early Roberts Cafe. That was where the robberies had ended.

Of course, the real issue was the Navigation Street Murder. And Stewart called witness after witness to talk about it.

The Navigation Street Murder was an uncommonly sadistic and unnecessary killing. Sierra, Vargas and Ruiz had walked into the Crescent Food Market and ordered everyone to lie on the floor. And Sierra had shot one of the employees in the chest.

Then, as Sierra was leaving, he shot an elderly patron in the left side of the body, for no real reason. The bullet burst both of the man's lungs as well as his aorta, and it exited just under the armpit on the opposite side of his body. The man was named Joseph Picinich, and he was called "Papa Joe." He was just a few days from his sixtieth birthday. He died almost immediately.

Papa Joe had lived in the neighborhood, just four blocks from the Crescent Food Market, and he had come here the night of June 22 to buy some cigarettes. As Sierra had finished killing him, he had walked out of the store, got in the car with the others, and drove away—to commit, next, the robbery that took the life of Ashokkumar Patel.

Stewart could not tell the jury about the Brady Street Murder, the Fort Bend County Murder, the Middle Street Murder, or the Murder in the County Jail—because none of those were admissible in evidence. But by the time he rested the case, the jury knew a great deal about the Navigation Street Murder. And the map with the little red flags looked like the map of a battlefield.

The defendant offered no testimony.

When it came time to instruct the jury, Judge Price again considered whether Stu Stewart's conspiracy theory was right. Stuart Kinard and his co-counsel Terry Gaiser, for the defense, objected to it with all the force they could muster; and Kinard got his objections into the record as grounds for his appeal. But the judge ultimately accepted the prosecutor's reasoning.

He instructed the jury that they should find Bernardino Sierra guilty if they believed, beyond a reasonable doubt, that the death of Joseph Picinich was an event that should have been anticipated as a result of the robberies.

The jurors had heard more than enough evidence to answer that question. They remained in the deliberation room less than 25 minutes before finding Bernardino Sierra guilty of capital murder.

CHAPTER SEVENTEEN
THE BRADY BUNCH, PART IV: BERNARDINO SIERRA'S PLEA BARGAIN

Before the jury returned its "guilty" verdict against Bernardino Sierra, Stu Stewart's map and little red flags had been the focus of everyone's attention.

But now the trial on the guilt-innocence question was over.

The penalty hearing was under way.

And in the penalty hearing, the focus of everyone's attention was on the witnesses Stuart Kinard began to call for the defense.

"We call Dr. Bowers to the stand," said Kinard, as he began to put on the evidence he hoped would save Bernardino Sierra's life.

Stu Stewart waited. He had no idea, of course, what the witness was going to testify to. The fifth amendment protected not only the defendant himself, but the defendant's case as well, from prosecution discovery. Kinard, like any good defense lawyer, had not tipped his hand to the State.

"Will you tell the court and the jury your name?" Kinard asked.

"William Bowers," the witness answered.

"And what is your business or profession?" asked the defense lawyer.

"I am a statistician," was the answer.

Almost immediately, Stewart recognized what the witness was going to say. Kinard was not going to focus on

Bernardino Sierra personally. He was going to mount a frontal assault on the death penalty itself.

The statistical profession is deeply divided on the capital punishment issue. Many statisticians believe the evidence indicates that the death penalty is not a deterrent to crime. Others believe that the statistical evidence shows that it is an effective deterrent.

It was not difficult to guess which camp this witness was in, since he had been called by Stuart Kinard.

The defense lawyer drew out the witness' scholarly background. It was impressive: degrees, professional societies, and the like. Then Kinard reached the crucial point.

"Is the death penalty an effective deterrent to the crime of murder?" he asked.

"We object, your honor," said Stu Stewart. The jury was not allowed to consider whether the legislature should have passed the death penalty statute, he argued to the judge. The jury was not even allowed to consider whether the death penalty was proper. All they were required to do was to answer two factual issues—deliberation and violence—that pertained to the individual on trial, Bernardino Sierra.

"That's sustained," said Judge Price.

"Dr. Bowers, you will have to step down," said Kinard. "I'm sorry." The witness left the courtroom, unable to testify.

But most of the story of Dr. Bowers' testimony had unfolded while the jury was in the courtroom, listening to every word. Whether the evidence was admissible or not, Kinard had gotten part of his message across.

"The defense calls Mr. Don Reid," said Stuart Kinard.

Stu Stewart recognized this name. Don Reid was editor of the Huntsville *Item*. The *Item* was the principal newspaper in Huntsville, Texas, the town where the Texas electric chair was located. Don Reid had witnessed, personally, over a hundred executions. He was a well-known writer on the subject of capital punishment.

It was a pretty good guess that he, too, like Dr. Bowers, was not going to testify about Bernardino Sierra. He was there to do what he was famous for—to attack the basic idea of capital punishment.

"Your honor, I would ask that the testimony of this witness be taken first outside the presence of the jury,"

Stewart said. He explained that it seemed clear Don Reid's testimony was not going to be admissible.

"Well, let's see what he gets into," said Judge Price, overruling Stewart's request.

Kinard asked about Reid's profession, his background, and his experience. Then he began to ask the witness about his beliefs concerning capital punishment.

"Objection, your honor," said the prosecutor.

"That will be sustained," said Judge Price, once again.

The witness was excused. But again, part of the message had come across, inevitably, to the jurors, who heard what was going on.

The testimony of the third defense witness was nothing short of amazing, even though it, too, was inadmissible.

"State your name for the court and jury, please," said Stuart Kinard, when the man was seated in the witness chair.

"Edgar Smith," replied the witness.

Edgar Smith, it developed, was a businessman from San Diego, California. He was Chairman of the City's Bicentennial Commission. He was obviously a solid citizen, successful and respectable.

Kinard asked him about his background.

"I was on death row, myself, in the State of New Jersey," the witness said.

At one time, Edgar Smith had been convicted of a capital crime and sentenced to death. He had spent time on death row for the offense. He had won a new trial, and in that new trial he had again been convicted and sentenced—this time, to a term of imprisonment. He had served a part of his sentence and had been paroled.

From there, he had gone on to make a success of his life. Now he was testifying on Bernardino Sierra's behalf. The point was already obvious before Kinard went into the issue of capital punishment. Stewart again objected, and again his objection was sustained. But again, the jury had heard most of what Kinard wanted it to.

Defense witness number four was Bernardino Sierra, Jr. This was the son of the defendant on trial.

He was there mainly to "humanize" the defendant in the eyes of the jury. Here was a young boy, the message went;

and he needed his daddy at home. Kinard had prepared the child carefully for what he was about to say.

"Do you know this man?" Kinard asked, indicating the defendant.

"Yes," Bernardino Sierra, Jr. replied. "He is my father."

"Do you know who these people are?" Kinard asked, indicating the jury.

The child looked at the twelve people. "Yes," he said.

"Do you know what they are here to decide?"

"Yes. They are here to decide whether my fathers lives or dies."

Kinard was asking his questions slowly, letting the answers sink in. Finally, he asked: "Do you have anything you want to say to them?"

"Yes," answered the child. "that I love my father, and I miss him—very much."

It had nothing to do with the proceedings and nothing to do with the issues in the trial. No one would have thought it proper had Stu Stewart brought in the son of "Papa Joe" Picinich, for example, to say that he loved and missed him, or the wives or children of any of the other five victims of Bernardino Sierra's crimes. It would divert the jury from what they were supposed to be considering; it would make them decide on grounds of bias and sympathy. But that was precisely the purpose for which the testimony of Bernardino Sierra, Jr. had been offered.

And Kinard was not finished yet.

Defense witness number five was Bernardino Sierra's mother. She testified that the defendant's stepfather was an alcoholic who beat him regularly and mistreated him in other ways and that Bernardino Sierra himself was a heavy drinker.

The sixth, and final, witness was named Dr. Richard Jones.

"And what is your occupation?" Kinard asked.

"I'm a clinical psychologist," Dr. Jones replied.

Stewart began to take notes. This witness was obviously going to testify on an important point: the probability of future violence on Bernardino Sierra's part.

"Do you recall how many tests you administered to Bernardino Sierra?" Kinard asked.

"I administered the Wechsler Adult; the Bender Gestalt

Test; the drawing test of Howstret, the person drawing test; and the Rorschach technique—it's commonly called the ink blot test," the witness answered. He also named several other diagnostic tests he had used.

Kinard asked what the findings had been.

"My primary impression," the psychologist answered, "was that of alcoholism. Habitual drinking; type, severe. The second diagnostic impression was that of personality disorder, antisocial type.

"The third diagnosis was that of borderline mental retardation."

This "third diagnosis," Stewart knew, was in direct conflict with the findings of the State's pscyhiatrists and psychologists.

And there were more conflicts as the witness' opinion emerged more clearly. Bernardino Sierra did, he acknowledged, have an anti-social personality. But he was only "moderately" antisocial, and that was not the primary reason for his violent acts. The primary reason was alcoholism. That, plus the beatings and mistreatment Sierra's mother claimed he had received as a child. So Dr. Richard Jones concluded.

Now Kinard was ready to drive his point home. "First of all, I would like to ask you if you are aware of the prison commissary selling alcohol?"

Everyone smiled.

"It is my understanding that one cannot," replied the psychologist, with mock gravity.

Kinard next asked whether Bernardino Sierra would be likely to commit acts of violence inside a prison, where alcohol was not sold.

"Well, as I understand, either circumstance would involve a structured environment, an alcohol-free environment," Dr. Jones said.

"I wouldn't predict anti-social behavior under those circumstances."

Bernardino Sierra would be an ordinary, docile, nonviolent member of the prison population, in other words.

Stu Stewart gagged in disbelief and consternation.

The psychologist was saying this, of course, about a man who had suffocated one person inside a jail and tried to kill two others by stabbing them with a pair of scissors. But for technical reasons, the jury could not be told about those incidents. The psychologist's opinion was going to be all the jury would hear, and Stewart would be deprived, by the rules of evidence, of the means to show it for what it was. That was the way the rules sometimes worked.

* * *

There was, at least, one thing Stewart might be able to do to combat this testimony from the defense.

He could call a psychologist who had examined Bernardino Sierra on the State's behalf, a man named Jerome Brown.

"We would call Dr. Brown," he said.

Stuart Kinard was on his feet immediately. He objected to the testimony of the state's psychologist being heard by the jury at all. This interview of Bernardino Sierra had been "done without his consent, and without counsel being present." Therefore, said Kinard, Dr. Brown's testimony would be like the repetition of an inadmissible confession. It would violate the fifth and sixth amendments to the Constitution of the United States, as well as article 38.22 of the Texas Code of Criminal Procedure.

Kinard made his objection without the jury being present.

In his chambers, Judge Price told the lawyers that he was persuaded by Stuart Kinard's argument. "They took him over there for the psychological evaluation, and it wasn't voluntary," said Judge Price. "Besides, it wasn't an interview about the death penalty. It was to determine his competence to stand trial and his sanity."

It was likely that the fifth amendment would be violated if Dr. Brown testified to the results of his evaluation, the judge concluded.

"I think I'm going to keep it out," he said.

That was the end of the prosecution's ability to counter the defense. Bernardino Sierra had, of course, consented to the interview by his own psychologist, Dr. Jones, so it was admissible. But the prosecution could not counter that testimony with its own psychologist because of the judge's ruling. And the prosecution also could not disprove the defense psychologist by showing the defendant's conduct inside the prison.

Worse yet from the prosecution's standpoint, Kinard had

succeeded in preventing the jury from knowing that these items of adverse evidence even existed. And by offering his own evidence before the jury, evidence about the deterrent value of the death penalty, which Judge Price had ruled inadmissible, he had forced Stewart to object in the presence of the jury. To the average juror, it must have looked as though Stewart, the prosecutor, was suppressing evidence—while Kinard, for the defense, wanted only to bring out all the facts.

* * *

Inside the jury room, the twelve people who had been brought together by the battle over Bernardino Sierra's life became divided. Almost immediately, there were two irreconcilable camps.

The first ballot produced nine slips of paper that answered both of the penalty questions "Yes." That was nine votes for the death penalty.

The other three votes were for life imprisonment.

For three days, these two warring factions glared at each other, sweated, and argued. The numbers on each side shifted from time to time. But they were still not able to agree.

And so the verdict was—nothing.

It was a hung jury.

After the trial was over, and the jury had been excused, both the prosecution and the defense interviewed individual jurors. Their efforts gave a unique picture of the jury's deliberations.

The three "No" jurors, who favored life imprisonment from the start, had offered their reasons to the rest of the jury. The prosecution, they said, had not shown any "pattern" of violence. The prosecution's evidence had shown the jury "only thirteen hours," and not Sierra's "entire past life." There might be "some good" in the defendant, these jurors said, and this one "spree" was only "a small part of his life."

Inside prison, the "No" jurors argued, Sierra would be "treated"—by both psychiatrists and psychologists—for all his ills, including his anti-social personality and his alcoholism. Prison would be an endless, structured, alcohol-free environment where Sierra could do no harm.

The "No" jurors also argued that Stewart had "suppressed" evidence. He had done this by objecting to the statistician's testimony. And the "No" jurors maintained, vigorously, that the State, through prosecutor Stewart, had "shirked" the burden of proof. "The State didn't present psychiatric testimony to refute Dr. Jones' testimony," they said. Of course, none of the jurors knew that Stewart had tried to present a psychologist, only to be prevented by Kinard's objection.

The jurors voting for the death penalty saw the case in a different light. What sort of person would do what Sierra had done? What sort of person would be released from his first prison sentence and then embark, within a matter of days, on a spree like this?

How many people did Bernardino Sierra have to rob? How many did he have to kill, before he could be stopped? Didn't that show he was dangerous?

No, it didn't, said the "No" jurors.

Sierra had a low I.Q. Dr. Jones had said so. "Could he have actually been the leader in such a state of mind?" the "No" jurors asked. With Sierra so handicapped, these jurors concluded, "Vargas must have been the leader."

The "Yes" jurors thought that argument was unpersuasive. After all, it didn't take a college degree to rob a store and shoot somebody.

The "No" jurors had an answer for that.

Sierra did the actual killing, but Vargas had influenced him. Vargas was the "real" killer. He was the one "responsible."

The first day of jury deliberations was a Thursday. It was occupied by discussion that seesawed back and forth.

On Friday, the second day, another vote was taken.

There had been a shift. Now, instead of nine to three for death, the jurors were divided evenly—six for life, and six for death.

On the third day, Saturday, the jurors discussed again an issue that had worried them throughout their deliberations.

The question they had to answer asked whether there was a "probability" that Sierra would be violent in the future. What did the word "probability" mean? If one wasn't sure, did that destroy the "probability?" How much of a "probability" did it take? And how could somebody prove "beyond a reasonable doubt" that a "probability" existed?

The jurors had read the question over and over. They had analyzed its sentence structure; they had dissected its words.

And they found, now, that they had gotten themselves thoroughly confused as to what the question meant.

In Saturday's vote, the balance finally tipped in favor of life imprisonment. The "No" jurors now numbered seven, the "Yes" jurors five.

The "No" jurors, and their arguments, made a fascinating study of the reasoning process of a criminal jury.

Here is a portrait of those jurors, with a brief sketch of each one, taken from Stu Stewart's investigation:

Voting No from the Beginning—Arnold White, a young man who felt a personal identification with Bernardino Sierra. White had himself had problems with a father who died of alcoholism. He broke down on two occasions and emotionally stated that he might have run with a gang, too, as Sierra had, if he had not had the luck to find a job upon leaving college. White repeatedly stated he believed Sierra would be thoroughly rehabilitated. He said, "Who can he harm in Jail?" and even asked, "Did we hear of any killings while Sierra was being held for trial?"

There had been one, the Murder in the County Jail, but Arnold White never knew about it—because it was inadmissible in evidence. So was the incident in which Sierra had stabbed two other inmates with smuggled scissors.

Voting No from the Beginning—Betsy Bagdikian, who also had an alcoholic father who "gets mean when he drinks." This juror said she, herself, could have done "the same thing under similar circumstances." Showing emotional sympathy with Sierra's mother, Bagdikian maintained that "without alcohol, he would be a different man. His antisocial personality could be treated in a liquor-free environment." And she asked, "How many people has he hurt while he's been in jail?"

Voting No from the Beginning—Andrea DeCarlo, who broke down, emotionally, on several occasions and said, "If I believe for a moment that without alcohol he can be rehabilitated, how can I kill him?" She argued that Sierra's murders were only short term, and did not describe his "general adjustment in life."

The rules of evidence had prevented Stu Stewart from telling Ms. DeCarlo any more about Sierra's "general adjustment in life" which included a number of other murders and a frightening psychological portrait, in addition to the escape attempt, the murder and two attempted murders inside the county jail.

Voting Yes, Changed to No—Phyllis Nardone. Another juror described Ms. Nardone as possessing a "remarkably dull mentality," and in any event she gave little argument to explain her change in vote.

Voting Yes, Changed to No—Edward Pennington. Pennington had difficulty with the terms "reasonable doubt" and "probability." Finally, he came to the conclusion that there was reasonable doubt as to the probability of anyone committing crimes of violence inside a prison.

Voting Yes, Changed to No—Marie Gessler, who had the same difficulties as Edward Pennington with the words used in the question and who felt that Sierra's "low intellect" made his "degree of guilt" such that he did not deserve a sentence of death.

Voting Yes, Changed to No—Janet Albedeck, who changed her vote in the last five minutes of deliberations. This juror apparently voted "No" in an attempt to resolve the case and prevent the necessity of a retrial. She said, "It would be a shame if all our time here had been for naught. And the man might be re-tried as effectively next time." She added, "Something is better than nothing."

What Ms. Albedeck was saying made sense, but it did not persuade the other jurors. They were convinced of Sierra's dangerousness. If this jury was too silly to see it, he should be re-tried—before another jury, which hopefully would be more sensible. This was a strange group, and the pressure of deliberations was affecting them. One juror, a grown woman, had sent a request through the bailiff for her Teddy Bear. It was brought to her.

At last, a note came out from the jury. It informed Judge Price that there was a hopeless deadlock.

Reluctantly, the judge declared a mistrial and excused the jurors.

The mistrial meant that the entire trial had been a waste

of time. The conviction—the guilty verdict—was wiped out too. The case would have to be tried again, from jury selection all the way through the end.

* * *

On Tuesday, July 6, the lawyers for the prosecution and the defense met in Judge Price's chambers.

This was the day set for the retrial.

Judge Price had set the case for trial, and he had been prepared to set his other cases aside. But it was clear to everyone that he was concerned about the time, the expenditure, and—above all—the uncertainty, that a re-trial would involve.

He had a point. The two defense lawyers were being paid by the government, at a minimum rate of $250 a day. That was $2500 a week. If there was a four-week jury selection, that alone would mean ten thousand dollars. Many times that amount had already been spent on the services of the defense lawyers, and if the presentation of evidence, jury arguments, punishment hearing and so forth had to be done again, it would boost the fee into the hundred thousand dollar range. Appeal would add tens of thousands of dollars to that.

And if one considered the cost of the courtroom, the salary of the judge, bailiff, court reporter, prosecutors and other personnel that were necessary for the process, that cost would be multiplied several times over.

The trial of Bernardino Sierra was going to cost the State somewhere in the quarter-to-a-half million dollar range, fairly estimated.

Of course, that much expenditure might be justified.

But there was more to it.

The judge had a heavy docket of other cases. Many of them involved accused robbers and murderers who were dangerous, too. A trial that lasted several months would hamper efforts to do justice in those cases.

And there was one other consideration.

"I admitted all the robberies and murders from that same day into evidence last time;" said Judge Price. "But we don't really know whether they were admissible or not, because the Texas Court of Criminal Appeals hasn't ruled on the question."

The judge turned to Stu Stewart, and he went on.

"I can just imagine what will happen if you retry Sierra, and the extraneous offenses are admitted," he said. "The Court of Criminal Appeals might reverse the conviction. And then we'll be left with a situation where you have to try him again, for the third time. That might be three or four years down the road."

Everyone knew what a retrial four years later would mean. It would be next to impossible for the state to get all its witnesses together. It might, conceivably, mean that Bernardino Sierra would escape conviction for any of the six murders he had committed.

Judge Price was not forcing Stewart's hand. "He never did that," Stewart said later. "He was just seeing the case from a perspective that was neutral."

Stewart discussed the case privately with Kinard. He knew that the judge was right; he had problems with his case. If the extraneous offenses were taken away, he might even have trouble getting a verdict of guilty. The defendant deserved the most severe sentence that the law allowed, but the rules of evidence stood as a barrier to achieving that objective.

"There's a possibility we could do this," Stu Stewart said to Kinard. "Accept a guilty plea to three of the murder cases, and recommend a life sentence on all three. Then we'd accept a guilty plea on the robbery indictments, and recommend concurrent sentences of fifty years on each."

That would impress even a reckless parole board, Stewart thought. It would assure that Sierra would not soon be free.

"I'd like to talk to my client about it," said Kinard.

* * *

That was the way that the Plea Bargain of the Century came into being.

Judge Price, after he had heard Bernardino Sierra's admission of guilt, received into evidence three sheets of paper that contained stipulations of the facts of the murders.

Those three sheets of paper became the only court records that showed what had happened to a man named "Papa Joe" Picinich on Navigation Street, a man named Jose Cruz Davila on Brady Street, and a man named Gilbert Moreno on Middle Street. They were all that was left of three innocent human beings.

There is an ancient prayer that reads, "God grant me the serenity to accept the things I cannot change, the courage to change the things I can, and the wisdom to know the difference." That prayer could have been written for a prosecutor. It expresses the soul of the prosecutor's dilemma, for the prosecutor can do as much harm, sometimes, by trying to change something he cannot as by failing to fight to change the things he can. And the wisdom to refrain from fighting invariably involves the most painful decision a courtroom lawyer ever has to make. Stu Stewart was feeling the full weight of it now, as he kept his bargain with Bernardino Sierra's lawyers.

"Your honor, the State recommends a sentence of life imprisonment on each of the three murders, and fifty years on each of the robberies," Stu Stewart said.

"On your plea of guilty," said Judge Price to Bernardino Sierra, "I find you guilty.

"I assess your punishment at life imprisonment on each of the murders and fifty years on each of the robberies."

The ceremony was over.

If he wanted to, Bernardino Sierra could take with him to the penitentiary a copy of his press conference. He could take the written confession in which he had admitted his participation in the most conscienceless killings that Houston had seen in some time. And so if anyone doubted that this had, indeed, been the Plea Bargain of the Century, Bernardino Sierra had the proof—for the whole world to see.

There was one final irony in this extraordinary case. It concerned Edgar Smith, the witness who attacked the death penalty on Bernardino Sierra's behalf—the man who had spent over a dozen years on New Jersey's death row, then lifted himself by his bootstraps to become a solid citizen and chairman of San Diego's Bicentennial Commission. The irony was that Edgar Smith's "rehabilitation" was incomplete. A few short months after Bernardino Sierra's Plea Bargain, Edgar Smith was arrested, convicted and sentenced to life imprisonment for attempted murder. Edgar Smith took the position that capital punishment was not an effective deterrent to crime. The death penalty had not, indeed, been effective in his case—primarily because it had not been imposed.*

---

*The following names in this chapter were changed, without alteration of the incidents in which the persons were involved: Arnold White, Betsy Bagdikian, Andrea De Carlo, Phyllis Nardone, Edward Pennington, Marie Gessler, Janet Albedeck.

PART FOUR

Of Barbarism—
And Justice

CHAPTER EIGHTEEN
THE DILEMMA OF CAPITAL PUNISHMENT

Early in 1977, convicted murderer Gary Gilmore became the first person to be executed in the United States in nearly a decade when his life was ended by a Utah firing squad. Gilmore's spectacular willingness to die led the Supreme Court to say, "This case may be unique in the annals of this Court."

Gilmore's case attracted so much of the attention of the national press that it almost came to symbolize the issue of capital punishment. But the question remains whether it was the proper case to bring the capital punishment issue into focus. In other words, was there anything unique about Gary Gilmore that bears on the capital punishment dilemma?

The answer to that question is a resounding "No."

Certainly, what Gilmore *did* was not unique. Both of Gilmore's murders could have fit into this book without adding anything drastically different. He killed two innocent strangers in Provo, Utah, one a gas station attendant and one a motel manager, by forcing them to lie on the floor and shooting them in the back of the head. Both of Gilmore's murders were carbon copies of what Richard Vargas did to Ashokkumar Patel in the Almeda Road Murder. And for sheer, execution-style murdering, Gilmore's crimes pale by comparison to Bernardino Sierra's Middle Street Murder or Kenneth Brock's homicide in front of six police officers, not to mention Ronald O'Bryan's cold-blooded elimination of his own son or Gerald Bodde's unbelievably senseless murder of an 81-year-old woman. It is a sad conclusion, but it is impossible to conclude otherwise: Gary Gilmore's crimes, for all their horror, did not qualify him for the death penalty any more than many others.

It has been said, on the other hand, that what was unique about Gilmore was his personality. For one thing, he is sometimes described as having been extraordinary in his manipulative abilities. He seems to have had an uncanny knack for "putting on" his prison keepers, so as to maneuver them into doing what he wanted. But compared to John Stiles Griffin, Gilmore was a novice at it. Griffin was the man who taught motivation classes in prison and convinced his case worker that he "definitely" could lead a clean life, but then embarked on a series of murders that made Gilmore's crimes seem almost pleasant by comparison. And for sheer straight-faced mendacity, neither Gilmore nor Griffin could match the Halloween Candy Murderer, Ronald Clark O'Bryan.

Gilmore is sometimes said to be unique in his death wish. But his suicidal urge was no more reckless than that of the members of the Brady Bunch, who proudly confessed on television and repeated, over and over, "They can only burn me once." Gilmore was not unusual in this regard. Death row is filled with men who do not care whether they live or die, because they do not care whether anyone lives or dies.

What, then, was unique about Gary Gilmore?

Entertainer Johnny Cash wanted to telephone Gilmore to keep him from becoming depressed on death row. The question arises whether Johnny Cash wanted to call the families of Gilmore's victims; most of America did not know their names. You could read *Time* and *Newsweek* that week without learning them, but you would find out a great deal about the murderer. And on NBC's Saturday Night Live, a troupe of comedians sang: "Let's give Gary Gilmore what he wants for Christmas."

"Cut Rona Barrett!" shouted the ABC newsman who circled over the Utah penitentiary in a helicopter during Gilmore's execution. Speaking into his microphone, the reporter added that from his vantage point, he could make a gripping television broadcast for the network's "Good Morning America" Show. That statement, especially the reference to Rona Barrett, sums up in a nutshell what was unusual about Gilmore.

It was sheer Hollywood hype.

And when all is said and done, the public debate over Gilmore's case had very little to do with capital punishment.

Unfortunately, that is frequently the problem with the debate about capital punishment today. Much of what is said is nothing but Hollywood hype. Those who favor the use of the death penalty and those who oppose it shout slogans at each other across a void, and neither side faces the issues that the other raises. In fact, neither side ever examines its own arguments to see whether they hold water.

Is the death penalty morally acceptable? Given the imperfections of our system of justice, can we tolerate the risk of using it? If we abolish it, will it lead to increased numbers of murders of innocent people? Will abolition cause Americans to lose faith in their system—and perhaps take the law into their own hands? Can justice be done without the death penalty?

Will there be a public reaction against the use of capital punishment a few years hence? If so, will it be of sufficient strength to induce a repeal of current death penalty laws?

No one really knows the answers to any of those questions. And the debate about capital punishment today is not likely to produce the answers. Each person must struggle to find them for himself or herself. Not only can we not afford to leave the issue to the experts; we have to realize that, insofar as the death penalty is concerned, there *are* no experts. That is why it is important that each citizen equip himself with sufficient knowledge to turn aside the sophistries with which he is assaulted daily from both sides. And that, in turn, requires that each citizen know something about the cases—the kind of cases that are subject to the death penalty. That knowledge is hard to come by, because stories about people like Gary Gilmore on the one hand, or reasoning that fails to come to grips with the issues on the other, account for most of what is available. That is why we have written this book.

* * *

This book tells the stories of six men who were accused of capital murder. Five of the six were convicted by juries, and one pled guilty.

The question might legitimately be asked: How representative are these cases? Can they be taken as showing something that is useful to know about capital punishment?

As of the start of 1976, there had been twelve completed capital murder trials in Houston. Eleven of the trials ended in convictions for capital murder. The twelfth ended in a hung jury, requiring a retrial.

Of the eleven convicted defendants, eight were sentenced to death. The other three were sentenced to life imprisonment.

And so the Houston cases, taken as a whole, show roughly the same proportion of convictions, hung juries, life sentences and death sentences as the cases in this book. And while these cases are sensational, there was at least one other Houston case—the trial of Ignacio Cuevas, for two murders during an eleven-day escape attempt at the Walls Prison Unit in Huntsville—that received more national publicity than all the ones in this book combined. In short, we believe that the cases in this book are representative. That is an unpleasant conclusion, because the cases are nightmarish. The point is that an examination would show that all of Houston's capital cases are nightmarish.

Furthermore, the rate of convictions and the ratio of life or death sentences does not change dramatically when the statistics are taken from the entire State of Texas. Evidently, there are enough Kenneth Brocks, John Stiles Griffins, Ronald O'Bryans, Gerald Boddes, Richard Vargases and Bernardino Sierras to account for all the capital cases in the state.

For that matter, it seems likely that there are enough people who are willing to commit these sorts of crimes to go around in every state of the union, from Maine to California. And so in most respects, we think that the cases in this book are a fair sample—and taken as a whole, they provide a good map of the Road to Death Row. They certainly have more to do with what capital punishment is all about than did the publicity surrounding Gilmore's case.

Of course, it is not enough to map the Road to Death Row and leave it at that. Some people think that the Road ought to be maintained or expanded, and there are others who believe that it should be torn down completely. What, then, is the case for capital punishment? And what are the best of the abolotionists' arguments?

CHAPTER NINETEEN
THE BEST OF THE ABOLITIONIST ARGUMENT

Representative Craig Washington is an impressive speechmaker. And for him, attacking the death penalty was the most important task of the legislative session. He put all he had into it.

The legislature had before it a bill that would re-enact the death penalty in Texas. The year was 1973, and the bill was the Texas capital murder law. As Washington wound up his argument, there were cheers from people on both sides of the capital punishment question—cheers for the eloquence with which this conscientious legislator had presented his views against capital punishment.

If death was a deterrent, Washington said, why not do it in public? Why not, indeed, at the State Capitol? Washington suggested amending the proposed bill so as to require the legislators themselves to vote on every capital case—and then to witness the execution. He predicted that there would "never be a majority of this House with the moral conviction to stand eye to eye with a convicted felon and watch him fry on the floor of the House."

What Washington was saying, really, was the simplest and most basic of the objections to capital punishment. It was that capital punishment is unacceptable on moral grounds.

Soon after Washington made his modest proposal, State Senator Jim Wallace proposed an amendment that would have required executions to be carried out by "smiting" the convict with "instruments of iron, wood or stone." The amendment was based upon Biblical scripture, from the Book of Numbers. Wallace was doing the same thing as Washington: through satire, he was trying to say that the death penalty was morally unacceptable. His amendment was immediately voted down.

Then the Texas House listened in silence while Representative Mickey Leland quoted a telling phrase from the Bible: "And God spake these words, saying, thou shalt not kill." It was the same message, but taken from another source.

And ACLU spokesman Wayne Oaks summed up all these arguments of the opponents by saying of the death penalty, "It's barbaric. It's unconstitutional. It's inconsistent with contemporary standards of decency and morality." Oaks added that in his opinion the problem of violent crime had nothing to do with the death penalty, but was caused instead by "sloppy and inadequate law enforcement."

These arguments did not prevail. The supporters of the death penalty in the Texas legislature were the ones who had the votes. In spite of an attempted filibuster by opponents in the House, a spokesman for the governor's office predicted that the new law would pass "going away." And so it did.

But the echoes of those arguments can still be heard today. And they are still disturbing. How do the supporters of the death penalty answer the claim that it is "immoral?" What do they say when capital punishment is called "barbaric?"

Two years later, a test case reached the United States Supreme Court—a test case involving the Texas capital murder law. And it provided a partial answer to the "barbarism" claim. When the Court heard from lawyers in argument, Justice Lewis Powell asked the attorney for the condemned man, Anthony Amsterdam, whether he could think of *any* crime meriting the death penalty. Amsterdam said no. He was opposed to capital punishment under any circumstances, on principle.

Mr. Justice Powell then asked whether the commandant of Buchenwald might have deserved capital punishment.

Amsterdam paused and thought about that one. Then he said, "My instinctive reaction is to say yes." But, he added, he was opposed to capital punishment on principle, on the ground it was unconstitutional, and therefore he was bound to say no.

Mr. Justice Powell persisted. "Suppose a terrorist destroys New York City with a hydrogen bomb?"

The answer was still no, Amsterdam replied. It was his positon that such crimes could be prevented by "police methods" rather than fear of punishment.

Within a few months of Amsterdam's statement, a terrorist placed a bomb in the baggage area of New York's Laguardia Airport. The resulting explosion killed eleven people, and if Amsterdam knew of "police methods" that could have prevented it, he failed to divulge them to the New York City Police Department in time. But in any event, the Supreme Court did not accept Amsterdam's argument. Justice Potter Stewart explained the reason: it is much easier to view the death penalty as immoral or barbaric in a purely academic discussion than it is when one is confronted with a crime so gross, so heinous, so brutal that anything short of the death penalty seems an inadequate response. Perhaps the basic human yearning for justice is itself "barbaric." But even if that is so, the morality of the death penalty ought to be decided by a citizenry aware of the kind of cases to which it applies.

They are cases such as the ones in this book.

Is it, then, barbaric or immoral to use capital punishment in Richard Vargas' case, or Gerald Bodde's, or Bernardino Sierra's, or Ronald O'Bryan's? Every person has to decide that question for himself.

* * *

Another of the arguments against capital punishment is that the chance of executing an innocent person is unacceptably high.

"You have to live with this verdict," Bob Carroll argued to the jury that sentenced Richard Vargas. "You can't change the verdict you render."

"It scares the hell out of me," said Frank Shepherd to the jury that sentenced Gerald Bodde. "If you make a mistake, you can't change it—if you pull the switch."

What are the chances of a mistake?

In the cases in this book, there are two examples of people who were falsely suspected of capital crimes. One was Walter Hixson, who was actually arrested in the wake of his wife's murder—a murder of which he was innocent, a murder that had been committed by John Stiles Griffin. The other was William Hudspeth, the man whom Ronald O'Bryan falsely identified as the man who had given him the poisoned Pixy Stix. Both of these suspicions were based upon superficially persuasive evidence. But the significant thing is that the falsity of the evidence in both instances was detected immediately; Hixson was released in a matter of hours, and Hudspeth was never arrested. It is inconceivable, given the processes that it would take, that either of these men could have been indicted, tried, convicted and falsely sentenced to death before a jury.

But, opponents of the death penalty argue, can one *guarantee* that a death sentence for one falsely convicted can *never* occur? If the United States maintains the use of the death penalty for the next fifty years, can one be certain that there will *never* be anyone executed who is innocent?

Supporters of the death penalty, if they are honest, have to answer that question no. It is as though they were asked, each time they boarded an airliner, whether they could guarantee absolutely that it was safe. The answer to that question would have to be no, and in the same manner, no one can answer absolutely that there is no chance of a mistake with the death penalty.

Of course, it also seems fair to turn the question on its head. Can opponents of capital punishment guarantee that their own position has not *already* cost the lives of some innocent human beings? Just to ask the question is to answer it; the answer is "of course not." But the focus is rarely on *that* kind of innocent lives, just as Hollywood's focus was on Gary Gilmore rather than on his victims. The innocent person killed in a murder is out of sight and out of mind—like the victims of a mass disaster, an earthquake or a flood, in a remote village with a foreign name on the other side of the globe.

This book shows what a capital trial is like. The lawyers for the defendant are charged with the responsibility of finding any argument—irrespective of whether they think the argument is reasonable, themselves—that would acquit their client or prevent a sentence of death. The jurors are instructed, over and over again, that they are to make their findings based upon the reasonable doubt standard. Supporters of the death penalty accept these protections as valid, but opponents do not consider them sufficient in a life-or-death case—and therein lies the difference between the two positions.

* * *

Another argument advanced by opponents of capital punishment is that it will lead to an increase, rather than a decrease, in murders. "Where the death penalty is still invoked, that is where the crime rate is highest," says Victor Blaine. "People are going to have a low regard for life if we take life."

There is some evidence that violence begets other violence. It is true, for example, that a child who watches violent behavior on television will sometimes imitate it. Social psychologists say that impressionable people can be induced to commit violent acts by "modelling" their behavior after other behavior they have seen. Could the same result follow from the death penalty? Could people be induced to commit acts of violence by "modelling" their behavior on an execution?

When Gary Gilmore was executed, the press wanted to be present, and a newsman brought suit against the Utah prison authorities seeking the right to film the execution for television broadcast. The court refused to grant this request, partly on the basis of testimony from a psychologist who said that there was a danger that impressionable people might see the execution, model their own behavior on it, and go out and shoot someone themselves. Perhaps, then, there is something to the argument. At least from this one case, there is expert testimony that says that the death penalty, if it were to be televised, could lead to other killing.

Of course, that does not really answer the question. The psychologist *also* said that if the execution were not televised, and only printed accounts of it were to reach the public, the danger of modelling would be much less significant. A person does not ordinarily model his behavior on a violent example unless that conduct is shown graphically and in detail—the way a television program is shown. Violent people, to the extent that they learn their conduct through modelling, learn it from acts they see—through being abused as children, through fighting, through watching television. At least, that is the position of those who favor capital punishment; their opponents disagree.

* * *

Opponents of the death penalty also argue that capital punishment is discriminatory, arbitrary and capricious. They point out that blacks, poor people and persons of low intellect are disproportionately represented on death row. "In Nazi Germany, Hitler tried to kill off all the people he thought were inferior," says Bob Carroll. He adds, "Maybe we should line up all the minority groups and kill them. All the people that have only a fourth grade education. I don't like the death penalty because I don't think it's fair."

And Adrian Burk told the jury that sentenced Kenneth Brock that the death penalty was "unfair from this standpoint, that you don't see any rich people getting the electric chair."

It is undeniably true that blacks, poor people and persons of low intellect are disproportionately represented in the ranks of those sentenced to die.* At the beginning of 1977, there were 57 persons on death row in Texas, and of those 57, 29 were white, 21 black and 7 Spanish surnamed. But it has to be remembered that the vast majority of capital crimes occur in cities, where black and Chicano populations are greater. For instance, the statistics are not out of line with the population of the city of Houston, which is approaching a fifty-fifty split between Anglo and non-Anglo peoples. When that fact is taken into account, the disproportion decreases—although it does not disappear.

The supporters of capital punishment look at another aspect of the matter. They point out that minority groups are disproportionately represented in nearly all crime statistics, not just in the death penalty. The relevant question, they say, is this: if a person is accused of capital murder, will his life depend upon whether he is black or white?

---

*This issue provides an example of one respect in which the cases in this book are not representative. Houston's early capital murder cases, for some unknown reason, did not involve the higher representation of blacks that usually characterizes death row. Consequently, all the defendants in this book are Anglos—except for the Brady Bunch, who are Chicano.

The answer to that question, from the statistics, appears to be no. In Texas, 55 percent of black defendants tried for capital murder were sentenced to death during the first two years that the present law was in operation. During that same period, 58 percent of Caucasian defendants tried for that crime were sentenced to death. Although the difference is not statistically significant, the figures are paradoxical. They show that, if anything, a black man accused of capital murder has a slightly better chance than a white!

The supporters and opponents will continue, undoubtedly, to place emphasis on different figures. Opponents will point out that there are more blacks on death row than there should be. Supporters will rely upon the data that show that a black man and a white man have virtually identical chances of escaping the death penalty once charged. Once again, the reader might well consider the cases in this book. When a crime such as Bernardino Sierra's, or Gerald Bodde's, or John Stiles Griffin's, comes before a jury, does the race of the defendant affect the outcome?

* * *

There have been dozens of other arguments offered against the death penalty. But these are the main ones—that capital punishment is immoral, that it risks execution of innocent persons, that it cheapens human life and that it is arbitrary and discriminatory. Still, the debate does not end there. The supporters have a case to make in favor of capital punishment, and the opponents, as might be expected, have an answer to each point.

CHAPTER TWENTY
THE CASE FOR CAPITAL PUNISHMENT

Supreme Court Justice Lewis Powell was one of the most outspoken of the nine justices during arguments on the 1976 death penalty cases. As the government's lawyer, Solicitor General Robert Bork, spoke in favor of capital punishment, Justice Powell asked him about deterrence of murder.

"While I recognize that deterrence may not be the controlling factor here," the justice said, "I invite your attention to the 1973 report of the FBI." Justice Powell then summarized what the report had to say: that murder had increased 42 percent between 1968 and 1973. "It is fairly obvious," he went on, "that we need some way to deter this slaughter of Americans. I say 'slaughter' because that word was used in describing the American death toll during our involvement in Vietnam. Comparing the records of Vietnam and the FBI's figures, it appears that, on an annual basis, more Americans are murdered in this country than were killed in Vietnam."

The Solicitor General agreed. It could not rationally be maintained, he said, that capital punishment was not a deterrent. "Respectable academic authority can be cited on this point," he said, "but I think common sense is sufficient to tell us that if we raise the cost and risk of certain conduct, the incidence of that conduct decreases." The Supreme Court would be taking an awesome responsibility, Bork went on, if it were to outlaw capital punishment. That, he said, would condemn thousands of potential murder victims in order to save a few hundred guilty people.

This exchange was significant. It led to the ultimate acceptance by the Supreme Court of the deterrence argument. For some crimes, wrote Justice Potter Stewart, "the death penalty is undoubtedly a significant deterrent." And the acceptance of this argument, in turn, was part of the reason for the Supreme Court's ruling upholding the death penalty.

But the deterrence issue is far from resolved. There is still vigorous debate, and vast difference of opinion, on the question whether the death penalty has any deterrent effect at all.

Could some future Ronald O'Bryan be deterred from a murder for money by the cold calculus of capital punishment? And what of a Bernardino Sierra—is there any possibility that he, or someone else in his position, may be prevented from murder by the death penalty? What of Kenneth Brock, who considered strategy before killing his hostage? The ordinary passion killing, of course, would not be stopped by capital punishment. But supporters point out that the death penalty does not apply to passion killings; it applies only to intentional and deliberate killings of types that are most likely to be deterred by it. They are crimes like O'Bryan's, or Sierra's, or Brock's. And they are in a period of rapid increase today.

The Texas Capital Murder statute, for instance, covers just five kinds of murders. They are murders of peace officers, murders of prison employees, murders during violent felonies, murders by escaped convicts, and murders for hire. Even in these instances, the death penalty is inapplicable unless the murder was deliberate and the killer can be proved to be likely to repeat his crime. Supporters contend that these are the instances in which the deterrent value of the death penalty is highest—and most necessary.

Opponents of capital punishment see the matter differently. They answer that there is no scientific proof that the death penalty is a deterrent. And they point out that there will probably *never* be any such proof either way. The usual way of examining the deterrent effect of the death penalty has been to compare crime statistics from states that have capital punishment to those that do not. But the results, by definition, are inconclusive. "The inescapable flaw," writes death penalty opponent Charles L. Black, "is that social conditions in any state are not constant through time, and that social conditions are not the same in any two states. If an effect were observed (and the observed effects, one way or another, are not large) then one could not at all tell whether any of this effect is attributable to the presence or absence of capital punishment." And so Black concludes that a scientific assessment of the deterrent effect of capital punishment "is simply impossible."

But scientists have tried anyway, and the results they have produced are interesting.

In 1975, a statistician named Isaac Ehrlich published the results of a study he had done on American murder rates and capital punishment. His results did not amount to scientific proof of the deterrent value of the death penalty, but they are fascinating nevertheless. Ehrlich used a sophisticated technique called multiple regression analysis, which produced a prediction that capital punishment would deter some murders. Since the multiple regression technique gives quantitative results, Ehrlich was even able to put a figure on the number of murders that an execution would deter: He predicted that the first execution would prevent eight homicides. The prediction is not scientifically exact, and Ehrlich is the first to admit it; for one thing, the deterrent effect could easily be miscalculated because of other variations—what scientists call "noise"—in the statistics. For another, the prediction can never be tested, for the simple reason that it will never be possible to identify and count the murders that are deterred by capital punishment.

And so the deterrence argument remains, thus—and science will probably never resolve it. This is not an issue for computers. This is an issue, like many other issues of law or government, that has to be resolved by each citizen. The supporters of capital punishment, agreeing with Solicitor General Bork, say that the evidence today is sufficient; but opponents demand more concrete proof, while at the same time pointing out that it is impossible to obtain.

* * *

There is one effect of capital punishment that is clear and absolute, and that is that capital punishment prevents future crimes by the same killer.

To Detective Carolyn Stephenson, this is one of the most important considerations. "How can they say it's not a deterrent?" she asks. "It deters that particular person from doing again what he's already been convicted of doing."

There can be no question that this is an urgent consideration. The cases described in this book provide an illustration of the reason. John Stiles Griffin, for example, escaped from custody and killed three women. Whether he would have killed his five Galveston victims had he had the time, or the police officer who arrested him in Port Arthur, is a matter of conjecture. But it is beyond conjecture that he is a dangerous man even inside a prison. The ease with which he smuggled escape implements and manufactured weapons in a solitary cell in the county jail is proof enough of that.

And in addition to John Stiles Griffin, there are the members of the Brady Bunch. Inside the county jail, Richard Vargas and Bernardino Sierra suffocated a fellow inmate; Richard Vargas attempted suicide by setting his cell on fire; Bernardino Sierra escaped from the county jail on one occasion, but was recaptured; and Sierra also attempted the murders of two other inmates with a pair of smuggled scissors. These men too are dangerous inside or outside of prison.

All told, the six men described in this book accounted for nineteen known murders or attempted murders. Six of those—four murders and two attempts—were committed while the killers were confined in prison or during escapes from custody. It is certainly fair to ask, as George Jacobs asked the jury that tried Gerald Bodde, whether there will someday be other killings.

And these six cases are not unique. Murders or assaults by inmates upon inmates are commonplace in prisons. Perhaps there are methods that could be used to reduce the incidence of such assaults, and certainly well-run prisons, such as the Texas Department of Corrections, have fewer than others. Can they be eliminated?

The opponents of capital punishment think so. "Who can he hurt in prison?" was the question the jurors in Bernardino Sierra's trial asked themselves. And one of Ronald O'Bryan's character witnesses put it this way: "If a man has been incarcerated, it is the state's job to rehabilitate him, not to take a life."

To death penalty supporters, that last remark betrays a lack of understanding of the problem. A prison cannot "rehabilitate" men like the six men described in this book. Opponents of capital punishment frequently conceptualize rehabilitation as a simple process—as though it involved a simple medicine that could be poured into a killer's head to make him refrain permanently from his conduct. But the fact is that there is no clear "cure" for the antisocial personality, and that is the affliction from which most capital murderers suffer.

Anthony Amsterdam suggests that the answer is "life imprisonment in solitary confinement and without benefit of parole." And perhaps that would be an improvement on today's "life" sentences.

But to supporters of capital punishment, the idea that a prisoner will not be dangerous because he is in solitary confinement is equally unrealistic. Day after day, year after year, the prisoner has to be kept securely, but human contact can not be eliminated entirely, and the necessities of hygiene can not be withheld, nor can dozens of other items that are potential weapons. Death penalty proponents are also skeptical about whether withholding of parole will really be done. The state Supreme Court in California, Professor Amsterdam's own home state, has already acted in at least one case to strike down restrictions on granting parole to a prisoner—on the ground that restrictions of this type are unconstitutional. And besides, if a prisoner could be kept under all these conditions, what is to be gained by it? Would not the regimen that the State would thus impose upon the prisoner be more cruel than death itself?

* * *

Capital punishment also involves a question of justice.

When the Texas capital murder law was tested in the United States Supreme Court, the matter of justice was a primary concern.

The case that the Supreme Court had before it was called *The State of Texas versus Jurek*. Jerry Lane Jurek had been indicted for kidnapping and attempting to rape a ten-year old girl, whom he strangled and threw in a river after she refused his sexual advances. Jurek had ignored the child's pleas for mercy, which were heard by several witnesses as he drove through the little town of Cuero, Texas. He was ultimately convicted of capital murder and sentenced to death. As Texas Attorney General John Hill argued to the Supreme Court that Jurek's sentence should be affirmed, he emphasized the brutal and callous nature of the murder.

"Do you mean to tell me," Hill asked the justices incredulously, "that the people have no means of taking care of such a crime?"

What Hill was saying—and the justices later agreed—was that sometimes the death penalty is the only sentence that can do justice to the case.

What sorts of crimes are there that require capital punishment for justice to be done? In Houston, the best example may be Elmer Wayne Henley—who participated in the abduction and murder of over two dozen adolescent boys. Many of the victims were homosexually raped and tortured, and the tortures included mutilation of their genitals while they were still alive, handcuffed to a board. Henley was sentenced to six consecutive terms of ninety-nine years. He was exempt from the death penalty because of a ruling of the Supreme Court.

There are dozens of other cases. There is Charles Tuller, the self-styled revolutionary who hijacked an airplane in Houston in an effort to promote "radical politics of change." He killed three innocent human beings in two different incidents. He too was exempt from the death penalty, and he was given a lengthy sentence of imprisonment. Then there was the case of Henry Jarrette, who was serving penitentiary sentences for two stabbing murders. He escaped, and within two days of his escape, he had kidnapped and raped a 16-year-old boy and robbed and murdered a 16-year-old boy. He told the arresting officer that he regretted being unable to kill him too. But all that could ultimately be done was to return Henry Jarrette to the prison from which he had escaped.

There is something more than deterrence involved in these cases. There is the question of justice.

Today, the cases continue to come—in the form of murders and trials such as those involved in this book. Can justice be done in a case such as Richard Vargas' without capital punishment? Can we as a society ask men like Officer Noskrent to serve in his job, and to see the exploded head of

Ashokkumar Patel in the course of that job, and then do less than justice in the case? How can an enormous crime such as Ronald O'Bryan's be dealt with by anything short of capital punishment, if justice is to be done? Or the crime of a Kenneth Brock, who executed a hostage in front of six police officers to gain a momentary advantage in his escape plans? Or the crime of a Bernardino Sierra, who bragged about his six killings on television?

Again, the opposition sees these questions differently.

The opponents of capital punishment do not regard the concern for justice as a valid argument. A death sentence cannot be based on the notion that the defendant has earned it, says Victor Blaine. "That's revenge," he maintains. And Frank Shepherd says that when a murderer is executed, there are "two murders instead of one." Justice, it appears, is a false issue in the eyes of the opponents—who regard the death penalty as "atavistic butchery that has run its course."

And so, apparently, it comes down to a simple but insoluble dilemma—the dilemma, that is, that one man's justice is another man's barbarism.